PCS to Corporate America taught me it is my personal responsibility to make things happen as a leader. Expectations tend to be "soft" in corporate America, and at times there are a lot of people working, but not getting the right results. I reiterate this same theme to the people I'm developing to become leaders over and over—it is the leader's responsibility to seek out the problems, take responsibility to solve them, and fight through all obstacles to get there. There are plenty of people willing to try, but companies are looking for those who can succeed. Roger taught me not only how to interview but also how to be a better leader!

> Alex Allen
> *Facility Manager, Cargill*

•

After reading *PCS* for the first of three times, I began to immediately understand how my success in the military could easily translate into success in business. Roger clearly lays out all of the rules of the road in order to (1) get the interview, (2) make a *great* first impression, (3) interview with skill and class (even if you have *never* interviewed before), and, finally, (4) get the offers rolling in! This book will not only get you into corporate America but also serve you well throughout your career. It still sits on my bookshelf in my office today, and I go back to it routinely. I owe so much of my success to this book!

> Patrick S. Dickerson
> *Sales Representative, Boston Scientific Corporation*

•

PCS is spot-on in explaining what corporate America expects from the JMO. Roger explains how to prepare and express your capabilities during the interview process such that the hiring company will clearly see your ability to immediately contribute in your new position, plus your potential as a leader within corporate America. In my global leadership role I use *PCS* as reference to ensure that our hiring process results in obtaining people with the right skills, professionalism, and motivation to drive results.

> Jorge R. Serrano
> *Director, Global Product Line Management*
> *Corning Cable Systems*

When I decided to transition from the military to corporate America, I felt that the ten years I spent between the Naval Academy and the Marine Corps had given me a strong set of leadership and team-building skills. *PCS to Corporate America* helped me translate those skills into terms familiar to corporate America, and it gave me a clear view of what corporate America wanted. Most importantly, *PCS to Corporate America* helped me understand the path that I needed to take in order to continue to grow as a leader.

Patrick M. McBride
Functional Engineering Manager, INVISTA

•

PCS guided me as a candidate, and today it guides me as a business executive. *PCS* will quickly teach you how to translate your experience effectively into the business world. Later in your career you will benefit by rereading *PCS* to prepare for interviews—as both an interviewee and interviewer. Roger's insights into self-awareness and preparation are invaluable and timeless. Read *PCS* now and reread it for years to come.

John Tunison
Director of Finance, Purchasing, and Administration
Univar, Inc.

•

PCS to Corporate America has been an indispensable resource throughout my career to prepare for promotional interviews and other assignments since leaving the Army. If you do nothing else before transitioning to the private sector, get this book, read it, and most importantly, apply its time-tested tips and tools to take charge of your career!

Kristopher S. Hull
Senior Vice President, TNS Custom Research, Inc.

•

PCS to Corporate America was the key to a new life that has been ever more rewarding with each year that passes. The ideas I found inside helped propel me toward greater personal opportunities, and even today I find myself reflecting on the insight and advantages I've gained through *PCS* and the Cameron-Brooks program.

Chris Moore
Plant Manager, Cardinal Glass Industries

PCS to Corporate America was the definitive road map for my transition to business, guiding my preparation, skill building, and overall readiness to move to corporate America. A decade later, I continue to apply the behavioral lessons I learned from *PCS to Corporate America*. Not only have they helped me rapidly advance my career—I also use them to train and develop my team members, most of whom have never served in the military.

> Trevor Bynum
> *Vice President and General Manager*
> *Strategic Growth Channels, Whitewave Foods*

•

When you enter the corporate environment from the military, it's a big decision. While you bring a lot of leadership experience that is valuable, you are simultaneously competing with a peer group that has been navigating in this environment for a few years. *PCS to Corporate America* gave me a broad overview of what to expect. It lent practical advice regarding basic expectations, business terminology, and the similarities and differences between the two environments. It made me more confident in my decision to transition and helped me compete effectively for that first role and the others that have followed.

> Fran Lawler
> *Human Resources Director*
> *Corning Display Technologies, Taiwan*

•

I continue to remember and actively use many of the lessons from *PCS to Corporate America*. My favorite is Roger's observation that being late for a meeting either shows that you don't respect others or are disorganized, neither of which is good. The other lesson outside of interviewing I learned from Roger and continue to apply is to always be polite and friendly to hotel maids, executive assistants, and facilities staff at work. They work just as hard as I do and deserve to be treated with respect. I recommend this book to military officers and enlisted men and women. If you want a straightforward preparation for your transition, read *PCS to Corporate America*.

> Jim Dillon
> *Vice President, Marketing, Cypress Semiconductor*

PCS to Corporate America was a wake-up call for me. I was a JMO who figured I'd get hired based on my resume, without any insight into how the recruiting world worked. PCS taught me that I had a long way to go to be ready to transition to the corporate world. Thankfully, I read it in time to avoid stumbling into a new career. PCS gets results if you're willing to work.

> Brian D. Vance
> *Director, Process Development, Boston Scientific Corporation*

•

PCS to Corporate America provided me with the framework I needed to understand how best to position my unique skill set to potential employers. This framework, coupled with incredible support provided by the Cameron-Brooks team, helped me secure a job with a Fortune 100 company.

> Scott H. Jones
> *Product Director, Ethicon*

•

I met Roger and the Cameron Brooks team while serving at Fort Hood, Texas, in 1988. As a young Army officer, I was not well prepared to face the transition from military service to the civilian workforce. By working with Cameron Brooks, however, I gained valuable insight into corporate America and how best to leverage my military experience. In short, Roger and the team prepared me for more than just an interview, they also prepared me for a civilian career that has been both fulfilling and rewarding. I would highly recommend Roger's book to anyone considering a career transition.

> David A. Hendrick
> *Senior Vice President, Sales Operation*
> *St. Jude Medical, U.S. Division*

•

I reflect back on my experience of working with Roger Cameron and the Cameron-Brooks team on a daily basis. All too often I've seen fellow military officers come into my company unsure of the career path they are truly interested in pursuing. Roger, his team, and his book, *PCS to Corporate America*, were key enablers for me as I determined the right roles to pursue. I feel strongly that I found the optimal career path with the right company as a result.

> Mick Boeing
> *Customer Team Finance Manager, Procter & Gamble*

PCS helped me navigate my way through the transition from JMO to a rewarding high-tech career in a Fortune 500 company. Roger's book helped me hone my interviewing skills and present myself with confidence to corporate recruiters. The book is still a great reference book I fall back on for successful approaches to interviewing.

> Ray Berzins
> *Director of Operations, Energy and Environmental Solutions*
> *Applied Materials, Inc.*

•

PCS to Corporate America was instrumental in my decision to pursue a career in the private sector after nearly ten years of military service. By helping me understand just how valuable my experience was to potential employers, it gave me the confidence to fully commit to the decision and to the work it would take to realize my vision of a career outside the Navy. Having made that decision, the value of the book only increased as it showed me how to best communicate my value to prospective employers.

> Tony Samer
> *Managing Director, Protiviti*

•

PCS helped to shift my paradigm from "what's in it for me?" to "what's in it for them?" I learned from this book how important it is to not come across as entitled or arrogant—it is a huge advantage to be neither of these. Each time I have interviewed for a new position in my company, I go back to the basics I learned from Roger's team and PCS: know my failures and be able to discuss them proudly, and prepare very carefully to share stories of success that are pertinent to the job in question.

> Natalie Friel
> *Senior Manager, Quality Systems*
> *Roche Pharmaceuticals*

•

We must prepare officers to lead industries, just as we prepare them to lead armies. Roger Cameron and his approach gives young officers the tools they need to accelerate an effective transition to civilian leadership.

> Dave Wagner
> *Vice President, Strategic Sourcing and External Partner*
> *Development, General Mills*

PCS to Corporate America is a must-read for any JMO preparing to make the transition to a civilian profession. While your background and skills are important to HR departments and potential employers, your ability to prepare and communicate your value is absolutely vital.

You need to learn the language and have a plan before going into this new arena. Speak too broadly about your experiences, and you will seem unprepared. Speak too specifically, and risk not being understood. The preparation and interviewing process is like a dance. Show up to the ballroom in your break-dancing gear, and you can expect to be denied at the door.

Roger has been successfully doing this for generations of veterans. I am so grateful for the coaching and mentoring that I received from him in this book.

> Nate Hemphill
> *Territory Sales Manager, Berry Plastics*

•

PCS to Corporate America was the first book I bought when I considered leaving the military. The knowledge contained within proved to be an excellent jumping-off point to beginning my second career in corporate America. The Cameron-Brooks process, *PCS to Corporate America*, the additional recommended reading, and the many other exercises outlined in the book mirror the training methodology of the military—train harder than you expect to fight. I would recommend Cameron-Brooks and *PCS to Corporate America* to any JMO, and I have also recommended them to my company as a source of talent.

> Bryan Phillips
> *Project Development, ConocoPhillips*

•

PCS to Corporate America was instrumental in preparing me for the "life-cycle transition" and transformation from the military to corporate life. Roger's transparent guidance allowed me to wrap my mind around the entire process, enabled me to prepare effectively for every stage, and set me up to execute with excellence throughout my journey from initial interviews, to early transition to corporate life, and throughout my 26 years in the business world. A must-read for those who desire a successful transition and "fast start" in the corporate world.

> Emory E. Zimmer
> *Director, Strategic Program Management, Procter & Gamble*

It has been about 16 years since I left the military, but I remember how *PCS to Corporate America* gave me a sense of calm about translating my military experience into success in business. As a guide to interviewing, there isn't a better reference manual for how to succinctly frame answers that effectively deliver a message. I keep a small number of business books on a shelf in my office, and this book has never moved off of that shelf.

    Bill Stewart
    Associate Vice President, Strategic Accounts, DePuy Spine

•

I read the original first edition of *PCS to Corporate America* in 1991 and started my corporate career, thanks to Cameron-Brooks. There are interviewing and conversational techniques that not only landed me a job but sustained me throughout a very successful career. I have even gone so far as to pull the old book out of the attic and have my 20-year-old son (born in 1991!) read and learn these techniques!

    Tom Cooper
    Project Manager, Corning Life Sciences Greater China

•

PCS to Corporate America was an invaluable tool and a great source of confidence during my transition. The book allowed me to clearly understand how my experiences as a military officer directly translated to those desperately needed by today's elite corporations. *PCS* taught me how to verbalize my military achievements clearly and concisely to hiring managers. I firmly believe that *PCS to Corporate America* and the Cameron-Brooks team were the cornerstones for my successful transition.

    Ed Lonsway
    Sales Operations, Medtronic Spinal & Biologics

•

This book is loaded with simple yet profound insights on ways junior officers can put their best foot forward in the transition process. It's tailored for JMOs, yet indispensable as a tool for managing a career once you're inside an organization. I've turned to it countless times over the years to help me market my skills, and I've used it to help coach countless others. *PCS to Corporate America* is a timeless treasure.

    Pete Burney
    Senior Vice President, Supply Chain & Business Enablement
    Hallmark Cards, Inc.

The book helped me enormously from the standpoint of understanding not only the transition process but what corporate America "looked like." I needed a lot of help in translating my military skills and background to relevance in the business world. This book helped me do that.

> Chris Sultemeier
> *Senior Vice President, Transportation, Wal-Mart Stores, Inc.*

•

PCS to Corporate America is the ideal playbook for junior military officers transitioning to corporate America. It provides the strategy and tactics of how to successfully earn the "Yes" from prospective recruiters and hiring managers. I attribute much of my success in transitioning to learning and applying Roger's 40+ years of strategy and tactics.

> Jesse Dubberly
> *Product Support Operations Manager, Joy Global*

•

PCS is an invaluable resource for the professional in transition. It codifies the expressed talents demonstrated through military service and brings to the forefront the implied attributes that corporate America is searching for in their leader development. *PCS* guided me in expressing my talents, honing my message, and establishing a match between my skill set and the needs of the hiring company. Initially, I realized I possessed certain attributes, but I was unfamiliar with how to transition those skill sets to a marketable package. *PCS* and the Cameron-Brooks team assisted in that transition. Even today, 14 years post-transition, I refer to *PCS* for guidance and clarity.

> Greg Beckman
> *District Sales Manager, Abbott Laboratories*

•

The tools, techniques, and insights in *PCS to Corporate America* are my competitive advantage as I prepare and interview for and assume new roles and responsibilities. I have been able to successfully transition between functions, business units, and levels of responsibility, delivering results and making an impact on day one. *PCS* is the most valuable book in my library.

> Steve Joachim
> *Director, Product Development, Ethicon*

Eight years post-transition, I still keep my copy of *PCS to Corporate America* on my bookshelf right next to my desk. It served as a guide during my transition and still serves me well today. Whether I'm looking to prepare myself for the next step in my corporate growth or wanting to help an employee understand some time-tested principles, *PCS to Corporate America* is a key resource for me in my professional library.

> Michael DeBock
> *Senior Director of Business Development*
> *NextEra Energy Resources*

•

PCS to Corporate America gave me much-needed insight into preparing for my military transition into a career. I regularly refer back to *PCS to Corporate America* when interviewing for new career opportunities, and it has never failed to get me prepared. The material in Roger's book is timeless and applicable at any transition in my career.

> Gary Smith
> *Regional Asset Protection Manager, Wal-Mart Stores, Inc.*

•

For those who have served our country in war time, you are so far beyond where I was when I left the USAF as a captain. I am incredibly impressed by the maturity and professionalism of those who have served in today's military. What you've done and who you are will be incredible assets for your future success. *PCS* and the Cameron-Brooks team will help you effectively prepare for success in your new life.

> Stephen Morse
> *Area Vice President of Sales, Boston Scientific Corporation*

•

PCS to Corporate America was my primary resource to prepare for a civilian career. It helped me understand what it would take to be successful outside the military, showed me what career opportunities are possible, and trained me how to effectively communicate my talents in an interview. Roger offers key insights into what it takes to be a leader and a professional in any career, and he helps candidates achieve their goals. Not only has *PCS* been a valuable resource in developing my own career, but I have also applied what I learned to more effectively interview new hires and mentor others in the company.

> Jim Ball
> *Senior Supervisor, Manufacturing, Genentech*

PCS to Corporate America is the foundation for building a plan for a successful corporate career and a must-read for any JMO. As a JMO, I was given more responsibility at the first stage in my career than any corporation would have likely provided me without my JMO experience. I used *PCS* to help me understand how to best leverage those experiences to launch a successful career in the corporate world.

Leo Watson
Area General Manager, Western Canada
Linde Canada, Gases Division

•

Roger Cameron understands the true-north principles of success in corporate America. Roger and his team took the raw talent I developed through service as an officer in the U.S. Air Force and coached me on strategy, personal branding, and execution of my PCS from the military to a Fortune 500 company. I am blessed with a thriving career and continue to follow Roger's wise advice every day in leading a global business. His wisdom is highly relevant in today's fast-changing business environment. *PCS* is a must-read.

Law Burks
Vice President and General Manager
ITW Medical Products, Illinois Tool Works

•

PCS to Corporate America was not the typical book on how to prepare for a job interview, but rather a comprehensive book to successfully launch my new career into the business world. The strategies and information not only opened doors for me as a JMO but also have assisted me in preparing for cross-functional and new company moves throughout the past 15 years. A big thanks to the Cameron-Brooks team.

Andrew Shipe
Vice President, Marketing
ARAMARK Sports and Entertainment

•

By applying the concepts and lessons in *PCS to Corporate America*, I was able to better market my skill set by understanding what the corporate world expected. Ultimately, I was able to land the career field and company of my choice, and the skills I learned continue to benefit me as a leader and a manager.

Alan Swanton
Manager, Strategic Category Management, Noble Energy, Inc.

It has been 16 years since I read *PCS to Corporate America,* and I still recall the confidence that its guidance and road map provided me in making my decision to pursue my career in industry. The book provides direct and grounded counsel on how to prepare yourself for the transition as well as complete the self-inspection required to leverage your strengths and talents in your new career. I still remind myself of key messages, such as "Always be connecting" in my career and personal life today. I personally appreciate the focus that *PCS to Corporate America* brought to my transition and, looking back, I would not have pursued it any other way.

> Jeff Kent
> *Technical Associate Director, Procter & Gamble*

•

PCS to Corporate America was an invaluable tool to help make the transition from military officer to corporate leader. It provides a road map to take the knowledge and skills obtained in the military and turn yourself into someone to be noticed during the interview process and rewarded in your career with exciting opportunities. I still use the interviewing skills and tips on how to improve my performance in my everyday routine. I appreciate Roger taking the time to create this highly effective tool on how to succeed in today's corporate world.

> Kevin Robles
> *Vice President of Operations, INVISTA*

•

To enter the business world successfully and sustain that success requires hard work and attention to detail. Roger's book puts all of the details together for you and just requires your commitment to work hard. And as your career grows, the wisdom you have taken from *PCS* will continue to resonate with you.

> D. Mark Wittschen
> *Consumer Sales Manager / Vice President, Regions Bank*

•

Since joining my company 16 years ago, I have used *PCS to Corporate America* extensively to prepare for interviews and new job responsibilities. Roger's book is fundamental to my success as much today as it was when I transitioned to corporate America—this book is about real success and it truly rivals some of the best business books out there.

> Todd Kinser
> *Vice President, Research & Development, Ethicon*

When I transitioned out of the U.S. Air Force, *PCS to Corporate America* was the single most useful tool I used to help prepare for interviews with Fortune 500 companies! After going through at least 14 interviews with prospective employers, there wasn't a single question I was asked that I wasn't prepared to answer after reading *PCS to Corporate America*. I even used *PCS to a Corporate America* to help prepare for promotional interviews within my company, and it helped me get promoted twice. I highly recommend this book to any JMO looking to transition out of the military and into corporate America!

Ryan Luecke
Divisional Manager, Ethicon

•

I find that most people are willing to do hard work. Unfortunately, the road map to success is not often very easy to navigate. *PCS to Corporate America* provides the best road map I know of for military officers wishing to transition to the business world—if the person is willing to work hard, the destination can be reached when you follow *PCS to Corporate America*.

Chris M. Sutter
Project Services Area Supervisor, ExxonMobil Development

•

PCS to Corporate America was instrumental to my successful and positive transition into a civilian career. Roger's book clearly articulated a proven process to support a major career change choice that cemented my decision to pursue a career in business. The book provided business skills and knowledge that gave me an edge while entering corporate America and continues to be valuable today in growing my career.

Greg J. Jensen
Commercial Program Manager, Operations-Americas Finance
Dresser-Rand Company

•

PCS to Corporate America provided a conduit for me to understand how best to connect my military experiences to the corporate world. Further, it created context and dialogue around the transition process that not only provided a framework on how best to tell my story in the interview process, but built my confidence as a future business leader.

Jason Derstler
Business Unit Manager, Johnson & Johnson

PCS to Corporate America is essential reading for anyone in the military seriously considering a transition to the business world. For me it proved to be more than a primer on interview preparation, but also a reference guide on professional behavior and habits consistent with the military ethos of loyalty, hard work, and commitment.

> Rob Mercuri
> *Manager, Financial Services Advisory*
> *PricewaterhouseCoopers LLP*

•

Leaving the Air Force was a huge decision in my life! It was scary because I had a wife and three children under the age of five and I had to declare I was leaving the Air Force before I had secured a job in corporate America. After reading *PCS to Corporate America*, it was obvious to me that Cameron-Brooks had the right leadership, process, and contacts in corporate America to make my personal transition successful. The tools and methods for interview preparation and execution that I learned with Cameron-Brooks during my preparation for the Career Conference were superb, and I still use them today.

> Robert Sackett
> *Vice President, Franchise Operations Development, Ethicon*

•

Read this book! It is the most direct information source positioned just for the military officer and provides what you need to know for the most successful transition out of the military and into corporate America. Questions you have now—like "Why would someone want to hire an officer?" and "What kind of position would I be best for in the civilian world?" to "What should I wear to an interview?" or "What questions will I be asked?"—are all answered in this book. It's a must-read. Since I transitioned from the military into corporate America, every lesson Roger and his team have taught me has not just been helpful but also critical to my success.

> Marla K. Bradbury
> *Associate Vice President of Marketing and Advertising*
> *Apollo Group, Institute for Professional Development*

PCS opened my eyes to a professional, structured approach for effectively translating and communicating my military accomplishments to the corporate equivalent. This book is unique in the recruiting community, and it provided the confidence needed for my decision to transition out of the military. Roger provides actionable information targeted against specific challenges faced by transitioning military officers. Since my transition, I have had the pleasure to lead inside two Fortune 100 companies. Through the years, *PCS* remains on my shelf and is the first resource I turn to for corporate transitions. Welcome to the first step in building the skills required for a career of transitions.

> Ed Barchak
> *Manager, FedEx*

•

PCS to Corporate America provided a paradigm shift in the way I thought about corporate America. Sales techniques seem foreign to many JMOs. However, I quickly learned from *PCS* that the skills I gained selling ideas to commanders could directly translate to medical device sales. I still think back to the many words of advice Roger has offered in *PCS* and use them every day. Listening skills, asking open-ended questions, building rapport, and cross-functional leadership are critical to success in sales and the business world.

> Ben Berkowick
> *Territory Manager, Biosense Webster, Inc.*

•

PCS to Corporate America removed some of the fear that I had when I made the decision to separate. I think we all wonder, "Will corporate America want me?" The answer you will find in the book is a resounding "Yes!" From there it will help you showcase your skills so that more opportunities than you thought possible will be presented to you.

> Steve Carney
> *Regional Sales Manager, Boston Scientific Corporation*

•

When I left the Army, I wasn't sure how to make the transition, or confident that anyone would hire me. *PCS to Corporate America* laid out a map for the journey. Get the right "map, compass, and provisions" for your journey. Read, listen, and make a successful transition.

> Kerwin Hoversten
> *Senior Director / Head, Integrated Semi Service Products*
> *Applied Materials*

PCS to Corporate America truly prepared me for every interviewing scenario and has also helped me broaden my professional development and inspired me to continue to develop throughout my corporate career. *PCS to Corporate America* is basically "How to Get a Great Career in Corporate America for Dummies." Everyone leaving the military for the business world should read it, even if you don't decide to utilize Cameron-Brooks.

>Mac Johnson
>*Professional Education Manager, Ethicon*

•

I read *PCS to Corporate America* four times from cover to cover, and my wife also read it. Because of this, we were in the right mind-set every step of the way: making the decision to separate, choosing the right recruiter, perfecting my resume, practicing for interviews, completing the reading list, buying the right suits, interviewing initially and in follow-ups, and finally accepting and declining offers. Even five years later, I continue to benefit from the advice, readings, and mind-set gained from *PCS* and the Cameron-Brooks experience.

>Alex Svetlev
>*Supply Planning Manager, Whirlpool Corporation*

•

Fourteen years ago, *PCS* helped me realize my skills were needed in corporate America and helped me land my dream job one year later at a Cameron-Brooks conference. Today, still with the same great company, I use *PCS* to prepare for promotional interviews as well as a quick review before I head to a Cameron Brooks conference to interview candidates! As you look to make the transition from combat boots to dress shoes, *PCS* is a must-read. Read *PCS*, take the advice of the Cameron Brooks team, and start a powerful career.

>Bill Bentley
>*Division Manager, Ethicon*

Since 1996 I have relied on the techniques and discipline I learned from Cameron-Brooks and *PCS to Corporate America* in order to develop and implement my career progression plan. Roger, thanks for what you did for me and what you and your team continue to do, helping our teammates in the armed forces make one of their most important PCS moves ever.

> Nelson Santini
> *Senior Vice President and General Manager*
> *Bridgeline Digital*

•

PCS to Corporate America provided me a reality check. It helped me not only to better understand how my Army leadership experience was valuable in the business world but, most important, to develop additional skills to be successful in corporate America. The book was of great value and Cameron-Brooks has developed a genius process to prepare any JMO to be a success in corporate America. I highly recommend this book to JMOs who are serious about their future.

> Wenqing Su
> *Offshore Installation & Project Logistics*
> *ExxonMobil Development Company*

•

PCS to Corporate America took away some of the ambiguity and myth around working in a corporate environment. It gave me confidence in my transition by providing subtle but important insights about everything from behavioral-based interviewing to dressing professionally for the corporate world. *PCS* still guides me when interviewing candidates and advising others on how to interview. It has also helped me as I interview for new roles at each stage of my career, giving me confidence every time I interview.

> Michael L. High
> *Onshore Management Information Manager, Royal Dutch Shell*

•

PCS to Corporate America is the playbook to make that transition and for success in business and life. Roger Cameron captures the essence of servant leadership and personal accountability that we all strive to emulate and instills in us the vision to move from aspiring military leaders to aspiring business leaders.

> Roland Tink
> *Contracts & Procurement Site Lead, Motiva Enterprises*

Perhaps the number one thing I learned from *PCS to Corporate America* and the Cameron-Brooks experience is that it is highly important to be prepared to succinctly describe your experiences and qualifications. Taking the time up front to know yourself and what you want and then translating that self-knowledge into crisp talking points will pay many personal dividends—even beyond your next interview. For 12 years this lesson has stuck with me.

> Phillip Bell
> *Product Line Manager, New Business Development*
> *Corning, Inc.*

•

I found *PCS* to be a very valuable resource during my transition. It effectively complemented the extensive Cameron-Brooks transition program, providing solid reference and additional context to many of the themes and key preparation points. *PCS* provides excellent guidance on translating military leadership experiences into the right business language for the interview. With anything in business, clear communication is critical. The book's approach helped me share my background and qualifications in "business terms" that were relevant and impactful throughout the hiring process. I highly recommend *PCS to Corporate America* to any JMO transitioning to corporate America—and as a dependable reference to support future promotional preparation.

> Jason Howe
> *General Manager, Global Accounts, Schneider National, Inc.*

•

While I knew I wanted to transition to the business community like most JMOs, I had no idea how to successfully do so. *PCS to Corporate America* provides a clear road map on how to transition to the business world. The recommended reading gives much of the terminology and concepts required to have a fair start. The interviewing strategy continues to aid in the difficult task of defining the challenges, action, and outcomes of what we do on a day-to-day basis.

> Peter Taczanowsky
> *Inventory Control Manager, Pyramid Tubular Products*

PCS to Corporate America was a critical resource as I prepared to transition from my role in the Army to my career in marketing. The interviewing approach provided in this book made the conversations I had with potential employers both efficient and effective. This is a great resource—leverage it to its fullest.

> Clint McClain
> *Senior Director, Marketing, Wal-Mart Stores, Inc.*

•

PCS to Corporate America provided me with a wealth of knowledge in regards to multiple facets of interview preparation along with communicating my military experience to corporate America. Still to this day I am able to articulate my experience in a way to executives and business partners that adds value to my personal brand. It's a great road map to begin the journey in knowing thyself, understanding what corporate America is looking for, and developing the confidence to get companies to say yes.

> Drew Burke
> *Joint Ventures Manager, Shell Oil Products U.S.*

•

PCS to Corporate America was the first book I read as I considered a transition from the Army. Roger's impressive knowledge and articulation of what it takes to exceed the high standards of entry into corporate America were evident, and I consumed the book in only a few short hours. As I naturally wrestled with the uncertainty of such a significant transition, I considered *PCS* my go-to manual or playbook before, during, and after my transition in order to help me achieve my transition goals.

> Mark Riegel
> *Brand Manager, Kraft Foods*

•

PCS to Corporate America did a great job of providing real-life examples of what officers can expect when transitioning to a corporate position. It helped to alleviate much of the fear of the unknown that I think many transitioning officers might feel. For me, the book was a very valuable resource throughout the transition process—from helping me to make the decision to leave the military, to interviewing for jobs, all the way through the first few years in my new role.

> Pete Eichhorst
> *Manager, Software Engineering, Boston Scientific Corporation*

PCS to Corporate America is thought-provoking, practical, and insightful. I love Roger's simplicity and wisdom to prepare the JMO in making a career-changing transition. Corporate America is starving for leaders, and Roger provides wonderful perspectives and tools for developing leaders at all levels. These concepts have been tremendously influential in shaping my leadership approach and in building my teams.

> Tom D. Anderson
> *Regional Vice President, Sales, Medtronic Spinal & Biologics*

•

From the age of 12, I have tried to live the motto "Be Prepared." *PCS to Corporate America* has been, and continues to be, one of the sharpest tools available in my pursuit of that ideal. *PCS* is truly the "secret sauce" that created a road map for winning every aspect of the interviewing process and translating my military accomplishments into relevant stories in business. Even today, it keeps people wondering how I manage to get such strong starts on a new assignment or recruit so thoroughly for the future of our company. Leaders are readers and this isn't a book—it's a kickoff to your career.

> Dom Alcocer
> *Marketing Manager, General Mills*

•

PCS to Corporate America was my personal "go-to" guide for everything related to my transition from the military. The book gave me many "ah-ha" moments, most of which I still use to this day. I can't imagine a smooth and successful transition without the nuggets of knowledge packed in *PCS*. Ten years after my original *PCS*, I look forward to the fourth edition as a refresher and reminder of the basics of corporate America.

> Robert Griffin
> *On-Site Plant Operations and Engineering Manager, Linde Group*

•

PCS to Corporate America is the best black and white preparation you will get when transitioning from the military to corporate America. Roger's preparation is the only way to get ready for *your career* beyond the service, and *PCS to Corporate America* is the guide.

> Isaac Nelson
> *Plant Complex Manager, Air Liquide*

Coming from the military, you already possess all of the critical attributes that companies value: work ethic, problem-solving, integrity, and leadership. Unfortunately, there is language barrier between corporate America and the military. *PCS to Corporate America* was an irreplaceable translation guide for me. It was the "workbook" that allowed me to be successful and begin a new career. The greatest value, however, was allowing me to visualize what the corporate world was. Roger's lessons are timeless and have become the foundation of a great journey.

Brian DeBoda
Vice President of Sales, Covidien

•

PCS is all about the fundamentals . . . and don't kid yourself: the fundamentals still matter. It is also about taking charge of your future. In today's business world, the transition from serving in the military to serving (leading) in corporate America happens at a faster pace than ever. Making that transition in a successful way requires your commitment and dedication (preparation, planning and execution)—something we are used to doing in the military. *PCS* is the GPS to get you started in the right direction and keep you going along the journey. Take Charge, Start Strong (with *PCS*). You'll be amazed where it can take you.

Philip Cobb
Sales Director, Ethicon

•

I have known Roger Cameron for over 20 years as both a candidate and recruiter. All junior military officers planning on pursuing a career in corporate America would be wise to read *PCS to Corporate America* and apply the lessons Roger so ably distills in this book. *PCS* is the "10" every JMO should study and apply to maximize their interviewing skills. In fact, it is excellent reading for anyone who wants to interview at their best. As a hiring authority, I have personally interviewed several hundred candidates over the years. I am no longer surprised by the poor interviewing skills exhibited by many candidates, but those who read *PCS* and partner with Cameron-Brooks are always extremely well prepared.

David J. Brady
Director, Integrated Planning & Operations
G3 Manufacturing, G3 Enterprises

Trust Roger Cameron and read *PCS*. It will prepare you more thoroughly for interview day than you could possibly prepare yourself. More importantly, you'll leave the military with a solid understanding of business language, priorities, and culture. By reading *PCS* and partnering with Roger and his team, I hit the ground running as a consultant and laid the foundation for a successful 11-year (and running!) career. If you're willing to push yourself hard, Roger and his team will help you reach your full potential. They are the best.

> Michael J. Scheller
> *Director, PricewaterhouseCoopers LLP*

•

With age comes wisdom, with wisdom comes knowledge, with knowledge comes the responsibility to impart it into others. *PCS to Corporate America* is a timeless resource for making not just a transition into the corporate world, but for truly thriving during the process and enabling success as the outcome. I thoroughly recommend this book to prospective junior military officers considering such a career change. *PCS* is one asset that will always be there for you.

> Bill Martin
> *Sales Support Director, Dell, Inc.*

•

Deciding to transition to corporate America was a significant life decision for me—a decision that carried great uncertainty. The Army helped build a solid foundation of personal integrity, decision making, and leadership. However, translating those military qualities into successful corporate attributes I found quite unclear. *PCS to Corporate America* and working with the Cameron-Brooks team enabled me to bridge those characteristics into the practical direction needed to immediately succeed in a new company.

> Charles C. Gunst
> *Business Analysis and Reporting Supervisor, ExxonMobil*

•

PCS is the *premier* preparation tool for candidates to manage their transition to corporate America. Seeking advice from trusted and proven experts is critical as we successfully navigate through life—medical, legal, financial. When managing one of the most important events—a transition to corporate America—rely on the advice from the most accomplished expert in the JMO recruiting industry: Roger Cameron.

> Mark Voss
> *National Sales Manager, Pactiv Foodservice*

PCS to Corporate America is a must-read. I still have certain pages bookmarked, and lots of pages are filled with highlights. The main take-away for me was how to analyze my military background, see my strengths and weaknesses, and use the real-life examples to show how my military experiences would translate to the corporate world. I've been asked many times over the past few years how I landed this position. Without a doubt, I owe Roger and his team the credit for preparing me for corporate America from interviews to post-transition. I still keep in touch with my Cameron-Brooks advisor. I consider him my "career mentor."

Lisa Schad
Market Development Manager/Field Sales Associate
American Medical Systems

•

PCS to Corporate America was an instrumental tool in helping me prepare my transition from the U.S. Army to corporate America. The book provided essential guidelines for taking that critical first step into corporate America. For me, the most helpful aspects of the book were its direct and clear language that told me, as a junior military officer, what I should expect from corporate America and what corporate America would expect from me. I continue to reference *PCS to Corporate America* to help prepare for interviews, either as the interviewer or interviewee. Its rules and guidelines are timeless.

Joseph Linn
Sales and Marketing Manager, Abbott Diabetes Care

•

PCS to Corporate America is a must-read for any military officer looking to transition out of the military. It serves as a lifelong guide to building a bridge between your accomplishments and how they can be used in corporate America. In addition, *PCS to Corporate America* is relevant beyond that military transition. I made my transition to corporate America three years ago and most recently used my copy to prepare for an interview for a promotion here at my company.

Porsche J. Wilson
Claims Manager, Regions Bank

PCS to Corporate America is a true road map to selling yourself. Through Roger's guidance and the information in his book, I was able to take the accomplishments from my military experience and relate them meaningfully to the corporate world. I would have most certainly been lost without it! These lessons still apply in my current roles. Whether selling myself in an interview or selling our products to a customer, I find myself using the techniques in PCS.

Steve Dean
Plant Manager, Cardinal Glass Industries

•

By reading *PCS to Corporate America* and partnering with Roger Cameron's team, I learned the value of knowing yourself inside and out prior to an interview and then looking for ways to connect on a personal level with the interviewer. I have prepared many others to interview using a similar process, and the results are always much better than for those who don't know the value of good preparation.

Jim Bourne
Franchise Operations Director
Advanced Sterilization Products

•

Leaving the military to join corporate America is unlike any change you ever experienced in your career and perhaps your life. PCS becomes your road map and pocket field guide, giving you valuable tools, real-life examples, pitfalls to avoid, and lots of practical advice that is useful in any situation. Decades of experience will be shared with you in this book, and you will be amazed when you witness firsthand the advice from this book playing out right before your very eyes, but to your benefit. You will underline and bookmark many pages and keep it handy even after you have started your new career. I reference it regularly when interviewing for internal positions and often refer to it when advising others on interviewing.

Steve Philips
Profit Forecaster, Procter & Gamble

I read Roger Cameron's book, *PCS to Corporate America*, in advance of the interviewing process. *PCS*, along with the practice question dialogue, helped to appropriately frame and communicate my value proposition to a company. I did not realize it at the time, but the extensive preparation really built skills for interviewing—skills I did not have previously. Not only was this important for my own interviews, but also as a coach to others. It has been great to use this skill to help others prepare for, compete, and win new roles within the organization. The book serves as a great reference.

Jamey Friel
Senior Manager, Planning and Logistics, Roche Carolina, Inc.

•

PCS to Corporate America was by far the most useful piece of information I had while transitioning from the Marine Corps to corporate America. It provided me with the much-needed "internship" I missed while doing my master's on active duty, and truly prepared me for the types of career paths that awaited me on the other side. Both as an interviewee and as an interviewer, *PCS* has provided me with more insight, knowledge and relatable skills than any other book I have come across for those having served. Over a decade later, it still remains the one book I consistently recommend to those seeking advice about leaving the military.

Dan Martin
District Sales Manager, Medtronic Spinal & Biologics

•

Roger Cameron is right. A military officer's strategic thinking ability, the drive to make things happen, plus being extremely well organized, energetic, intensely curious, and approachable are strongly sought after in corporate America—and not just at hiring time. These characteristics distinguish the top performers throughout a civilian career. Roger knows this, and he knows how to help a military officer clearly show these traits during an interview. *PCS to Corporate America* is an absolute "must-read" for a military officer preparing for a transition to a civilian career.

Anita Riddle
Sourcing Manager, Procurement
ExxonMobil Global Services Company

For JMOs leaving the military, this is the must-read book. For anyone leaving the military, this is the must-read book. For anyone looking for a job, looking for another job, looking for a promotion, or looking to better themselves in preparation for a promotion, this is the must-read book. Roger and his team expertly provide what has been called a "mini MBA." And you are now holding his syllabus.

Eric Olsen
Maintenance Manager, Cargill, Inc.

•

PCS to Corporate America and the entire Cameron-Brooks team were instrumental in helping me prepare for my transition to the corporate world. *PCS* and the Cameron-Brooks recruiters asked me questions I needed to ask myself to ensure my decision to leave the military was sound and then guided me through the journey of preparing myself for what companies would be seeking in a junior military officer. Not surprisingly, the preparation they guided me through 15-plus years ago is still applicable today in my business career.

David Tomasi
Marketing Director, Procter & Gamble

PCS

TO CORPORATE AMERICA

FOURTH EDITION

PCS

TO CORPORATE AMERICA

From Military Tactics to Corporate Interviewing Strategy

by Roger Cameron

with Chuck Alvarez and Joel Junker

SHEARER PUBLISHING
FREDERICKSBURG, TEXAS

Shearer Publishing
406 Post Oak Road
Fredericksburg, Texas 78624
Toll-free: 800-458-3808
Fax: 830-997-9752

www.shearerpub.com

CIP Data on file with publisher

ISBN 978-0-940672-85-7

First edition 1990
Second edition 1994
Third edition 2000
Fourth edition 2012

Printed in Canada

Contents

HOW TO GAIN THE MOST FROM THIS BOOK

I n 1990 I wrote the first edition of *PCS to Corporate America*. Since then I have received very positive feedback from JMOs regarding the book's value in helping them prepare for corporate interviews and a transition to the business world. However, the interviewing world is very dynamic—a world in which better methods of identifying and selecting talented employees are constantly evolving. I rewrote *PCS* in 1994 and 2000, identifying changes that had occurred, clarifying points, and bringing up new issues. Again, I received positive feedback both times I rewrote it. Due to the changes in both the business world and military environment since September 11, 2001, I am excited to work with Joel and Chuck to write the fourth edition of *PCS*. I feel confident that this updated edition includes new information that will benefit you and increase your opportunities for interviewing and business career success. As always, you must take *action* to gain the full benefit of this book.

My intent for this book is to address the bottom line. You won't find any fluff. I felt it best to write a book you could get into immediately, one that focuses on what you need to do to be successful in interviews and to make a successful transition to the business world.

You won't find in this book what you, as a military officer, already do so well. Many things are so innate to you that I don't need to discuss them. Often after having gone through Cameron-

Brooks interviewing workshops, military officers come away feeling as if they will never do anything right. In this book we address only the issues you have a tendency to miss or approach incorrectly. Reading a book about things that are natural to you and that you already know how to do would be a waste of your time and mine. Some of the suggestions in *PCS* may challenge you. However, I feel strongly that it is my responsibility to cover topics that could prevent you from making a successful transition. I am proud to be one of the originators of the process that transitions military officers successfully to the business world. My goal is to help you do just that.

Throughout this book I recommend ways of addressing specific questions. It is not my intent that you repeat the verbiage word for word. Instead, use the suggested ideas and develop your own answers. Be yourself. If you allow a company to hire you while you hide behind a facade, it won't work. Ultimately, the company will wonder why they hired you. Make sure a company hires you for who you are rather than what you might pretend to be during your interviews. If some of the concepts in this book are new to you and you agree with them, begin immediately to use them at work and in your life. In this way, by the time you begin interviewing, you will be giving credible information to the recruiter.

Hopefully, you are reading *PCS* long before you make your transition. While the book is valuable at all times, its value is enhanced the earlier in your military career you read it. I often talk with officers who share with me the value that *PCS* added to their successful transitions and business careers. Without fail, each of these officers recounts a systematic approach to reading the book, along with specific points that enabled them to retain and apply what they learned. I want to share the following three steps with you to help you, too, gain the most from *PCS*.

1. Read *PCS* cover to cover over two to three days. Do not stop to do the recommended exercises. It is important to understand all the points the book covers and the significance given to different issues.

2. Slowly reread *PCS*. If you are reading this in the printed version, use a highlighter or multiple highlighters of different colors to highlight issues of their unique importance. If you are reading this as an e-book, use the highlighter function so you can refer later to key notes. Whether you are reading a digital or printed version, stop and take notes. I highly recommend you do it right in the book versus on a separate pad so all of the information is right there in one place. You can also make special remarks and notes relative to your situation and development.

3. Now read the book again. Practice all exercises using a recording device (in many cases a video recorder is ideal) and a notebook for additional reference. Evaluate each exercise. Listen to and watch the recordings with study partners whose judgment and constructive feedback will be of benefit. Take advantage of all material in the book, including the information in the Appendix. Practice, practice, practice!

PCS will become one of the most important books in your library. As your career progresses and you interview for promotion, do not assume you will automatically recall your interviewing techniques. Reread *PCS*. As you gain the responsibility of interviewing and hiring for your company and are required to identify individuals and recommend them for hire, your credibility is on the line. Reread *PCS*. Utilize *PCS* long-term and make it your primary career resource.

Most importantly, I caution you in loaning out your copy of *PCS* to anyone. You may not get it back! The value of your remarks and references represents an extensive amount of dedicated time, along with important development notes that will make a difference in your career. Direct your friends who want to borrow your copy of *PCS* to our Web site at www.cameron-brooks.com where they can place their own order.

ACKNOWLEDGMENTS

I want to give a warm thanks to the members of the Cameron-Brooks team who have been "cornerstones" assisting me in writing my books. Each has traveled thousands of miles with me during their careers, offering quality insight and advice. It would have been impossible to experience success without them.

I especially want to thank Chuck Alvarez and Joel Junker, who helped me write this fourth edition. Chuck joined Cameron-Brooks in 1994 and has had a tremendous impact in growing Cameron-Brooks. He is the current president of Cameron-Brooks and future CEO. His insight and depth of experience from his work with our client companies added a lot of value to this edition. Joel joined Cameron-Brooks in 1999 right out of the U.S. Army. He worked closely with Cameron-Brooks client companies for over 10 years and now leads our candidate recruiting effort. He has interviewed thousands of military officers, providing advice on their business marketability and helping them reach their personal and professional goals. The future of Cameron-Brooks is bright with their leadership.

To my friends, business associates, clients, and Cameron-Brooks alumni who continually encourage and support our organization and me, a special thank-you and appreciation. I have had the best job in America, having the opportunity to interact with so many exceptional people.

Those of you who have written words of praise as readers of

PCS deserve a special acknowledgment. It has been inspirational to hear from thousands whose lives have been and continue to be impacted positively as a result of this book. I cannot count the number of individuals who have told me they consistently refer to *PCS* for promotional interview preparation and furthering their careers. These individuals espouse the long-term value of the many lessons taught in this book.

I am appreciative of the Cameron-Brooks alumni in corporate America who are passionate about hiring JMOs and hiring them from Cameron-Brooks. At every one of our Career Conferences, it gives me great satisfaction to work with the many alumni who attend our conferences in search of hiring talented JMOs and to hear of their successes in their business careers.

Thank you to the many business leaders in corporate America for believing in the quality of our military officers. Many of our client companies have been hiring junior officers from us for over 45 years and have watched the JMO move up the corporate ladder to the very top.

Finally, thank you to all of the military service members for your selfless service and sacrifices for our great country. I have met so many officers and their spouses who have made tremendous sacrifices as we continue to fight the war on terrorism throughout the world. I am grateful for your leadership, courage, and fortitude! Our country is in your debt.

INTRODUCTION

You are likely reading this book to learn more about a business career, or if you have already made that decision to transition, you want to develop a plan and strategy. Regardless of where you are in this thought process, I want you to first understand your leadership advantage and why companies value the military experience. Our clients value your abilities and experience—in developing teamwork, adapting to change, exercising cross-functional leadership, improving processes, solving complex problems, managing projects, changing behaviors, counseling and mentoring others, focusing on results, and applying a make-it-happen attitude. These qualities are your leadership advantage. Compared to those who graduated from college and have been working in business for four to eight years, you typically have more leadership experience. More and more companies see the value in hiring you for your leadership qualities and then teaching you the fundamentals of their business.

Even though there are many companies who hire junior military officers, not all companies value your military experience for the same reason. Not all companies know how to fully utilize your JMO background. Generally, there are three ways for JMOs to transition from the military to the business world:

1. Transition *down* into a business career. In this case the JMO takes a position with a company that does not value the JMO experience and therefore ends up in a position that

11

has less responsibility than he or she had in the service. I am sure these companies have good intentions, but to value your experience means the company knows how to utilize the JMO's unique skills and abilities developed while in the military and offers the JMO positions that build on top of that experience. To transition down, the JMO usually interviews and accepts a position that he or she could have earned right out of college or a few years after college without the military experience. You might ask, "Why would a JMO do this?" Every career choice you make has trade-offs. Most often I see JMOs make a decision to do this because they want a specific geographic location or perhaps because they want an industry that predominantly recruits off the college campus. Unfortunately, I hear from a few every year wanting to start a career search all over because they are not fully utilized. It's a tough way for a talented young leader to launch a new career.

2. Transition *across* into a business career. In this case the JMO takes a position with the responsibility and career upside that is equivalent to what he or she had in the military. Companies who hire these types of military backgrounds will hire any JMO, regardless of how successful the JMO was in the military. In other words, the company places value on the JMO's military experience (unlike the first situation), but does not distinguish between different-caliber JMOs. While this type of career will utilize your skills, it will take time to move into a position that is considered developmental, and potentially you might not ever have the opportunity to get into a development track. Very often we see this type of hiring in positions that require security clearances. The company is not interested in your military track record, but rather, it just wants to take advantage of your clearance. These are usually easy transitions, but seldom provide much career opportunity.

3. Transition and *accelerate* into a business career. In this case the JMO takes a development position with a company who values the military officer experience, starts in a position that will build on top of the JMO experience, *and* offers significant promotional opportunities based on performance. The companies who offer these types of opportunities value top-caliber JMOs because of their leadership track record and leadership potential. These are extremely competitive positions to obtain, and companies look for the best of the best. While these types of positions are highly desirable, they also require the highest level of preparation and skill development.

Cameron-Brooks recruits only for development positions in corporate America, positions that will allow you to *transition and accelerate*. Therefore, our clients are selective and require us to partner with officers who have the demonstrated *ability* and *desire* to grow into senior leadership positions in a company. Military officers who form a career transition partnership with Cameron-Brooks read numerous business books, increase their communication skills, improve their objective skill base, and prepare for competitive interviewing. It seems the better the candidates are, the earlier they start their preparation. They are not procrastinators. They know it takes a lot of time and preparation to be at their best and to transition and accelerate.

In order to earn an employment offer from a company where you will accelerate into your next career, *you must be at your best by the time you start your interviewing*. These types of leading companies expect you to interview at 100 percent. After all, they can be very selective because they have highly desirable career opportunities. To be successful in this type of a transition, you must start early in your transition process to prepare to be at your best. It is critical that you understand this concept. Companies will never believe you are better than what their recruiters see or hear in the interview. *Your goal as you prepare for a career transition is to prove you have the ability and desire to be a future leader in business.*

How do you achieve "being at you best"? Preparation. Hard work. Realistic preparation. Recruiters have said to me, "Roger, if an individual won't work hard to accomplish one of his or her own objectives (a great career), why should I assume he or she will work hard to accomplish objectives that we give them?" I have to agree. Amazingly, some officers will come to the marketplace assuming success without preparation. This is like having an annual inspection on Monday morning but starting preparation for it on the previous Friday, or expecting to be successful in a deployment without first conducting diligent and realistic training. You know what will happen. You will fail. You may say that you should be natural interviewees. That would be great, but it won't work. Most officers I interview want the opportunity to transition and accelerate their career, but not every officer is willing to commit to world-class preparation to accomplish this goal. You have to prepare for tough objectives. And, as you know, the more time you invest in preparation and the more realistic it is, the more successful you are.

You learned this early on in school: The more time you invested in studying and the more you focused on the areas you needed to master, the better you did on the exam. Everything in life is based on preparation. Not one of us is natural at everything we do. I put Cameron-Brooks' success for facilitating transitions to corporate America against any other recruiting firm or recruiter in America. I have listened to what great companies are looking for, and I have seen the kind of individuals they are hiring to lead their companies into the future. I have seen the individuals who have gone to the top of corporate America. I recognize the pattern. It is a pattern created from day one—the pattern of preparation and diligence—of people who do their work thoroughly. It is gratifying to watch the career progression of those officers we have helped transition to the business world.

To transition and interview into positions that will allow you to accelerate also requires strong communication skills. Rarely do company recruiters read your military evaluations. Instead, you must communicate in an interview what you have done, how you have done it, the results you achieved, and how this relates to corporate America. Unfortunately, some people who are probably very good performers are not going to be hired because of their inability to communicate. Company recruiters will evaluate your interviewing skills to determine if you will have the ability to communicate, to persuade, and to convince or persuade your peers, superiors, team members, customers, and competition to see your point of view. People say, "Roger, if they would hire me, they would see that I'm a good performer." Sometimes I feel the same way. If they would just hire some military officers, they would discover how talented they are. Unfortunately, recruiting just doesn't work that way. You will need to be a good communicator to interview successfully.

I am frequently asked, "What is the bottom line, Roger? What is corporate America looking for in development candidates?" This is a good question.

Corporations want people who possess the following:

- Leadership. In general, this means the ability to catalyze actions in others in order to achieve results. The type of leadership (Team, Cross-Functional, Up, Idea, Change, etc.) depends on the position.
- Ability to get real-world results. What do companies mean by "real world?" They mean results that impacted the military's bottom line (readiness, fighting capability, mission success) and achieved the required results by overcoming obstacles or challenges.
- Self-development. They want military officers who are constantly striving to improve themselves both objectively and subjectively and who lead and develop others to do the same.
- Ability to control their environment, use their time effectively, and are extremely well organized.
- Knowledge of exactly what needs to be done, when it needs to be done, and how to get it done.

Cameron-Brooks recruiters and I have accepted approximately 15 percent of all the officers we have interviewed. We are looking for those qualities listed above. Often people say, "Roger Cameron and Cameron-Brooks recruiters are tough." We are tough because corporate America is very demanding. Companies come to us to hire their future leaders. They want to see only the best of the best. We listen to our client companies. We bring them what they tell us they want. We are selective because our clients are selective.

This book is written in a very direct way, but that is pretty much the way corporate America thinks. I have watched recruiters decline individuals I felt were very capable. In fact, I knew they were good because I had read their performance evaluations, but because they did not have the ability to communicate their successes, recruiters walked away from them.

Even though the book is direct and to the point, I encourage you to read with a positive attitude. Say to yourself, "I'm going to listen to an individual who has worked with military officers and helped transition them successfully to the business world for over three decades."

This book will help you interview for any position in any organization. I would like to put my plug in for the profit-oriented world, the world of capitalism. It is a world that is exciting and challenging. When I think of how young America is, I realize that our greatness is based on the innovative nature of the United States. We have been leaders in numerous areas for many years. Sure, it is true that some countries have copied products we originated and made them better because of circumstances in their countries, such as cheaper labor. But I will still put America against anyone else. I will put our leaders, engineers, finance people, and information technology experts up against any in the world.

Officers we assisted—10, 15, and 20 plus years ago—are still using many of the techniques our team and I taught them. I am very proud of our alumni. Each time I recruit an individual for corporate America, I ask myself the question, "Do I want to put my name beside this individual as he or she transitions to the business world?" This is important to every member of the Cameron- Brooks team. We want to be proud of every candidate we help transition to the business world. And, of the overwhelming majority, we can be. We have had very few failures over the years.

People have often asked how I could stay in this business for over 45 years. I always give the same answer. In all these years, I have had thousands of jobs presented to me, yet I have never seen a job that interested me enough to take more than a casual look at it. I'm not so sure that there is a more exciting business than that of recruiting talented young men and women for top development positions with some of the best companies in corporate America. It has been exciting to watch these young men and women move up the corporate ladder, have their successes, and become key leaders within their companies. I have received thousands of letters and e-mails of appreciation over the years, and every one of them made me feel good. They made me realize how fortunate I am to be in this business.

Working with the quality of companies I have represented over the years is very exciting. I have companies today who have a 10 percent growth rate, and some of them even higher. When you take a highly sophisticated company that has this kind of growth, you need to have outstanding people to accomplish and manage it. The military officers I have introduced to the business world have loved the fact that they are not practicing but are, in fact, *doing*. What they learn on a daily basis, they can apply. When they go home at night, they can measure the fact that their company has been able to take a step closer to its objective. It is challenging but also satisfying to be in an environment in which you know you must constantly be changing and improving. It is also gratifying to work with positive-minded people who come to work in the morning because they *want* to be there, who are excited about what their company does and what their products can do for mankind, and who find it exciting to be paid and promoted based on performance.

Recruiting military officers for corporate America has always been interesting. I cannot say it has always been fun. I remember when I helped originate this business; I talked to companies about why they should hire military officers. I also remember some of their comments: "Excuse me, Roger, you're suggesting that we should hire somebody who operates in the world of nonprofit, in the world of appropriation instead of the world of profitability?

Roger, what are we supposed to do with this individual who, for the last five years, has been involved with tanks, guns and artillery, airplanes and ships? I'm a little confused as to why we should hire this person. We should hire someone who is proud that he or she spends the entire budget? As a matter of fact, they even put it on their resumes."

That's the way things were when the military recruiting industry started. Interestingly, it has grown over the years—grown to the point where today military officers have demonstrated their value to corporate America. Today we can point to military officers who are presidents and CEOs of some of the nation's top companies. Suddenly, corporate recruiters who have been cynics over the years about military officers are starting to take a very hard look at them. Today companies are calling us rather than us calling them.

You've been good. As a matter of fact, you've been great! I don't know of any individual who has had more impact on corporate America than the military officer. We admit to you that we made a lot of mistakes over the years in evaluating military personnel, but today we know you very well. We know what makes you successful and what your weaknesses are as you leave the military. We have developed programs that will bring you up to speed quickly in areas where you need more development. We know where to recruit to find a particular background. We know what you need to do in the military to make yourself successful in business. Today we know the kind of private lifestyle you need for success in your business career. You were an unknown when we started this business. It has been fun to watch the progress of our candidates and yet agonizing to observe some of their failures. Fortunately, these failures are at a minimum in relation to what they were when we first started recruiting military officers.

I ask many of the Cameron-Brooks alumni who have been in the business world for a while what, if anything, they feel they have gained or lost by transitioning to the business world. Typically their comments pertain to three significant positives that never seem to change.

The first positive is the improved quality of life—the ability to tell your sons or daughters with confidence that you are going to be at Little League at 6:00 p.m., to tell your family you'll be home for dinner, to know that evenings and weekends are yours, to set a vacation six months down the road and know that you will be there. I have rarely seen a vacation canceled by a company in all the years I've been associated with corporate America.

The second positive relates to the input and control you have over your career. Companies ask you: "What is it you want to do? What kind of positions will enhance your career? What do you expect your company to do to ensure that you have a successful career?" You have a lot of input—veto rights for locations, positions, and the timing of promotions. When this veto right is exercised, it will *rarely* have a negative influence on your career.

Third, our candidates have told us that they have more ability to affect their compensation. Why? Because companies promote and pay based on performance; they have exceptional retirement plans such as 401(k) plans, with company-matching, and other savings vehicles as well. Now, this should not be the main reason you should make the transition, but it is a fact that business rewards are based on performance, and companies have much less rigid processes for promotions and compensation increases than the military's time-in-grade promotion program.

We get many other positive comments, but these three comments are the most significant in encouraging officers to make a career transition to the business world.

The Cameron-Brooks Alumni Association, made up of thousands of our candidates who have successfully transitioned to business, is a powerful influence in making the transition easier for our candidates. It is virtually impossible for you to come to corporate America without being touched by Cameron-Brooks, either by being hired, mentored, or managed by one of our alumni. This alumni network offers tremendous support to newly transitioned officers, their spouses (or significant others), and families. Our alumni will go out of their way to help make the transition as smooth as possible for you. One of the major reasons we have become such a powerful force in our industry is our alumni. Cameron-Brooks alumni are adamant about hiring junior officers for their positions and about hiring them from Cameron-Brooks.

As I've always said to military officers, it's not that one environment is good and the other bad. They are different. Some of you will determine that the military is better for you than the business world. We understand that. We like to think that as some of you read this book, you will feel more confident that corporate America is where you want to have your career. For those of you who make this choice, here's a word of caution. Do not think that corporate America is going to be a cure-all for the problems you might have had in the military. We have our problems. Some of the things we do are not always smart. We are influenced by economic conditions and have our ups and downs, just as the military has its own challenges.

There is no ideal company, job, or environment. However, I feel it is critically important that you come to corporate America as an individual who intends to go to work for a great company and have a career with that company. I know that this is considered the old-school way of thinking. However, I have seen way too many people leave companies at the wrong time, for the wrong reasons, without ever discussing the decision with their boss and thus not having all of the information. I am a strong advocate of conducting thorough and proper analysis to determine which company is right for you. I do not encourage moving constantly from one company to another. Sometime during the course of your career, some personal challenges will arise that will divert you from your job. These challenges will cause you to need special focus on your family. You want to know that your company will support you during these difficult times. Too many times people switch from one company to another, looking for that better situation, only to find greater difficulties. If you expect the company to remain with you during the difficult times of your life, it is only fair that you stay with the company during difficulties it might have. Many employees want to leave a company when they see the product lose market share. They reason that it is okay for the company to support them during *their* difficult times, but they don't want to reciprocate when the *company* has difficult times. That is not fair. I encourage you to be loyal. Switching from one company to another will not always advance your career. All you have really done is to change the problems. Every time you make a move, it is difficult for you and your family emotionally, and it says many things about you that you may not want said.

I hope you find this book a valuable tool for preparing for corporate interviews and a career transition. Anytime you have a question on an issue discussed in the book, feel free to contact Cameron-Brooks at candidates@cameron-brooks.com. I wish a book could cover everything, but I know it can't. It's similar to the preparation prior to our Career Conferences. We try to prepare for every question we think a candidate may encounter in an interview, but after years of experience, I have found corporate recruiters can still surprise me. I think you will find the major issues for military officers considering a transition to business covered in this book.

PCS is a career reference book. It is a book we hope you will read, refer to, reread, and refer to again as your career progresses. Do not loan it or any other reference book from your personal library. Throughout your career these books should never be out of arm's reach. There are some books I reread every year to remind me of valuable points. Every quality book should be read, referred to, and reread. Have fun reading it, and the best of success to you in your career search.

Chapter 1

THE EVALUATION PROCESS

In the early days of recruiting military officers, corporate America believed that the officer would have a difficult time being competitive in the business world as a Development Candidate. There were three basic reasons for this belief.

First, when we first started recruiting the military officer, most were leaving the military five to seven years after their age group graduated from college and entering the business world. That meant officers spent five to seven years in the nonprofit world (the military) and were then entering the world of profitability. Given the difference in experiences, how could the military officer realistically catch up to his or her business world contemporaries in minimal time?

I compare this situation to a track race in which you are competing with recent college graduates. To be considered a winner, you have to finish in the top 10 percent. No problem, you say. But when you get to the track and you're in the blocks, I reach down to tap you (the military officer) on the shoulder and I say, "By the way, when I pull the trigger, you stay at the blocks. Wait until all the college graduates in your age group get a fifth of the way around the track. Then you may start." Undoubtedly, you would stand up and say, "Come on, Roger, that's not realistic." Similarly, it makes sense that you, the military officer, would have a hard time catching up with your age group as you entered the business world. You notice that I said *age* group, not *year* group.

In the military you need to be concerned about being competitive with your *year* group. In contrast, when you begin a career in business, you are measured by your *age* group.

Second, as we examined the bulk of officers coming out of the military, we discovered that the majority had never used their college education as it was designed to be used. In other words, the military was not taking advantage of officers' education. For example, you could be an engineer in a military operational role that does not build on your engineering education. Additionally, many officers either did not plan for a career after their military commitment or believed they would make the military a career and did not earn a degree relevant to business. This was a second strike against you, especially compared to your peer group in business who were building relevant experience on top of their education.

The third reason companies believed military officers were going to have difficulty being competitive in the business world was that we had a difficult time making a connection between many of your positions in the military and what you had to offer corporate America. What could a Surface Warfare Officer, Field Artillery Officer, Infantryman, or Intelligence Officer do in the business world? We knew there existed some relatable knowledge, but we were not sure it was enough to overcome the disadvantage of time.

Corporate America Discovers the Military Officer

What forced recruiters to rethink this situation? The Vietnam War. During the Vietnam War corporate recruiters discovered that when they went to the college campus to hire Development Candidates, there weren't enough students available due to the draft. Suddenly, recruiters had to reassess the military officer as a potential hire. Corporations started hiring officers, but reluctantly, because they felt officers would have a hard time competing with their age group. Because of this, officers interviewed for only a small fraction of the positions they see today. But as corporate America measured your performance in the business world against the very best from the college campuses around the United States, they discovered you were catching up very quickly.

This was an exciting discovery for the corporate world. All of a sudden, companies had another source for hiring Development Candidates—the military. It's proven so successful that many companies today have made recruiting military officers a strategic talent initiative. They have witnessed military officers effectively transfer their military skills to the business world, immediately make an impact, and assume higher levels of leadership responsibility.

Over the years, interest, enthusiasm, and excitement for the military officer have grown. Corporate America increased its interest in the military officers after the first Gulf War in the early 1990s. This awareness significantly increased again during the wars in Afghanistan and Iraq. The junior military officer was even highlighted in the March 22, 2010, issue of *Fortune* magazine with the picture of a JMO on the cover and a cover story titled "Meet the New Face of Business Leadership." The article described companies like Pepsi and Wal-Mart having a shortage of leaders and hiring JMOs for their leadership and potential to assume higher levels of responsibility. This article noted that companies specifically seek out military officers to fill unique leadership roles with more responsibility, more opportunity for upward mobility. We completely agree, and today we see more military officers starting their careers in a wider range of job positions and career fields than ever before.

I cannot tell you how proud we all were of seeing a JMO on the cover of *Fortune* (one cover featured a Cameron-Brooks alumna). Being one of the originators of this recruiting channel, I knew firsthand how far the industry had come since the early days in the late '60s. The credit literally belongs to the thousands of former military officers who have made a big impact on the business world.

Types of Career Paths—Development and Nondevelopment

Not all career paths are the same in the business world. Industry to industry and company to company, there are differences in the way a company will structure a career path. Fundamentally, there are two types of career paths—development and nondevelopment.

The *development* career is designed for candidates who will be future leaders in a company. While you will always fill specific jobs as a Development Candidate, the company will expose you to various functions within a corporation to develop you as a generalist. Regardless of where you start your development career, as your career progresses, the company will provide you opportunities to develop broad knowledge in finance, accounting, information technology, supply chain management, manufacturing, sales, marketing, human resources, etc. The intent of such broad knowledge is to develop your skills to be a future leader in the company. Without these general management skills, a person cannot lead a company (just as a general or admiral cannot lead in the military without excellent knowledge of or experience in a wide variety of military functions and operations).

A Development Candidate needs to have the ability and desire to rise to the top leadership positions of leading commercial corporations (those that earn their revenue from selling or providing a product or service primarily to other businesses or consumers). As you enter the business world, it is important that you understand how you, as a commissioned officer, fit into a major corporation. Corporate America will spend a lot of time, money, expertise, and effort getting you, the Development Candidate, to the point where you can have a major impact on the direction of your company.

A *nondevelopment* career is designed for people to fill jobs in a specific area of expertise. These managers are not targeted to be the future top leaders of a company but rather are oriented toward developing an expertise in one functional area of a company. It is not that they can't be Development Candidates but rather that their goal is to develop along the line of a specialist. Regardless of where you start your career as a Nondevelopment Candidate, your career path is designed to make you a future expert in one area of the company (engineering, IT, finance, HR, etc.). As an example, let's say you begin your career in finance. As your career progresses, you will learn more and more about a company's financial structure, perhaps specializing in reporting, compliance, tax, or accounting. As a Nondevelopment Candidate, you will stay within a specific area and not move up into positions leading other people or broad-ening your responsibilities like a Development Candidate would. These positions are important in any company because experts ensure that the organization executes at a high level, but the key is that functional experts rarely get promoted to lead divisions or entire companies.

I am not saying that one career path is more important than the other, but rather that they are radically different. As you consider your options in the business world, it is important that you determine the type of career that interests you. Remember, not all companies hire Development Candidates. Some companies and industries have no programs in place to develop future leaders and thus have no interest in recruiting Development Candidates. These industries and companies "pool-promote," which means all hires jump into the pool and whoever floats to the top when a management spot becomes available gets promoted. Many (but not all) new companies start out this way, as they do not have the depth of personnel to develop leaders from within the company. However, as companies mature and become more sophisticated in their talent management, they tend to move toward the hiring of high-potential Development Candidates as a means of developing future leaders within the company.

Career progression in a company is not an overnight venture any more than it is in the military. Advancing from O-2 through O-3 to O-4 and up the ranks takes time and a considerable amount of investment. There are many things you need to learn and expe-riences you must have to become a top-level leader in a company. It is important to realize that these steps are necessary, and it takes time for them to happen. No matter what the size of the company or the type of business, there are few "overnight sensations" in corporate America. The media has popularized this quick-success notion. Nothing could be further from the truth. My belief is that business schools have acted irresponsibly, promising students that their two-year classroom curriculum can ensure a fast track to leadership. Can you imagine going to school for two years and learning how to be a Brigade Commander in combat? Leadership is learned and earned by executing consistently over time. People follow leaders they trust.

The business world wants Development Candidates who understand this mind-set. This is what having that "burning desire" to be a top leader is all about. In other words, *you understand the investment that it takes to be a leader in a successful organization.* Hoping for or simply wanting success is worthless without the burning desire to prepare for it.

Over the last 45 years, I have interviewed literally tens of thousands of JMOs. So many of them will say they want to be successful, but, unfortunately, only a small percentage realize the investment in personal growth that it is going to take to get there. Find any group of the top leaders in the business world, and I promise that you will find people who are constantly reading and expanding their knowledge base and skill set. These individuals know the importance of a diverse skill base, and they work on becoming knowledgeable in all areas of a company, not just their specific position or function. They seek higher degrees as they advance in age, keeping their formal education current so they remain competitive and in position for promotion. They know there is no substitute for knowledge, so they are constantly in the learning mode. They have outstanding leadership ability and interpersonal skills. They are mission-oriented leaders with a track record of making significant contributions to their past organizations. This is what I mean when I talk about having a burning desire to be one of the top leaders of a company.

Should You Use a Recruiting Firm?

Anyone reading this will feel it is a biased, opinionated statement. To a degree, it is. Nevertheless, the answer is "yes." Without fail, the first thing you should do once you have made the decision to enter the business world is to become associated with a quality recruiting firm.

Why? The answer is simple. You are a nontraditional hire for the business world. Many traditional sources (like friends and family networks or online application tools) are designed for traditional resumes. There are simply too many gatekeepers using these sources to find the top developmental opportunities. Plus, most military officers are too busy and often in more remote locations (or at least not in locations where they want to stay) to invest the hundreds of hours that it takes for effective networking. Bottom line: if you are making an industry change (i.e., DoD to the private sector), you are going to benefit from a good quality recruiting firm.

A quality recruiting firm will help you get through the "filters" a company puts up to screen its candidates. Absolutely, you can go out on your own and apply for positions, but recognize that you will have to clear several hurdles in the evaluation process before a real human being thoroughly evaluates you. Because companies receive so many inquiries for open positions (especially online), they set up a series of filters to screen people out (see Figure 1).

The first filter is posting or uploading your resume to a company's Web site. If you are lucky, a human will actually review this, but most likely some software program will search for key words and phrases or experience that most military officers do not have. If you are fortunate for a human to view it, it will likely be for about a minute or less, which also puts nontraditional resumes like a military officer's at a disadvantage. The second filter is the application, which is again there to screen out applicants and, once again, likely evaluated by a software system. The third filter is an interview. However, this is not the "real" interview. In fact, I like to call it an interview with a small *i* because it is a screening interview typically done by a talent acquisitions person or contract recruiter. This type of interview is usually completed in 30 minutes and over the phone. Its purpose is to further weed out. Finally, you get to the real interview, what I call the interview with the capital *I*, where you interview for positions in which you are interested and for which you are qualified, the timing of the open position fits with your potential start date, *and* you are interviewing with the decision makers. A high-quality recruiting firm will get you right to the Interview—the one with the capital "I."

I recall one time when a Fortune 500 telecommunications

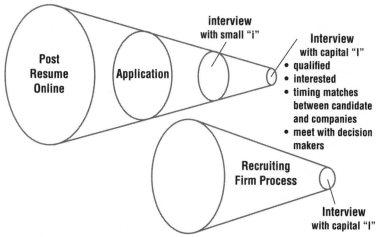

Figure 1. Comparison of candidate screening processes

company interviewed and *verbally* offered two Cameron-Brooks candidates Project Engineer positions. In order to make them the written official offer, the company asked the two candidates to post their resumes on the Web site and apply for the open positions. Once they did this, they would receive an e-mail of their written offer. You know what they received first? A rejection e-mail! They didn't make it through the filter system of this company! Now, because this was all administrative, they still received their written employment offers, so it worked out fine for them. However, the story illustrates that if they had been applying on their own through an online filter system, the company would not have seen the unique value in their military backgrounds from their resumes or applications. This is the true value of the recruiting firm for both the company and the candidates.

In fact, many companies prefer to hire through recruiting firms. If their normal ratio for hiring is one out of 200 interviews, the company is going to invest a lot of time and money to get to this point. They would much rather attend a Career Conference and interview 10 to 15 high-quality people over two days who meet their specific qualifications. Additionally, a company is going to be very reluctant to turn down 199 people who are going to be out on the street and have a negative impression of the company's product or service. For the company, it's much more efficient to have a recruiting firm say no to the majority of applicants and present them with a group of well-qualified and interested candidates.

Quality recruiting firms are evaluated by the client company's success in terms of the number and quality of talent the company hires. The measuring tool companies use to judge recruiting firms is based on the factor of 10 interviews. When a company seeks the help of a recruiting firm to fill its openings and interviews 10 people, on the average how many do they say yes to? Of every 10 people they pursue beyond the first interview, how many receive offers? For every 10 who are offered jobs, how many accept? And for every 10 who accept, how many are successful and promotable? Companies judge recruiting firms very carefully. In making your decision, it will be important for you to determine the recruiting company with whom it will be best for you to partner (depending on your needs, interests, situation, openness to location, etc.). In making your choice, I encourage you to use a recruiting firm that has developed outstanding relationships with its client companies.

As I said, you can make your career search on your own and find some success getting through the filters. However, there will be other challenges. For example, it will be difficult for you to verify that a position matches your background and interests and allows you to accelerate your career by growing into higher levels of responsibility. I'm not sure how you would do this. If you ask, and I would, you would probably want further verification.

Other disadvantages to conducting a search on your own are that (1) it is difficult to explore as many diverse opportunities as a quality recruiting firm will show you and (2) as you interview with companies individually and receive offers individually, you will be able to evaluate only one offer at a time. In other words, it's hard to tie your career search together when you are going at it on your own. There is simply too much guesswork on the timing of interviews and offers. Most companies won't allow you to consider an offer for a long period. A good recruiting firm can show you several opportunities at one time and help facilitate the timing of your interview results. Also, quality recruiting firms will work closely with you during the follow-up interview process (the weeks that follow an initial interview in which companies invite candidates for second and third interviews and extend offers to those candidates who best fit their criteria and culture). During the follow-up process, quality recruiting firms will help you evaluate your different offers and arrive at the career decision that is best for you.

Some officers will not earn the right to be represented by a recruiting firm. That's not a harsh statement—it's an honest statement. Every recruiting firm that agrees to represent an officer must ask itself, "Do my client companies need to pay me a fee to find this person?" Unfortunately, many times that answer is "no." We are not suggesting that the person is not a quality person and a potential good hire for a company, but client companies are very specific about the skill set of individuals they want to hire through a recruiting firm.

Using Multiple Recruiting Firms

Some candidates come to us suggesting that two or three recruiting firms represent them. We understand the reasoning that sometimes it feels good to spread risk over two or three recruiting firms. It's just that some recruiting firms that work with candidates over an extended period of time and prepare them for corporate interviews invest a tremendous amount of time and effort on each candidate's behalf. Obviously, these recruiting firms are not willing to develop individuals so they can interview on their own or through another recruiting firm. If you're going to choose one of the best recruiting firms, it is to your advantage to be loyal to that company until it has had the chance to show you to its client companies. I know of no recruiting firm in America that asks for 100 percent exclusivity. If they do, walk away from them. However, for a quality recruiting firm to ask for exclusivity until after they have shown you to their client companies is simply good business.

At our recruiting firm, we have said over the years, "We

have the knowledge and capability to show candidates many high-potential positions in the business world for which they are qualified and in which they are interested. We know how to guide candidates through successful transitions, and we know how to develop them so their start in the business world is on a track accelerating their careers." Candidly, it is fair then that our client companies have an equal opportunity to pursue the candidates with whom we partner.

If you apply to a recruiting firm, it is important that you present a quality picture of yourself to the firm. Officers sometimes make statements that cause me to rule them out. They will rationalize, "Well, I wouldn't say that to a company." Let me emphasize: "You have just said that to a company." You must remember that a recruiting firm is retained by the corporation. If you make the statement to us, it's like making it to the company. We can't ask you not to make a statement. We can't be unprofessional and suggest you cover up the statement by saying, "Don't say that in front of the company."

Before Companies Invest in You, They Want to Know You're Committed

Officers have told me they're not sure whether they want to go into the business world as a Development Candidate, remain in the military, pursue other government employment, enroll in law school or other full-time graduate education, or perhaps pursue other options in the world of nonprofit. In other words, they really don't know their career objective, and this will make any high-quality private sector company nervous. I'm not saying these other options are bad, but it will make a company question your commitment. The business world and the Development Candidate path are not for everyone. Can you imagine a company saying, "Roger, we want to pay you to find us an individual who's not certain whether he or she wants a career in the private sector or something as different as the nonprofit world." We can only agree to partner with you as you transition if you are someone who has a burning desire to enter the profit-oriented private sector and rise to the top. Our clients must hear that desire before they will make an investment in you.

Some of you may want to explore the business world while you also apply to defense contractors and government agencies such as the FBI, CIA, Department of Homeland Security, etc. I do not believe that this is fair to your recruiting firm or its clients. As I stated earlier, being a Development Candidate means having the burning desire to be a leader in the private sector. You either have this desire or not. There is nothing wrong with a career with government agencies or defense contractors, but they are very different careers from the Development Candidate business career. Sometimes candidates tell me, "Well, it is my backup plan." I understand wanting a backup plan, but the companies do not view it this way. It makes them question your long-term commitment. When companies hire a Development Candidate, they are committing time and money to the candidate's development and growth. They want the same level of commitment in return. Over the years, before the recruiter has made the offer, I have been asked easily over a thousand times, "Roger, is this candidate committed?" With pursuing options in government or defense, neither the candidate nor the recruiting firm can honestly answer, "Yes."

I recall a specific company recruiter requiring Cameron-Brooks to ensure the candidate had "burned the ships." When he first requested this, I had no idea what he meant by this phrase. Then he went on to give me a history lesson about Spanish explorer Hernán Cortés. The story goes that when Cortés landed in the New World, he set his ships ablaze right in the harbor to prevent his men from returning home. He sent a message to everyone that there was only one path forward and no going back. The recruiter's point was that his company would commit to and invest in the candidate and wanted the same commitment from him or her. Submitting applications or resumes to government agencies and defense contractors is the same as "leaving the ships in the harbor." There will be challenges and difficulties in switching from the public sector to the private sector. Company recruiters want candidates to be focused on and committed to moving forward, and not run back to the comfortable and familiar ships anchored offshore.

Some individuals say to me, "Several years down the road, I want to have my own business." I have to decline individuals with this objective. You wouldn't want someone to walk into your place of business and say, "I want you to invest in me, develop my skills, educate me on your business and industry, and pay me a good salary. Then I can go across the street, open my own business, and go into competition against you."

I'm not asking you to be dishonest and game this answer. I am asking you to evaluate what you want to do with your professional career. If it is to open your own business or to stay in the public sector by applying to government agencies or defense contractors, I respect that. After all, I own my business. But don't use somebody else to do it. Just go open your business or apply on your own to the other agencies and be successful. To start a high-potential development career with a company knowing you're going to leave them in the near future to start your own business is unprofessional. If you want a career in corporate America, then commit to that as your objective and work your heart out achieving it. Use all of the development opportunities companies will offer. Be a leader within that company. Go to the top.

Be Thorough with Your Applications

Online applications are a big part of the recruiting process. Be thorough as you navigate these applications. Give the recruiting firm the information it needs to professionally represent you. Produce quality applications and supporting file material. Never refer to your resume on your application. Companies review thousands of resumes and applications every year. It is time consuming, and they don't have time to review dozens of different resume formats to find the information. Companies and recruiting firms deliberately design their applications to elicit the information they want. You need to be deliberate in completing it. Take time to fill out your application and other forms thoroughly, carefully, and accurately. Show us you believe your application material is important. Don't wait until the last minute to get your academic transcripts. Get everything ahead of time. Document everything you send to your recruiting firm or a company, and keep a copy yourself. Watch your spelling and sentence structure. Your career transition is too important for you not to be extremely organized, timely, thorough, and willing to work with the recruiting firm regarding the material in your file so it can best represent you to its client companies.

WEAK APPLICATION & SUPPORT MATERIAL = DECLINE

Cameron-Brooks and our clients will decline candidates for poor applications. I say to myself, "I don't even want to take the time to write a decline e-mail or call the candidate." This file doesn't warrant our time, but, as a professional courtesy, we do it anyway. When sloppy application material is sent to us, we say to ourselves, "Obviously, this wasn't very important to the candidate because it is so sloppy." These applications could misrepresent you—on the other hand, they may not!

If you want to work with a quality recruiting firm, check out the firm. Ask to speak with former candidates with whom they partnered and successfully transitioned to business. Ask the recruiting company about their program and success rate. How do they prepare candidates for a transition? What percentage of the candidates are successful at a conference? You have every right to know this information. It's important for you to select a recruiting firm that works in partnership with you. Unfortunately, some recruiting firms send only your resume to different companies and hope they respond. Unless a recruiting firm is doing a lot for the company—screening your background thoroughly and working with you to educate you about business and to build your skill package—it is doubtful the recruiting firm represents much value to a company. The great companies in corporate America are smart. They put their money where they get the best value.

I've heard officers say, "I've already been accepted by another recruiting firm." I say, "When were you interviewed?" They answer, "I haven't been interviewed in person. I've only talked with them over the phone." High-quality companies want their recruiting firms to do face-to-face interviewing. I assure you that when it comes time to interview with the company, they will do it in person. If a recruiting firm isn't willing to commit the time and expense to come to your base or post, meet you, and work with you over a period of time, what message are they sending to you about the investment they are willing to make in you? Plus, do you really need them in your search?

Many of you tell me that recruiting firms don't want to talk to you unless you're within three to six months of getting out of the military. Do you realize what these recruiting firms are saying? They don't want to do the work it takes to develop you and set you up for success in the business world. They don't want to look into your background and help you do what you need to do to transition "up." They don't want to invest time and effort into developing officers; they simply want to place you with a company. They're saying, "No, we just want to show you to a company, hope you get placed, and receive our fee."

Make sure the recruiting firm is willing to do the kind of work it will take to develop you over a period of time. You don't need a recruiting firm that looks at you with a dollar figure in mind. Unfortunately, too many recruiting firms do just that. When you know major companies are paying top dollar to recruiting firms to select, interview, develop, and bring talented people to them, you have every right to demand certain standards. It is your professional future you are placing in the hands of a recruiting firm, and you owe it to yourself to work with a recruiting firm that is going to give you the best possible start and future in a business career.

Evaluating Three Categories of Your Life: High School, College, Military

Each year Cameron-Brooks recruiters travel around the world looking for Development Candidates for our client companies. They interview an average of 2,000 officers from the Navy, Air

Force, Army, and Marine Corps annually. Out of these candidates, they only accept and bring to one of our Career Conferences approximately 15 percent. This is not by design but by normal evaluation of each candidate's credentials and interview results against the needs and requirements of our corporate clients. Why do Cameron-Brooks recruiters accept only 15 percent of the officers they interview? Let's look at the evaluation process.

If you were to look at the profiles of the top 10 percent of management in business today, you would find certain commonalities (behavioral traits, attributes, skills) that go all the way back to high school. If you come to an interview talking only about what you have done in the military, you're attempting to stand on only one of three legs, the other two being your high school and college careers.

We evaluate the performance factors in your high school, college, and military careers. First, we evaluate high school records on quantifiable factors: the grade point average, the size of your class, your ranking within that class, and SAT/ACT scores. This gives us a good indication of how your performance compared to that of other students. We look at the difficulty of the curriculum. Was it an honors program? Did you challenge yourself all four years of high school? Then we look at extracurricular activities. What did you do outside of academics? In extracurricular activities, our most important questions are "Were you elected to leadership roles by your peers or superiors?" and "What contribution did you make?" We would also like to see the beginning of a positive work ethic, including summer employment. Overall, we look to see how motivated you were to do more than only what was required of you.

After looking at your high school accomplishments, we evaluate your college years. We cover the same areas and questions used in evaluating high school performance, but we add two critical factors—the reputation of your college or university and the quality of your curriculum.

What is the first thing we look for in the military? The positions you've held. In your particular branch were these positions career enhancing? Did you get them at the right time? Did you hold them for the right length of time? We then proceed to your officer evaluations. We look for impact statements—statements that indicate high achievement and set you apart from your peers.

Each of you is familiar with the evaluation inflation factor in the different branches of the military. So are we. We know every nuance, every idiosyncrasy, of individual statements made in your officer evaluations. We also look at your academic performance. Remember that corporate America is an academic environment. Therefore, your performance in military schools is important.

Then we look at more subjective factors. This is the conversational portion of the interview. Here are some of the factors we evaluate:

1. Interpersonal skill
2. Rapport-building skills
3. Communication skill (verbal and nonverbal)
4. Professional development and growth

We start with poise, self-confidence, and interpersonal skill. This is important because you will be placed in a new environment and be expected to make an immediate impact. You must have the poise, confidence, and people skills to move into an unknown situation and perform quickly. You need to be able to get buy-in from people across the organization (your team members, peers, and superiors) and have the ability to create a positive work environment.

You must be able to communicate succinctly and persuasively in order to make an impact in as short a period of time as possible. Show us you use time effectively. There are many ways to make that determination, even though, for the most part, it is a subjective evaluation.

Finally, we look for a person who is constantly striving to grow. Sometimes when we evaluate an officer's high school and college experiences, we find extremely outstanding credentials. We ask ourselves, "How did they get it all done?" However, when we get to the military, we discover they do *nothing* but their job. We don't see the growth outside the job. The military encourages you to design your life around your job. We're not saying the military is wrong in that. We're simply saying that's not what we're looking for in corporate America. We seek individuals who have continued to develop their family interest, extracurricular activities, and life outside the military. We want to see continued academic growth. We have little interest in a person whose age has advanced but whose formal education has not.

We look for people who have developed outside interests. We like to see a good balance between intellectual and activity-oriented interests, but we don't care whether it's running, hiking, golf, family outings, reading, computers, writing, chess, flying, boating, camping, Boy Scouts, Girl Scouts, Young Life, or Big Brothers/Big Sisters. We like to see a diversity of activities. We're not looking for carbon copies. We want to see people who are involved—people who are growing. We are interested in your personal life as well, so when you are discussing extracurricular activities, be honest with us. Tell us what you do. Don't create an answer for us. Don't tell us what you think we want to hear. Tell it the way it is. We want to know about all aspects of your life. Learn to be comfortable with yourself as an individual as well as with your ability to perform and make an impact.

Companies cannot mandate that their employees work well with others. At any time, employees can resign and walk out the door. Therefore, we look to hire people who are professional and have good interpersonal skill—people who are respected by others, who work well with others, and who are eager to come to work each morning. Companies want individuals who have the ability to create positive work environments. We're not interested in the cocky person whose self-confidence controls them. We want people who have total control of their self-confidence. They don't have to wear it on their sleeve. They know they're good. They don't have to act as if they're the best.

I have learned that the really good people do not inflate numbers. The confident officers are not afraid to tell me that on a scale of 1 to 10, they're an 8 in leadership ability, a 6 in computer and information technology skills, or a 5 in mechanical aptitude. Only those who lack self-confidence feel they must tell me they're a 10 in everything they do. We want people who know themselves and can honestly identify their strengths and weaknesses. They want a company to hire them for who they are, not what they pretend to be in an interview.

Do we always get a perfect candidate? In all my years of recruiting, I probably have not seen one, though some have been very close! We take an individual's entire history of background material from high school through the military and put the positives on one scale and the negatives on the other scale. We do, however, want the positive side of the scale to crash to the floor. This is the type of talented individual who makes it to the top of corporate America and gets us very excited about recruiting.

Developing Specific Business Knowledge

Since beginning my career in business in the late 1960s, I have never seen such speed of change or degree of competition as I see today in business. Companies have many more competitors and customers due to globalization. Those companies who react and adapt to the market the best are the leaders. To do this, companies have to have leaders who can make decisions and lead efforts with minimal guidance. Today's leaders understand information technology tools and other concepts such as Six Sigma, Lean, and project management. I highly encourage any military officer wanting to transition to business today to become familiar with these concepts and start applying them in his or her military career in order to discuss them knowledgeably during an interview and apply them immediately in his or her new career. Below are recommendations to help you build your objective skill base.

Information Technology

Microsoft Excel is a great tool for gathering and analyzing data. You can develop formulas, graphs, budgets, and more. You should become comfortable enough with Excel that you can utilize the Pivot Table tool to analyze and manipulate data. Learning how to use the Excel statistics plug-in tool is also time well spent. You can use Excel to identify the root cause of maintenance problems, improve work flow, reduce bottlenecks, and improve results. In an interview you will then be able to demonstrate your knowledge of Excel using a specific accomplishment.

Microsoft Access is a database application used by many companies. You should learn to become at least an intermediate user with this application. Once you learn some basics, you should learn how to link Access tables with other relational databases. Access is very often a front-end database tool for aggregating data in a company's Enterprise Resource Planning (ERP) system. You need to learn how to write simple Access queries and be able to move data between Access and Excel for statistical analysis.

Microsoft Outlook is a front-end application that organizes your e-mail, contacts, appointments, tasks, and calendars and syncs with your smart phone as well. It is a feature-intensive application that you will most certainly use consistently if you leave the service. Learning this is time well spent. Although Apple computers are popular for personal use and e-mail applications like Gmail are prevalent, most of the private sector uses Windows and Microsoft Exchange.

Once you have developed knowledge of Microsoft's Excel, Access, and Outlook, I recommend you move on to the other subjects listed below. However, if you have extra time, you can take time to learn programming languages as well as networking.

Project Management

Companies will expect you to have a good understanding of project management and ask you questions regarding project management during your interviews. A project, defined by the Project Management Institute (PMI) is "a temporary endeavor undertaken to produce a unique product, service or result." Dr. J. M. Juran, a quality guru, defines a project as "a problem scheduled for solution." Based on that definition, you can see why companies need all Development Candidates to lead projects. Companies constantly have to deliver new or modified products, implement new processes to reduce costs/increase efficiencies, deliver better service, and reinvent themselves to meet customer needs and stay ahead of the competition.

Leaders add value by leading projects in addition to carrying out their traditional responsibilities. Tom Peters, business author and project management proponent, says people must think, "I = My Projects." Companies recruit Development Candidates who can lead peers, build teams, maintain a budget, and take initiative in order to lead projects. They also want to know if you can work with change, manage risk, be customer-oriented, and maintain enthusiasm for projects. During an interview, you can expect questions probing into all of these areas. Reading about project management is a start but will not provide the depth you need for the answers. You will have to identify projects at work, assume the lead, and drive them to completion.

I highly recommend you study project management. At a minimum, I recommend reading *Fundamentals of Project Management* (4th ed.) by Joseph Heagney. You can also take classes on military bases and posts on project management, as well as earn educational certificates in project management from various institutions. My team and I often recommend Villanova University's Executive Education for Veterans, a distance learning program. You can earn an Executive Certificate in Project Management from Villanova or other institutions, and then take exams from the Project Management Institute (www.pmi.org), the governing body for project management professionals, to earn professional certification. PMI is also the author of *A Guide to the Project Management Body of Knowledge* (known as The PMBOK Guide). It's a great guide for those who are really into project management and have a lot of time before the transition to dive deep into the subject.

Six Sigma and Lean

Companies put a lot of emphasis on continuous improvement to streamline operations, become more efficient, and improve quality. Six Sigma and Lean, sometimes put together and called Lean Six Sigma, are widely used concepts throughout the business world. You will want to be familiar with these topics, and ideally learn about them and apply some of their concepts or principles in your military environment *prior* to a transition. I talk to more and more corporate recruiters who ask candidates, "What do you know about Lean or Six Sigma? What have you done that relates to these?"

Six Sigma is a quality management initiative that identifies and reduces the number of defects and errors in a process. You will want to learn more about Six Sigma because almost every company is trying to better serve its customers and achieve the highest quality. This applies to all career fields—manufacturing, supply chain, engineering, sales, etc. You can use Six Sigma methodologies to solve problems while in the military and be ready to deliver answers that connect with Six Sigma and follow the DMAIC problem-solving methodology.

To learn more about Six Sigma and DMAIC, you can choose from many books. One of my favorite books is *What Is Six Sigma?* by Pande and Holpp. It is short and straight to the point. For those with more knowledge of Six Sigma, this book will be too basic for you.

Lean is the practice of adding more value and eliminating waste in a process. Initially, Lean was applied to manufacturing processes in order to eliminate non-value-added work. Today Lean is applied to production, supply chain, and service work. It is a much broader business practice that is used to improve the flow and efficiency of work, eliminate waste, and deliver a product or service that the customer wants. A great book on Lean is *Lean Thinking: Banish Waste and Create Wealth in Your Corporation* by Womack and Jones.

Many military officers today are taking the initiative to get formal education in Lean and Six Sigma. Numerous military installations offer classes through the education center, and some units invite instructors to provide courses; often the opportunity to earn a Yellow Belt or Green Belt certification is also offered. For those who do not have the military option, Villanova University also has Executive Certifications in Lean and Six Sigma.

Only you can improve your knowledge and skills. No one can do it for you. Do not rely on what you learned four or five years ago in school. It is outdated. If you are not able to leave the military for several years, make sure you are getting good advice about how to keep up with cutting-edge technology. Develop a plan to improve your skills while you are in the military so you remain on par with your peers in the business world. You will dramatically improve the number of development opportunities with which you can interview upon leaving the military. As mentioned, get with a high-quality recruiting firm that can provide guidance that helps you build your objective skill base and prepare for a successful transition.

Immediate Impact

As you enter corporate America, you will be expected to bring your leadership and problem-solving skills to the job immediately. Officers often say, "Roger, could you tell me how a company in the business world is going to train me?" I encourage you to be cautious in overstating the need to be trained.

Corporations *train* fresh college graduates. Corporations do not expect to spend a lot of dollars or time to train military officers. You received training and a lot of real-world experience in the military, and you bring that valuable training to corporate America. There's no reason why you shouldn't be able to have an impact on profitability (the bottom line) instantly. You've learned how to accomplish difficult objectives. You've learned how to prioritize, organize, and effectively manage time, to break tough objectives down into component parts, and to motivate your team members and peers to help accomplish those objectives. Whether you're applying your expertise to solve a problem in the military world or a problem in the business world, the methods are the same. You need to suggest that, as a military officer, *you can make an immediate impact.* Companies will pay you more than a recent college graduate and other entry-level hires, and you will expect to be promoted faster than they are because you already have had "training" that is valuable and costly. Most other entry-level hires do not bring this training and experience to the table.

After all, if you're going to catch up with your age group, you'll want to get in and get started immediately. The less time you take to become effective, the more quickly you can move ahead of your age group into significant management roles.

Most companies provide you with some orientation to the new work environment, but orientation is different from training. Orientation is basically what is considered as "on the job training" in the military. At the same time you are performing, you also are learning.

So, rather than emphasize the need for training, show that you, the military officer, have the flexibility to adapt to the ever-changing, highly competitive corporate environment. You have the right attitude, and you will succeed in making an immediate impact in this environment. Give a recruiter proof and evidence of these qualities in your interviews.

Throughout this book I talk about characteristics or competencies, such as problem-solving skills, flexibility, and a positive attitude, which companies look for in Development Candidates. This does not mean you need to possess all or be strong in each of the characteristics I mention, and not every company looks for the same characteristics or competencies. Every candidate is unique, and every company and position is unique. I mention them to you to get you to think about the characteristics and competencies you possess and to know which ones are important to bring to light in an interview. As you read this book, refer to Appendix A for a list of key competencies that recruiters look for in the Development Candidates they interview.

Chapter 2

THE CRUCIAL FIRST IMPRESSION

What is the *first impression* you make to a prospective employer? In the hundreds of presentations I've given around the world, I've often asked my audiences this question. And in the many years I've been in this business, I have rarely heard the answer I believe is the correct one.

People say it's the appearance you make as you step into the recruiter's office: your suit, your dress, your grooming, the sparkle in your eyes, your voice inflection, your walk, your handshake. I emphatically believe all these factors make up the second impression.

The first impression is your resume or application. In 99 percent of these cases, the resume is seen even before an application.

POOR RESUMES / POOR APPLICATIONS = DECLINE

Recruiters, believe it or not, are human beings. As they evaluate your resume, they form an impression. It can be one that generates tremendous interest—or no interest at all. Unfortunately, many times when I look at resumes, they do little to interest me. Let's focus on what a resume should do for you.

Resumes: The Vital Information

Gathering Information

Before you start the process of building your resume or filling out company applications, you should gather together all pertinent information. Create a file containing your high school and college transcripts, all of your academic and performance evaluations, past employment history, social security and driver's license numbers, etc.

Availability Date

First and foremost, a resume should tell a recruiter your date of availability. A position is open or will be open on a certain date. The date you are available will need to coincide with that time frame. You may be the best candidate going, but if your availability doesn't coincide with the appropriate time for the company, then you're of no value to that company. Many corporate recruiters are confused regarding the military's exit process—understandably so. Don't let your availability date be a guessing game for the recruiter.

Level of Education

Next, show your level of education. It's important because positions often call for a specific educational background. If your education isn't right for this particular position, the recruiter must move on to the next resume. I want to caution you to put accurate academic information on both your resume and any application(s) you are asked to complete. What your resume and application state must be identical to what is stated on your transcript(s). Frequently, officers will tell me their transcript is wrong. If there is an error on your transcript, get it corrected immediately and certainly before you begin a career search. I assure you this is considered a serious breach of accuracy, and you need to be on top of any such situations.

Accomplishments

When you list *significant accomplishments* (which is basically what resumes should do), remember that in corporate America no accomplishment is considered significant unless it impacts the bottom line. Your ability to communicate your significant accomplishments both on your resume and in your interviews is most important. If you cannot describe past accomplishments, you will have a very difficult time having a successful career search.

Recently, for example, an officer asked me my opinion of his resume. "Are you sure you want me to comment?" I asked. He said, "Yes" (his curiosity piqued). I said, "I'm amazed you would build a resume that suggests you've been a failure."

Why, in fact, was there strong proof of failure in his resume? After all, his resume told what his responsibilities were. It gave his job title, dates of that position, and the duties assigned to him. He was a commander, had 120 subordinates, and was responsible for their combat readiness, operational success while deployed, health, and welfare. There were several lines of this information, and then he went on to his previous position. He wrote down his entire military career. But here is the point—his resume failed to list his accomplishments. *It listed his responsibilities, but, remember, with any responsibility, you can fail or succeed.* You can fail to certain degrees. You can succeed to certain degrees. A recruiter could only assume he had no successes with his responsibilities. What we want to know on your resume, more than anything, is this: *When you were given a responsibility, what did you do with it? What were your accomplishments?* On your resume state the back end of a responsibility rather than the front end. Recruiters are interested in results.

We also are interested in the bottom line. In your descriptions of your back-end results, refer to the bottom line of the military— combat readiness and combat effectiveness. Every action you take, regardless of your position, should further this cause. Also keep in mind that the military wants you to achieve your objective at minimum cost. You need to be able to talk about your accomplishments in terms of the bottom line and the military's push for doing more with less, because this is exactly what a recruiter wants to believe you will have the ability to do for a company in the business world.

Stating Your Objective

You must have an *objective* on your resume. Don't be vague or general in your objective. "Position in management, building upon an ability to balance multiple projects while still attaining overall goals by virtue of detailed planning and thoughtful delegation of responsibility." This tells most recruiters that you don't know exactly what you want to do. Furthermore, you have used the words "position in management." Most of the top companies in corporate America develop management from within. Consequently, you have just eliminated yourself from many top companies. Be careful of the word "management" when, in fact, you mean "supervision." *Caution: Officers working with a recruiting firm should follow the firm's specific guidelines on objectives.*

Frequently, officers make the statement that they want to start in one of the following:

- A mid-level management position
- A lower mid-level management position
- An upper mid-level management position
- An entry-level management position

In the many years my company and I have been recruiting military officers, we have rarely facilitated a career transition directly into a management role, even though the job title may have had the word "manager" in it. Our client companies rarely hire management from outside, and certainly not someone without business experience. Imagine yourself working for a company for a four- or five-year period. A management spot opens up above you, and then the company goes outside to hire someone for that position. You would not be very happy. You would be demoralized, and that company would have a morale problem on its hands.

Frequently, the word "management" is misused. It is confused with the word "supervision." Here's how we succinctly articulate the difference between management and supervision. In the military you're not a manager until you reach the level of O-5, because managers set big-picture objectives. Supervisors motivate the members of their team to carry out the objectives that management establishes. We would suggest that a company commander, flight commander, or department head is a supervisor carrying out the objectives that higher-level unit or upper-level management, 0-5 or above, establishes for him or her. This is not to say that one is good or one is bad—it just clarifies where you are in the hierarchy of a company. So if officers would use the word "supervisor" to indicate that they are looking for a supervisory position instead of a management position, they would find that their resumes would be read and the odds for pursuit would increase.

Give an objective that is directed, such as "sales leading to management," "staff engineering," "management information systems," "line operations," "manufacturing," "operations," etc. Be specific. Tell a recruiter you are a person who knows what you want to do. *Demonstrate that you have done a thorough analysis, studied the business world, and have a good feeling for where you will fit best.* When you leave the military as an officer, you are behind members of your age group who went straight from college into business. Therefore, in order to catch up, you must have conviction plus a definite career objective.

It is better to build two, three, or even four different resumes, based on different objectives, than to have one resume with an objective that attempts to cover everything.

Supporting the Primary Objective

One of the most critical points in a resume is that your accomplishments must support the primary objective of the position you held.

Let's consider the commander with 120 subordinates. What do we want to know more than anything else? We want to know that his or her troops are ready for combat or, if deployed to a combat zone, that they were successful. That's most important. Once a company commander told me his best accomplishment was that his Combined Federal Campaign raised the most money of all the companies in his unit. But the Combined Federal Campaign is not a responsibility that impacts on his unit's combat readiness or operational success. It is not a primary responsibility. If this had been stated after several primary accomplishments, it would have been better received.

If you expect to be a successful supervisor in corporate America, then you should highlight among your accomplishments what you did with your supervisory experience. Tell about your successes in motivating members of your team. Understand that some supervisors (to achieve an accomplishment) burn up their people. They mishandle their people. They use negative motivation and, therefore, have a heavy turnover. The focus must be on the people themselves. The accomplishment of the objective in a professional manner is important. We are interested in hiring Development Candidates who understand that keeping turnover low and morale high are extremely important. Again, you must be careful. You cannot tell us you do this. You must show us, quantifiably, how you motivate and interact with the people you supervise.

If your primary job objective is an engineering position, then show the recruiter your technical accomplishments. Always remember that your accomplishments must draw as close a parallel as possible to the position for which you are interviewing.

Quantifying Your Successes

As you build your resume, the extent of your success, the quantification of it, is the key factor. In order to judge this quantification, we have to know what the goal was. For example, if you reached a vehicle maintenance readiness factor of 95 percent, let us know this was 5 percent above objective, or whatever the case may be. Too many officers, as they interview with me, prove by their rhetoric that they probably should stay in the world of nonprofit. They constantly want to tell me how they developed a new training program. But they never bother to tell me what the training program actually accomplished. *Once again, we are not interested in the front end of the accomplishment, only the back end.*

At one of our Career Conferences several years ago, a corporate recruiter declined his favorite candidate. He said, "Roger, I can't believe it. I just declined my favorite candidate of the day." When I asked him why, he went on to explain, "He had the perfect credentials and the best resume, but he can't see the bottom-line impact or the big picture. When I asked him about a significant accomplishment, he told me about this great project he managed building a bridge in Iraq. He never told me why he built the bridge, so I asked him. He just sat there and looked at me, and then went into further detail on how he did it and how the bridge was one of the best in the area. I still don't know why he built the bridge!" This candidate, and many others as well, put the emphasis on the "doing" and not on the purpose or the results. This candidate could have said something like, "This bridge allowed the U.S. soldiers to cross the river more freely and provide increased security, or provided the Iraqi civilians more freedom of movement, and over 200 vehicles passed over the bridge each day." These show purpose and impact. So be careful that you learn what is important to the business world when developing your accomplishments. Everything we do in industry must impact the bottom line of the company—saving work-hours, increasing profitability, lowering cost, etc.

Often officers tell me, "I improved the morale of my unit." You need to show how it was done. What percent increase did you have in reenlistment? How did it improve your promotion rate among your enlisted? How did this improve readiness or operational performance? You must give quantifiable proof and evidence of what you say. Rhetoric alone won't suffice.

Some officers also tell me, "But, Roger, I spent $75 to get that resume built by a resume service." I'm sorry if I step on toes here.

Too many times resume services are more interested in making a resume look pretty—focusing on how it's printed and the kind of paper used. I maintain that if these resume services charged you according to the success the resume produces, they might get more serious about the information they put on your resume.

Your resume must represent bottom-line qualities if you want a high degree of success in attracting companies to you.

Resume Format Suggestions

Most resumes today are sent to companies via e-mail or posted on a Web site. I recommend that if you e-mail the resume, you send it as a PDF file that cannot be modified. This will ensure that it will look the same as it did when you created it, regardless of the computer or operating system used to view it. If you post it or upload it to a Web site, you will use Microsoft Word or copy from a Word document and paste into a template.

Most resumes should be held to one page (even those listing the backgrounds of LCDRs and Majors). But don't be afraid to go beyond that if the information is relevant and presented in an articulate, succinct manner. Here are some additional tips for formatting your resume:

- Use ½-inch margins for each side.
- Begin approximately 1 inch from the top of the page. (If you are working with a recruiting firm, you may need to start lower to account for the firm's letterhead.)
- Single-space your resume.
- Do not add more than one line between sections of the resume.
- Leave at least ½ inch at the bottom of the page.
- Use a 10-point professional-looking font.

You will also want to have hard copies of your resume. Many officers feel their resumes should be on the best bond paper. I agree, but the *content* is what's important. I've had recruiters tell me, "I don't care if they write it on paper grocery bags, as long as the content is right and we can get the information we need."

I recommend two different resume formats. If you're leaving the military interviewing for a nondevelopment position, it might be better to exclude extracurricular activities in high school and college. However, the majority of you will want to come to corporate America and get into a development position. The major difference between the two resume formats is that one shows extracurricular activities in high school and college; the other does not. If you're interviewing for a development position and hope to be a top manager, keep in mind that most companies find top managers have successful traits in common, even in high school. As a Development Candidate, it's important, therefore, to show the extracurricular activities you had in high school and college. Over the years I've discovered these activities are very important as they demonstrate the candidate's track record of success.

The sample resume in Appendix B is for a development position and is the product of the many years I've spent recruiting officers and working daily with companies. I asked firms the following question: "What do you want to see in a resume to obtain the information you need?" I want to note that I have been in a business in which I am paid only for bottom-line performance, not for my opinion. This fact lends a lot of credibility to this resume format.

Use this sample resume and the following guidelines to determine how to organize your resume. Be careful and thorough.

Personal Information. At the top left of your resume, place your full name, address, city, state, zip code, cell or home phone number (whichever gives the caller the best access to you), including area code, and a professional e-mail address. I see too many candidates with poorly created e-mail addresses. Some are way too long or have their military call sign, university nickname, or mascot. Your e-mail address should be professional and easy for the recruiter to remember and use.

Availability Date. One space below the Personal Information section, place your availability date, written as month, day, and year. Your availability date should be determined by subtracting your total amount of terminal leave (which you continue to accrue while on terminal leave) from your ETS, or last date of official service. *Be sure to use the earliest possible date.*

Education. This section should include all your undergraduate and graduate degrees and any additional coursework. Place your undergraduate degree(s) on the far right across from your personal information. If you have a graduate degree, place this one space below your undergraduate degree. Your resume entries should match your college transcript entries for the degree(s) you were awarded. Many graduates have shortened their degree titles for convenience. *Refer to your transcript(s) to be sure of your degree title(s).* If you took a lot of courses in finance, that doesn't mean you had a minor in finance. If your transcript doesn't show it, don't put it on your resume. Some companies request transcripts, and if there is a discrepancy, it will be a significant strike against you.

Activities. Many of the candidates with whom we work have distinguished themselves not only academically but also in extra-curricular endeavors. List both high school and college activities on the resume.

For both high school and college, list the following: all scholastic honors and scholarships (except ROTC scholarships); honorary societies; student body government; class organizations; clubs; publications; assistantships; community, civic, or church memberships; and offices to which you were nominated or elected. For any society, student body, class government, organization, or club in which you held an office or had a unique organization-specific accomplishment, include that office or accomplishment in parentheses following the entry. For example, "Debate Club (President, First Place State Forensic Tournament)."

For any athletic activity, annotate with "varsity," "junior varsity," "freshman," "club," or "intramural status" (mention only the highest level achieved). If you received awards or honors, enter them parenthetically as above. For example, "Varsity Football (Co-Captain, All-Conference, State Champions)."

Experience. In this section enter your *military* experience. Provide the dates of your active-duty service, your military rank, your specialty, and your branch. Next enter your military work history. This is the most important part of your resume. Describe your duties and accomplishments for each position you held, starting with the most recent job. For each position, enter four key elements:

1. *Date*. Enter dates of service by month and year.

2. *Job Title. For the vast majority of jobs, enter the technically correct title.* Refer to your evaluations. Some job titles are not helpful to a recruiter, and you can't afford to spend your interview explaining what a title means. Therefore, you need to find a balance between what is technically correct (on your officer evaluations) and what is descriptive. *However, do not attempt to civilianize this or any other part of your resume.*

3. *Job Responsibilities*. Enter three to five lines of information about your specific responsibilities for each job you have listed. (Refer to your officer evaluations.) Be sure to include your supervisory responsibilities—number and type of personnel supervised. Be as specific as possible. The terms "mechanic," "electrician," "machinist," and "clerk" are more effective than "soldier." Also discuss the amount and type of equipment for which you were responsible.

4. *Accomplishments*. Enter the accomplishments you achieved for each job you have listed. Each accomplishment should stand on its own in a "bullet" format. Describe your accomplishments with action verbs. *Quantify your accomplishments;* in other words, make your accomplishments measurable. For example, "Achieved a higher operational readiness rate" is too general and a matter of opinion. In contrast, "Developed new maintenance program that achieved a 96 percent equipment operational readiness rate, 6 percent above objective" is a quantifiable accomplishment. It is specific and objective rather than general and subjective.

Civilian Experience. Below your military experience, enter any jobs you have held as a civilian that may enhance your marketability. Begin your civilian experience as you did above for the military section. Enter the dates, your title, and where you worked. Then enter a description of your duties. (Do not detail your accomplishments; there will be no room for bullets in civilian experience.) Include the following areas: engineering, co-ops, lab assistantships, running your own business, computer work, or any job that relates to your experience. While we do not want to diminish the importance of these types of jobs, in terms of market-ability, they are less relevant than your military career.

Always carefully proofread and check your resume for errors (do not rely solely on spell-check). Check all dates, making sure there are no time gaps or overlaps. Finally, read over your resume. Ask yourself this question, "Would you be interested in hiring this person to lead your company into the future?" If your answer is no, go back and reword your significant accomplishments. I am not suggesting you falsify accomplishments; I am suggesting you use language that is going to spark the interest of a corporate recruiter—language that will "sell" your ability to make an impact.

I consider your resume to be one of the most critical aspects of your job search. It's the primary factor, so build it first. You must have documentation on paper, listing who you are and what you're all about, along with your past performance. Too many individuals spend very little time on their resumes. What they produce simply isn't enough.

When you step in front of a recruiter for an interview, you want to know your resume has created a positive *first impression* about you and that the recruiter already has a positive attitude about you.

The Cover Letter

If you distribute your resume (by e-mail, regular mail, or any other way), it is crucial to send a cover letter along with it. If you send it via e-mail, you can either attach a cover letter to the e-mail or put it in the body of the e-mail. I recommend putting it in the body of the e-mail because it is more likely to be read, especially if it is forwarded to another person in the company. Also, many companies will want you to upload your resume to the Web site, and some do allow you to add a cover letter. Regardless, the letter must be written specifically to that company. Do not send generic cover letters. You're telling the company all they need to know to decline you.

The resume must be able to stand on its own. Often your cover letter will be removed from the resume or overlooked when the resume is forwarded to hiring managers. The managers will be unaware of any cover letter. If you've put important information only in this letter (and not duplicated it on your resume), it's likely to stay with the personnel director to whom you addressed it. Your resume will now be void of important data.

Make powerful statements in the cover letter. What can you offer that is relevant to that particular company? What are your abilities and career accomplishments? Why do you have a real interest in this corporation? Remember, keep the letter company-specific.

Applications

Your application to a company (the actual application form) is a document that will represent you for the balance of your career if you go to work for that company. *Think about that.* It must be completed in a manner that you would always want in your permanent records.

This form may be the first impression a company representative has of you. Don't underestimate its importance. Think carefully as you complete the basic form. *Applications are designed to eliminate.* No company can interview everyone who fills out its application. However, I encourage you not to help the company in the elimination process. I recommend you put yourself in the shoes of the corporate recruiter as you fill out any application. Reread it, asking yourself, "Would I hire this person to lead my company into the future?" It could save both you and the company a lot of time going through a wasted interview.

Follow these basic rules:

1. Carefully follow the specific instructions on the application.

2. Almost all applications are now submitted online through a company's career section of its Web site. This is much easier than in the past when applications were hard copy. However, I sometimes hear about data not being saved or submitted. I recommend you hit the Save function frequently when filling out the application so you do not lose information. Print out a hard copy for your records if the application process allows you.

3. Check for correct spelling, correct grammar, and correct punctuation. Do this *before* hitting the Submit button! I once ruled out a Naval Academy electrical engineering major who misspelled the word "engineering" three times on his resume. How could I confidently accept this person into our program and represent him to our clients knowing he doesn't pay attention to details?

4. Don't leave blanks or skip questions. If a question doesn't apply to you, put a short dash in the space, write "None," or write "N/A" (Not Applicable). Complete the entire form.

5. Fill in the entire space provided for an answer. If, for example, there are three lines to list school activities, fill in all three lines.

6. *Never write "See Resume."* Company representatives know they can look at your resume. Your application must be able to stand alone and apart from your resume. It must clearly represent your entire experience and qualifications. Put all the information where the company wants it: on the application.

7. Avoid attaching or uploading an addendum or an additional document. Although a form may state, "Feel free to attach supplemental information," if it is ever printed out, the attached sheet can become detached—and then vital information will be lost. Also, most company recruiters review hundreds of applications for many open positions in their company. They want to find the needed information in the application. If there are four spaces provided for work history and you had six jobs in the military, use two of the spaces for two jobs each. *Your entire military background should be divided so that all of your positions are included in the spaces provided.* Do not use just one space to indicate several years of military job experience, then the remaining three spaces for less notable work.

8. If asked to state "Reason for seeking change" or "Reason for leaving" a past or a present position, do give an answer. In the military, it may be due to promotion, change of duty, normal rotation, etc. But your reason for leaving your current military position should be carefully worded. Don't say, "Completed military obligation." That shows no interest or conviction to make industry your career. State a positive, goal-oriented answer, such as, "Desire to pursue a career in major industry." *Use your own words.*

You'll find four caution areas that are especially sensitive subjects on many applications. Here's how to deal with them.

Salary. Answer "Open" or "Negotiable." Please note this is not the way you would handle this question in an interview itself. But an application cannot elaborate. It can't modify. You don't dare allow the application to get you ruled out because you put a dollar figure that doesn't provide latitude. This gives you an opportunity to discuss the entire subject of compensation in person, with the company representative. It indicates salary is just one of many items you'll consider when making a career decision. If you must give a salary figure, I recommend that you give a range, but hold it to $10,000. No one wants to see ranges of $30,000 to $50,000.

Location. Always state "Open" on the application. *Again, this response is completely different from what you would give in the interview itself.* If the word "open" is used in an interview, it will frequently disqualify you. If this question has two parts—"Do you have a preference?" and "Do you have any restrictions?"—answer the first by stating a broad geographical preference, such as "the Northeast," "the southern United States," "east of the Mississippi

River," etc. Answer the second question with "None." If you know the location of the job for which you're interviewing, you can tailor your answer to that area. For example, you can state a preference of "east of the Mississippi" with no restrictions. It is reasonable to have a preference, but when the preference becomes an eliminator, then you should not plan to interview as a Development Candidate. National companies hire people they can promote without severe geographical restrictions. If you want to be a Development Candidate, you and your family must have a good attitude regarding multiple locations. If you were to suggest you wanted to go to the top 10 percent of any branch of the armed forces, you know you could not do so from a single location. Similarly, you can't get to the top 10 percent of corporate America from a single location.

Position Desired/Objective. Always state precisely the position title/objective. State only one objective per application, even if the application provides space for more than one position title.

Full Disclosure. Almost all applications will have a section inquiring about criminal charges, i.e., arrests or misdemeanors beyond simple traffic violations. Make sure you read the question on the application thoroughly. Sometimes an application asks if you have ever been arrested (without asking what the outcome of the arrest was). If asked on an application, we believe you should declare any arrest from the time you were a legal adult. After all, almost all companies will do a background check on you in the offer process. You are much better off with full disclosure on the application rather than having a surprise on your background check. Full disclosure is the best policy. Believe it or not, your driving record over your last three years is becoming more significant, especially if you are going to drive company-owned vehicles or equipment. Do yourself a favor and slow down so you can conduct your career search with a clean driving record. More than two speeding tickets in the last three years could complicate your employability. It's just the world we live in now.

The application is tangible, permanent evidence of your ability to answer specific questions and organize your ideas accurately and concisely.

Chapter 3

PREPARING FOR THE INTERVIEW

What makes successful interviewing? That's simple—preparation. Preparation includes the following:
- A thorough understanding of yourself
- A thorough analysis of what has made you successful
- The ability to communicate in a fluid, persuasive manner

Sounds easy, doesn't it? But it isn't. Many people feel they have the ability to take any subject matter and speak about it—"off the cuff"—in an articulate, concise, convincing manner. Unfortunately, few actually can. As a matter of fact, I'm not sure I've ever met anyone during my recruiting career—over 2,000 officers a year—who found a position in the business world without serious interview preparation. Corporate recruiters are adamant that individuals prepare well for interviewing. Recruiters reason that if people do not work hard to prepare for something as valuable as their own careers, why should any company believe they're going to work hard to accomplish an objective for their employer? I believe this reasoning is very accurate.

If you want to succeed in your interviews, you will need to dedicate time to prepare for them. This can be very difficult in today's high OPTEMPO military environment. Set aside a specific period of time—an hour a day, two hours a day, five hours a week, half a day a week, Saturday morning, Sunday afternoon—well in advance of interviews with corporate recruiters. Use this time to read books, to do work assignments, and to prepare for the key questions you know will be asked of you. I often use this example: If you knew you were going to have an inspection on Monday morning, you wouldn't begin preparing for it Friday evening. If you did, you certainly would know what the outcome would be. You wouldn't prepare on Friday evening for a six-month or a 30-day deployment knowing that you're leaving on Monday morning. Preparation is mandatory for quality results.

Fortune 500 and other leading companies want to and can attract the best of the best candidates. These are the same companies who will interview you. You have to be at your best. You must meet their criteria and effectively communicate your track record. There's nothing automatic in the hiring process. The fact that you were good in high school, college, and the military does not automatically guarantee you a career in the business world. There's just that little thing called an interview that stands between you and success.

Think about it for a moment. You're over 27 years old and in an interview. You are being asked to communicate your life—your successes and failures, your strengths and weaknesses, what you are all about, and what you can offer a company—in a 30- to 45-minute period of time. *You do not have unlimited time in an interview to communicate your abilities, key connecting points, and interests.* No matter how old you are or how much experience you have to convey, company recruiters do not give you more time in an interview. It sounds absurd when you think about it, but this is exactly what will happen.

If you don't know what part of your experience a company is interested in (and chances are, you won't), it stands to reason you must be prepared to give specific information on any part of your background at any time. It is the specific information that gets people without solid preparation into trouble. While you can talk in a general sense, you are rarely prepared to give the specifics of how you accomplished a particular event or objective.

Too many people feel being successful in an interview is about getting a resume together and buying a great suit and shoes, but that's only a very minor part of it. *The most important aspect of interviewing is being able to convince a recruiter that you have the objective and subjective skill set to make an immediate contribution to the company and the potential for future promotions to higher levels of responsibility.* It is only when you communicate your skill set that the recruiter will see you as a good fit for the company, now and in the future. You cannot expect to do this without having a thorough understanding of yourself and of what has made you successful as well as an ability to concisely and persuasively communicate this to the recruiter.

I've talked to many officers who interviewed for Development Candidate positions with leading companies without adequate preparation and never received offers. Consequently, without really wanting to, they stayed in the military. I honestly believe that, in many cases, they were declined by companies not because of their credentials, but because of their inability to communicate those credentials. It would be nice if you could get hired on the basis of a resume or an application, but it's just not possible. I've never known one of our client companies to hire a candidate sight unseen. So, please, dedicate yourself early in your career search to preparing for a very difficult venture—interviewing.

Objective and Subjective Assets

It is important for you to understand your objective and subjective assets as you prepare for interviewing. Highlight or flag this section so that when you begin your actual preparation, you will start with this topic.

The cornerstone of self-evaluation is an understanding of your objective and subjective assets. When I ask officers during the interview process what assets they will bring to an employer on the first day, they often have no answer. Recruiters will ask this question in one form or another. It's important for you to understand the concepts in order to respond intelligently. Comprehension is critical to marketing yourself effectively.

Objective assets are points of fact regarding your background.

This includes things like your college degree, GPA, job experience, amount of time in leadership roles, number of people supervised, certifications, military schools, size of budgets you managed, etc. Objective assets are easily verifiable and make up the content of your resume.

Subjective assets are a different matter. Your subjective assets are characteristics, competencies, or behavioral traits, such as leadership, team building, initiative, self-confidence, integrity, attitude, organizational skills, creativity, problem-solving ability, adaptability, perseverance, drive, out-of-the-box thinking, etc.

The business world conducts interviews to evaluate objective and subjective assets. If we were only concerned with objective assets, we would hire candidates simply from their resumes (a good representation of your objective assets). I see candidates all the time who have good credentials but weak subjective skills. These candidates struggle in their career searches, especially if they are competing for development positions.

All companies want a different collection of subjective and objective assets. These requirements change with different positions. A company will value an objective or subjective asset only if it is a requirement for the position. Many times, candidates make the mistake of emphasizing the wrong assets in an interview.

Objective Asset = Objective Value

When the Company Requires the Asset

To more fully understand objective value, let's say Company XYZ calls Cameron-Brooks to recruit engineers with leadership experience. In essence, Company XYZ is stating that, "objectively speaking," officers must have an engineering degree and leadership experience to interview with them. These two required assets are an objective value to Company XYZ. In addition to these two required assets, Company XYZ states that strong information technology (IT) skills will be helpful but not required. If you have an engineering degree and leadership experience, you have the objective assets required to interview with Company XYZ. Now, let's say you have a very good knowledge of software, hardware, and networking, but your skills are not comparable to those of a computer science major. Your IT knowledge will be considered objective value-added. Realize that what is value-added for one company may be required by another.

Let's consider this scenario: Ms. Hildebrand from ABC, Inc. wants us to recruit Development Candidates for her company. My first question is, "What are your requirements?" She says, "I need candidates with business degrees and GPAs of 3.0 or above—individuals who have managed budgets and are also familiar with Six Sigma and who are able to start work by September 15." If you have these objective assets, you now have the qualifications to interview with ABC, Inc.

Ms. Hildebrand then reviews the subjective assets her company values. She says, "We're looking for individuals with a strong work ethic, willing to work hard to get results. We insist on goal-oriented, 'make-it-happen' types." Ms. Hildebrand explains that goal-oriented, make-it-happen individuals are those who have a track record of setting demanding goals and who have the discipline to fight through adversity to accomplish those goals. In addition, her company wants people who are team players, who are creative, innovative thinkers, who are consensus builders, who have vision, and who have pleasant personalities. These are subjective values. This scenario is just one example. There are numerous variations of objective and subjective values, depending upon the company and the position.

To prepare for the interview process, list all of the assets you possess that will be of value to companies. Remember that if the asset is required, it becomes valuable to the company. For most positions, your objective assets determine your functional value in the business world. Your objective assets get you in the door and allow you to interview. The more objective assets you have, the broader your marketability. It is really very simple:

More Objective Assets = More Doors of Opportunity

Exceptions to this rule are sales positions that may require fewer specific objective assets other than a demonstrated track record of success in high school, college, and the military. In other words, the type of academic degree you have might be immaterial. It could be any degree. In fact, the company recruiter may not even bother with objective assets but will concentrate only on your subjective assets. For some sales positions, a specific degree is important to have—for instance, when the product is very technical. In that case, a corresponding technical degree might be required. It would then be necessary for you to have an objective asset (technical degree) before you could interview with the company.

While objective assets will get you in the door, communicating subjective assets will get you hired. You could be a perfect objective fit for a company and still be ruled out in the interview (this happens all the time). In other words, you could have the perfect academics and work experience, but if you cannot communicate the required subjective assets, you will not succeed in the interview. Therefore, your preparation for interviews also must include analysis of your subjective assets and, most importantly, practice in communicating them. You should be able to describe your subjective assets with examples of accomplishments that illustrate the use of these assets. This is how you help company recruiters understand your methodology (your thought process behind getting things done, as well as behind the actual execution of goals and objectives), personality, attitude, and motivation.

What do you consider to be your strengths and distinguishing characteristics? Think in terms of what is most important to company recruiters. Refer to Appendix A for a list of key competencies (a compilation of subjective strengths and traits our client companies look for in Development Candidates) to help you determine your subjective assets. Companies want certain assets in potential hires, such as initiative, creativity, enthusiasm, being a team player, ability to communicate persuasively, conceptual and analytical skills, and interpersonal skills. Make sure your subjective assets are valuable to companies. Remember who "owns" the interview—the recruiter. If you want to be successful in the interview, as the interviewee, you want to be empathetic to the needs and interests of the recruiter. Put yourself in his or her shoes and ask yourself if you would hire you. Do you possess the subjective assets to get you hired? Help the recruiter fulfill his or her needs. Too often interviewees fail in the interview because they are focused on what they want rather than on what the recruiter or company wants.

After developing your list of subjective assets, take your five or six most important subjective assets and practice illustrating them in your answers to interviewing questions such as, "Tell me about a complex problem and how you solved it." "Tell me about a significant accomplishment and how you achieved it." Your answers to these questions should show your methodology—in other words, a recruiter should be able to visualize your method for doing things, your thought process behind accomplishing objectives and motivating others; from your answer, a recruiter should be able to determine your subjective assets. To be successful in doing this, your answer must contain specifics. This is why preparation is so important. For you to go back two to five years or more and discuss specific details of how you accomplished a major objective is impossible without a lot of thought. Additionally, to articulate this in a persuasive and succinct manner (remember your time in an interview is limited) is impossible without a lot of practice.

The best way to practice articulating accomplishments and assets is to speak into a recording device and evaluate yourself, or work with a partner and ask him or her to listen to the recording to determine how well you illustrated your assets. If the illustration is not clear to you as you listen to the recording or to your partner, it will not be clear to the recruiter. You will find that to deliver your answers clearly, concisely, and effectively will take many tries. I emphasize the necessity to practice verbalizing, speaking out loud, and not just "thinking" about what you want to say in order to be succinct and to the point.

Remember to be yourself in interviews. Maintain your individuality. Your experiences are yours. Your assets, objective and subjective, are yours. You are unique. You must be believable. The recruiter must see your strengths and be able to determine how well you will fit into the company. You must verbally create a picture that effectively illustrates your ability to join the company and make a significant contribution.

While the foundation of a successful interview is knowing your subjective and objective assets, you cannot get away with simply "laundry listing" those assets to a recruiter. The key is to show these assets in your examples of accomplishments. You must be able to consistently and persuasively articulate your assets by the examples you give in the interview. You also should carefully evaluate the recruiter's questions and tailor your answers to fit the specific job requirements. This means determining quickly in an interview which of your experiences is most relevant to the position for which you are applying.

General Store Exercise

Cameron-Brooks developed an exercise called the General Store that is very effective in taking successes from the military and transforming them to successful interview answers. This preparation tool takes you to the next step by defining a method to effectively market your assets in the interview, much like a general store owner markets products in a store.

Think back to the western movie that showed a general merchandise store. The assorted products, such as nails, gloves, tools, buttons, thread, etc., were arranged in various drawers and cubbyholes in a shelving unit. The general store owner assisted customers with their shopping lists, matching their needs to products in the shelves. Each customer had a different request, and the owner was the product expert who would determine the best product for each individual need. No one knew the products better, and no one had more to gain from the sale. Customer service was the priority—a commitment to making sure customers were satisfied and their needs were fulfilled.

Now picture your own general store. The product line consists of your objective and subjective assets. You have actually taken your asset list and stocked the shelves. You have many assets supported by examples and evidence to ensure your inventory is very marketable. Your customer (the company recruiter) enters your store with needs that you (the store owner) must fulfill. You must evaluate and select the "best" product that matches or fits the company's requirements. Your selection and evaluation of the best product is critical. Just as the store owner reviews and evaluates the customer's needs, so must you evaluate the recruiter's needs. After all, the store owner would not sell a hammer to someone who wanted to paint a fence.

Your examples and evidence, concisely articulated, sell the products (your assets) to the recruiter. Remember: No one knows the product better, and no one has more to gain from the sale. Just as the general store owner wants to satisfy the customer's needs and sell the store's products, you want to "fit" the recruiter's needs and sell your assets!

Your ability to effectively match your assets to the recruiter's needs in approximately 45 minutes will be a key factor for success in your interviews. You see, the recruiter knows exactly what he or she is looking for in terms of a perfect "fit" for the company. You must have the ability to persuasively convince the recruiter that your total product (your objective and subjective assets) is exactly what the company needs!

To prepare for an interview, right now you should be "stocking" your "drawers" with examples and evidence of your objective and subjective assets (see Figure 2). How many team leadership examples/products do you have? Project management examples/products? Process improvement examples/products?

Most people try to force the exact same objective and subjective assets on every recruiter. This works no better than the general store owner trying to sell the exact same merchandise to every customer. Customers all have different and specific needs—just like the recruiter. The general store owner must evaluate and identify each customer's needs in order to make the sale. You, too, must

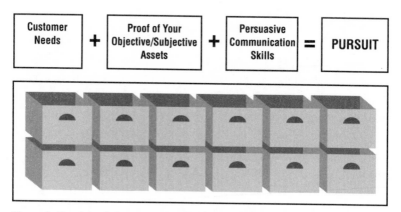

Figure 2. Candidate's "inventory" of objective and subjective assets

evaluate and identify each recruiter's needs to ensure a good "fit" and sell your assets. When you understand and apply this concept to your interviewing skills, it has a powerful impact. Investing time and thought into the general store exercise can help you achieve a very smooth-flowing exchange of quality and relevant information between you and the recruiter in the interview.

Developing Self-Insight

Our client companies constantly ask me to bring them individuals who have the ability to look in the mirror, see exactly what's there, know who they are, and have the self-confidence to be able to tell a company what they're all about.

I am reminded of a time when I was evaluating an officer who, on his application under career objective, wrote "CEO." Obviously, the minute he put this down as an objective, it was my job to see if he could offer proof and evidence that he could accomplish his objective.

I went back to his high school information to check how many times he had been evaluated number one. He hadn't graduated from high school as number one—he had a 3.1 GPA. I looked to see how many times he had been elected to leadership roles. There were none. His college GPA was 2.7. He was not class president, student body president, or, for that matter, captain of any athletic teams. I said, "Surely I'll find number one rankings in the military." I went to his military evaluations expecting, of course, to see only top-block evaluations. Again, there were some, but they were rather sporadic. I asked this individual one question: "What do you feel are the odds you would be promoted to LCDR below the zone?" He laughed and suggested it would be very doubtful. With that, of course, I had to decline him. After all, if you can't be promoted below the zone to O-4 where the statistics are more likely to be in your favor, it is unlikely you're going to leave the military and become CEO of a great company like Kraft Foods, General Mills, Corning, Boston Scientific, or PepsiCo.

When I declined this individual, he said, "Roger that's not fair. You're suggesting that I shouldn't have high objectives." I looked at the young officer and said, "Please don't say that. You must have high goals. You must have goals that make you perspire—goals that make you use every asset of your being to accomplish them. But they must be realistic goals." To become a CEO can be a personal goal, but, in this case, it should never have appeared on the officer's application. It will do you more harm than good. Remember, there is nothing wrong with ending up in the top 10 percent of a company's management structure. You do not have to be number one or two in the company to be successful. Have high goals, but be realistic and objective regarding your ability.

Some officers I interview feel it necessary to say they are a 9 or a 10 in everything they do. If this assessment is not accurate, you could get yourself into a job you're not going to be able to handle. I encourage you to be realistic. The business world has the ability to recruit the very best from college campuses such as Harvard, Penn, MIT, Stanford, Northwestern, Duke, and other top schools across the country. Remember, we're accustomed to having the very best. You must compare yourself and your skills accurately to those people who are coming out of top schools with top GPAs. We know you have a great ability to perform, but we still want you to be realistic about the assets you bring to the business world.

Companies are looking for people who are realistic about their abilities regarding job performance. *I can't count the number of officers I've seen ruled out because of inflated self-value. Remember this point.* Ambition is good, but keep it in perspective. We want to see confidence, not ego.

Discussing Your Weaknesses

Naturally, you will prepare to talk about your positive attributes (strengths) during an interview. Yet recruiters also will want to talk about your less-than-perfect attributes (weaknesses). Personally, I have never hired someone for Cameron-Brooks who could not answer the question, "Tell me about a weakness." The ability to discuss weaknesses demonstrates honest self-insight and a focus on self-development. Unfortunately, many candidates do not prepare to discuss this topic, assuming that discussing accomplishments, strengths, and positives will be enough. Your inability to discuss weaknesses or negatives will cause you to be declined in an interview if they are not handled correctly.

One way to think about weaknesses is to analyze your strengths in relation to others. As you can see in Figure 3, there are two strength lines: your normal strength line and your age group strength line. Your normal strength line is higher than the strength line for most people in your age group. There are those in your age group who did not finish high school, did not attend college, and have not had quality successes. The graph illustrates that any characteristic you would describe as "less than a strength" still would not qualify as a "weakness," as it would for most people in your age group. Those characteristics that are described as "less than a strength" are those that do not cause us to fail in the accomplishment of an objective. Recruiters won't ask you for a characteristic that is "less than a strength." They will ask for a weakness (or weaknesses). If you have a *consistent* weakness, do you really think they will hire you?

Now, how do you answer the question, "What are your weaknesses?" First, be honest. Hopefully, you can honestly identify a weakness. When you discuss it, use qualifiers such as "on rare

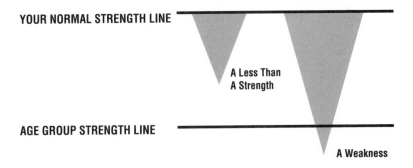

Figure 3. Comparison of your strengths with those of your age group

occasions" and "very seldom." For example, if you feel you have an occasional problem managing time effectively, you could say, "On rare occasions" or "very infrequently." "There have been a couple of times I feel I could have better managed my time." You've been candid but, in reality, have described an occasional "less than a strength" as a weakness. *By using strong qualifiers, you are leaving an important impression—that your weaknesses "rarely" or "seldom" present a challenge to the achievement of your objectives.* Again, the key in discussing weaknesses is to emphasize the fact that you experience them infrequently.

Equally as important as using qualifiers to modify a weakness is to identify specifically what you are doing to overcome the weakness. Using the example of a weakness in time management, you could suggest a definite process you have established to ensure good planning. You might say, "I can specifically remember a couple of situations during my four years in the military that could have been more effectively managed. Now, each time I find myself in a planning mode, I walk through three specific steps. First, I focus on the objective of the event. Second, I coordinate the event activities to coincide with the time the event must be accomplished, and, third, I put solutions in place for any common problem that could interfere with the timely completion of the event."

Remember that the primary reasons recruiters ask you to discuss your weaknesses are to determine your ability to be honest and candid and to identify what you are specifically doing to correct your weaknesses. To communicate that you are always perfect is to be less than honest and will cause a recruiter to determine that you are not an open communicator (because we are all human and have imperfections) and could be cause for decline.

When you discuss your weaknesses, be careful that you do not preface your remarks by saying, "One of my weaknesses . . . " or "One of my biggest weaknesses . . . ." People do this frequently. When it occurs, a recruiter is forced to ask about and examine the other weaknesses that are implied by these statements. This, obviously, will take away from the amount of time in the interview that you have to emphasize your achievements because the recruiter is focusing on a discussion of your weaknesses.

When a recruiter asks about weaknesses, they want subjective weaknesses rather than objective. Examples of potential subjective weaknesses could be receiving criticism, listening with the intent to truly understand, focusing on tasks too often versus the strategy, addressing those who failed on a promise, etc. Objective weaknesses—such as choice of a college major, lack of a master's degree, low GPA, etc.—are not what the recruiters want to hear.

When asked the weakness question, be thorough, be practical, and be prepared to discuss three of them just in case the recruiters asks for more than one. It is important to confront a negative. Don't brush it off. Don't push it to the side. Take time to examine the negatives and prepare your response.

Preparing to Discuss Failure

It is critically important that you go into any interview prepared to discuss a failure; it is probably best to have two prepared just in case. Remember that a failure is simply not accomplishing an objective or goal. It isn't necessarily earth-shattering. It won't necessarily wind up on the front page of USA Today.

"Roger, I got caught off guard," a candidate sometimes says to me. "They asked me for a failure. I couldn't come up with one." Don't let this happen to you. There can be no excuse for that.

You will be asked to discuss failures. There are two key factors about a failure that are important:

1. Companies want to see that you have enough self-confidence to be honest and forthright in describing a failure.
2. They also want to know what you learned specifically from the failure and what broad application this has for your future.

Companies will think that if you have never failed, you've probably set your objectives too low. Before hiring, companies want to know how a candidate reacted to an adverse situation. More than one recruiter has told me that they want to see candidates who have crashed into a brick wall. Companies want to know how they've reacted—if they've *learned* from the failure. They have actually asked me not to show them candidates who have not failed. I absolutely agree, so be prepared to discuss a failure. And don't be talked out of it. When you deliver your answer, accept responsibility for your failure, even if the failure was due to someone who worked for you. *Never attempt to justify the failure.*

The best example of failure you can give is one for which you were primarily responsible. It came from your lack of performance, inefficient time management, lack of organizational planning, lack of prioritizing, or overall ineffective management. *Remember, leaders do not justify failure—they learn from it.*

Your failure also needs to be an operational failure. It should be about failing an inspection, missing a deadline for a deployment, having less than 100 percent accountability for equipment, or going over budget, whether that budget was money, time, ammunition, fuel or range time, etc. It should not be a personal failure, such as your GPA, dropping from flight school, not getting the desired assignment or award. The company wants to see what you learned from operational failures and your lessons in leadership, and personal failures do not demonstrate leadership lessons.

When you discuss a failure with a recruiter, explain why you failed, how you reacted, and what you specifically *learned*. What you learn should have broad applicability in the future.

State how the failure encouraged you to improve skills in planning, organizing, communicating, analyzing, and delegating, but be specific. A recruiter wants to know that you can take an adverse situation and analyze how you would improve it, with or without a supervisor to tell you what to do. Recently an officer told me that what she learned from a failure was that the next time she purchased specific component parts for her computer department, she would be sure to check with her boss to determine her pricing latitude. While it may have been the policy for her to check with her supervisor, she also could have analyzed her skills more thoroughly. She might have determined that she needed to be more detail-oriented or that she needed to improve her planning skills. The latter analysis is much more broad-based and can have a continuous positive impact on her career.

What Do You Do When Confronted with Failure?

This question trips up candidates more often than any other I know. I encourage you to look hard at it. It is a question that is similar to being handed a stick of dynamite with a one-inch lit fuse. Be careful of it. The key word in this question is "confronted." The common response to this question is, "Well, the first thing I would do is analyze why I failed." Our response is, "But you haven't failed." What you've just told the company is, "The first thing I would do is proceed to fail; then I would turn around and analyze it." We don't think that is very smart.

Let's look at this situation for a moment. I explain to you, "You're coming to my hotel to interview with me. The road that you normally travel is blocked. Maybe it's being torn up to put in a new sewer system. Maybe a tanker truck turned over on it. What would you do?" You might say, "Well, if I couldn't go down the road, I'd turn around and go back home." Would you really? I doubt it. I think most of you would determine an alternative route to accomplish your objective. If I pointed that out, most of you would say, "Of course, that's what I would do." Yet when we ask you what you would do, you talk about the failure.

The best answer to this question I have ever received came from an Army captain from Fort Bragg, North Carolina. I'll never forget her answer. She looked at me and, using hand gestures, said,

"I can tell you one thing, Mr. Cameron—I wouldn't fail. If I can't get up the hill one way (she used her left hand to point), then I'll come up the other way (using her right hand to point a different direction)." Whatever the specific words were, her answer was beautiful. She wasn't going to allow any barrier to stop her.

Recruiters from all of our client companies have said to me that they want people who can *make things happen*. They explain, "I don't want you recommending people to me who, the minute the going gets tough, simply throw up their hands and accept the failure. That is not what we're looking for. We want people who can work through difficult situations, solve problems, and drive an objective through to successful completion."

Many years ago, on a trip to the Norfolk, Virginia, area, I asked this question of an officer I was interviewing there. The officer looked at me and gave me an answer that I hear far too frequently. The individual said, "The first thing I do when I am confronted with failure is reanalyze the objective." In other words, he will analyze his objective and lower it. If all we had to do was to lower our objective every time we were confronted with failure, nobody would ever fail.

Another frequent response is, "Well, the first thing I do when confronted with failure is let my boss know." Basically, you are stating you let your boss know that you have a "pending failure." My response is always the same: "Be glad you do not work for Roger Cameron, because that's only going to happen one time. I hire people to lay solutions—*not problems*—at my feet."

To go through this book and simply learn answers to questions isn't what this book is all about. I expect you to analyze yourself and ask, "Am I really a make-it-happen type of person? When I confront failure, do I do something about it? Does my mind automatically find an excuse to rationalize why it is okay to fail? Or do I figure out a different solution to accomplish the objective?" If it isn't the latter, do yourself a favor and stay out of the business world. It is an extremely competitive environment—more competitive than ever today. Those people who do not have the ability to find solutions to difficult tasks will fail.

Imagine a Fortune 500 company or any other leading company coming to me and saying, "Roger, we would like to pay you a fee to travel around the world and find us people who, when confronted with problems, give them back to us." Wouldn't that be absurd? Quite the contrary, companies come to me and say, "Roger, bring me people who can put in place solutions for difficult issues." I can never comprehend hiring anybody and paying him or her an outstanding salary to lay problems at management's feet. Don't miss this loaded question. Be careful. The question can be asked many ways using many different words. It won't necessarily be asked as obviously as I've asked it. It's the concept you must understand.

How Have You Dealt with a Disappointment?

Sometimes candidates confuse a question about a disappointment with one about a failure. They are similar, but the recruiter's intent with a question about disappointment is different from the one about failure. Most often the question "Can you tell me about a time you were disappointed?" or some version of it is asked during an interview for a sales position. Sales recruiters ask it because they want candidates who are goal oriented and driven, who don't like to lose a sale or take "second place." The disappointment question is not about an operational failure, but rather about a time when you had your sights set high on some accomplishment, achievement, or goal, and you just did not reach it. You might not have done anything wrong or necessarily failed. The circumstances changed or someone clearly outperformed you. Instead of the lesson learned, the recruiter wants to know *how you reacted to the disappointment* and how you set another goal, worked harder, made some changes, and ultimately succeeded.

A Word about GPA

Everyone we hire in the business world can't have a grade point average of 3.8 or 4.0. It would be nice, but it's unrealistic. Is there anything wrong with a low GPA? Maybe. If you have a low GPA and you don't have outstanding military performance, then, yes, there's something wrong with it.

I want you to realize we consider GPA to be an *indicator*. It's not absolute proof of your ability to perform. It's an indication that you're going to be an average or above-average performer, depending on the GPA. But the real proof of your abilities lies in your performance evaluations as an officer. We ask this question: "Despite the GPA, can this officer achieve bottom-line performance?" Unfortunately, I've seen officers with high GPAs who were unable to do this, and I have worked with some absolutely outstanding candidates who had relatively low GPAs. One young man, for example, had a 2.0 GPA, but every one of his evaluations was outstanding. He was consistently rated by his superiors as the best they'd supervised. He was able to convert the knowledge he gained from academics to bottom-line military performance. Under no circumstances am I suggesting you be casual about a low GPA, but I want you to understand how corporate America uses GPA to evaluate candidates. In the business world, education is considered a tool, not a ticket, and, therefore, a relatively low GPA will not necessarily prevent you from coming to corporate America as a Development Candidate.

Never justify a low GPA. I recall an officer I interviewed many years ago at Fort Lewis (now Joint Base Lewis-McChord), Washington. When I asked about his low GPA, he said his priorities were simply in the wrong place. I said, "If you were to go back and do it over, would you do it differently?" He replied, "No, I don't feel I would." And with that I declined him. Here's the analogy I drew: A young man worked for me. I sent him out on a job to accomplish a given objective. Then he came back with average to poor performance. We had a conversation as to how it could have been better. I asked him, "Now, if you had the opportunity to do that job again, would you do it differently?" He told me, "No." I said, "You've got to be kidding." *So be careful with suggesting that, in retrospect, you would still achieve only poor or fair performance. Never defend poor performance.*

We gain different perspectives as we mature and grow older. Therefore, you wouldn't go back and do everything the same. We realize, for example, that the purpose of college is academics, not extracurricular activities. Square your shoulders and simply admit that you didn't accomplish what you had the capability of doing. You'd like the opportunity to go back and redo it. But that's not possible, so explain (and give evidence) that you've been able to convert your low GPA into quality performance on the job. Some of you also can point to more recent academic achievements (advanced degrees, certifications, etc.) that demonstrated a better ability to apply yourself intellectually.

Handle your GPA head-on. Don't back away from it. And don't say you went to college to be "well-rounded" and therefore your social life and extracurricular activities necessarily detracted from the effort you put into your studies. I've known many outstanding individuals with GPAs of 3.7 and higher. I can assure you they were extremely well-rounded. It won't work to suggest that because you have a low GPA, you're well-rounded and the person with a high GPA is not. That's an alibi that will not stand up in the eyes of a recruiter.

Don't explain away a low GPA. Confront it. It had to be either a question of poor judgment or a question of intellect. Let's hope it was the former.

Asking Quality Questions

Asking quality questions proves you have an interest in the position, company, and industry. A company will not pursue you or give you an offer for employment if you do not show an interest. You could be the most qualified candidate the company interviews, but if you do not ask excellent questions, the company will assume you don't have interest and will not go to the next step with you. Asking quality questions shows intellect. Quality questions exhibit your intellectual curiosity and your ability to comprehend the position, company, and industry. They demonstrate your desire to learn (a key Development Candidate trait). In addition to proving interest and intellect, quality questions also build rapport with the recruiter. After all, we all like people who are interested in us.

Think about it this way. If you were interviewing someone

for a position, what kind of questions would you like to see from a potential hire? Naturally, you would judge the candidate by the quality of his or her questions. Does the candidate show a genuine interest in the company and this type of work? Does the candidate seem intrigued with the company and enthusiastic about the opportunity? Please don't shrug this off. Don't think questions will come to mind when you get into an interview. I can tell you this gives candidates as much or more difficulty than any other aspect of interviewing. You have to prepare quality questions before you go into the interview.

Good questions can be formulated from the job description and corporate recruiting literature (sometimes given to you prior to the interview or available on company Web sites). These are great sources for developing questions. Make a practice out of reading everything for both what it tells you and what it doesn't tell you. One of the best ways to do this is to write down questions as you read information on the company. If you don't do it this way, you might run into an embarrassing situation by asking a question that has been answered in the literature. This can be devastating to a quality interview, as it is a detrimental indicator that you did not do your homework. The recruiter says, "The candidate doesn't have the professional courtesy to prepare for this interview." Be careful! Read the literature. Study the company's Web site. Both will prompt you to think of several relevant, quality questions.

I recommend that you prepare three to five open-ended questions before you go into an interview. When the opportunity to ask a question arises, you will be prepared, but you need not solely rely on this list. By open-ended, I mean a question that requires a detailed explanation for a response versus a one- to two-word answer. Here's an example of an open-ended question: "Can you tell me about the recent new product launch and how it affected the manufacturing team leaders?" This would require a lengthy answer by the recruiter. An example of a closed-ended question is "How many manufacturing team leaders does the plant employ?" It's a closed-ended question because it requires a one-word response from the recruiter. Now you have to quickly ask another question, whereas after you ask an open-ended question, you will listen and focus on what the recruiter has to say, and more questions will come to mind. Most people ask one question, and then as the recruiter is responding, they are trying to recall the next question on their list. Wrong, wrong, and wrong! You must listen and then ask one or more questions based on the recruiter's answer, just like you would in a normal conversation.

Let me create a good interview scenario for you. Lisa, a company recruiter, describes that the plant is going through change. She states, "The plant has to make numerous changes to reduce the production cycle time and also improve quality. We are developing Kaizan teams and having some of our key leaders take Six Sigma courses. It has already reduced the cycle time." Now watch how a person with curiosity can develop a point by asking good questions (which is exactly what you must do when you get to your interviews). The candidate asks, "Lisa, that's impressive that it is already having an effect on the cycle time; what specific changes were made that impacted the cycle time?" Lisa responds to the question. The candidate's next question: "Do you see a similar fast impact on quality, and what are some of the specific improvements for quality?" The recruiter responds; the candidate listens and then asks the next question, "In this position for which I am interviewing, how could I learn Six Sigma as it applies to the plant, and what kinds of improvement projects will I be involved with?" Lisa responds; the candidate listens. And the process continues. The candidate stayed focused on Lisa's answers; by asking more questions, she developed a picture that had depth. By the time the conversation was over, the candidate also had valuable information. Lisa was pleased because of the candidate's sincere interest and ability to listen. Demonstrating interest through quality questions is key to successful interviewing. Rapport was further developed between the candidate and Lisa. Practice asking good questions. Engage yourself in what others have to say and get information out of conversations.

During initial interviews, ask only those questions related to the position you are seeking. You want to show interest in the position (after all, if you ever go to work for the company, this job is what you will do every day). Ask open-ended questions that will help you understand the nature of the position. Your questions about benefits, locations, and promotions are self-serving and should naturally be provided to you in the follow-up interview process. If you have questions of this kind, they are better asked after you have an offer. Other non-job-related issues should also be reserved for follow-up interviews or after you have an employment offer.

Take the position and break it into its component parts. For example, if you were interviewing for a procurement/contracting position, you might want to ask questions about the company's contract negotiation process, its relationships with vendors and suppliers, and how you would support the internal organization through optimal purchasing and procurement methods. By doing so, you will uncover the specifics on the type of work you will do and thus help you connect your abilities and experiences to the job requirements.

For a sales position perhaps the breakdown could include questions about products, customers, and competition. For manufacturing, questions could focus on equipment, maintenance, team members, and quality initiatives. In an interview focus on one subject at a time, then move to the next subject. Your questions should follow a natural progression or sequence of thought. Remember, all questions you ask should strictly relate to the particular job for which you are interviewing.

One way to develop good questions is to picture yourself going to work the first day. Think of all of the things you don't know about your new job. Focus on details. Develop questions that will clarify this picture in your mind. Another method I like is to assume that the recruiter is in the current position for which you are interviewing and you will start work one week from the day of your interview, but the recruiter will not be there, and you cannot call him or her. What would you need to know to be successful in the position and achieve the desired results?

Your questions should never be generic. They should be company-specific. It is very impressive in your interview to show due diligence in your homework. For instance, the following remark shows the candidate did her research: "I read in your company literature that last year the company successfully implemented several Lean and Six Sigma initiatives. Can you tell me more about these initiatives?" You can see the positive impact this statement of fact (and something that could not be said to any other company) would make on a recruiter. When you do this, the question is being asked specifically about this position at that company.

Candidates have asked in interviews, "What new products are you bringing to the market?" They've got to be kidding. Companies will not take somebody off the street and tell them what they're doing in research and development. New products are the biggest secrets companies have. This kind of question shows poor judgment. Can you imagine going to a foreign military and saying, "What new weapons are you developing?" They would laugh at you. You're smart enough not to do that. You must also be smart when you interview with companies.

You might find it useful to use numbers in forming your questions. Here are good examples: "Can you tell me the two biggest process improvement initiatives? Can you tell me the top two challenges your company faces in keeping its market share?" In other words, by asking about one or two factors, you really are inquiring about the most frequent or most significant.

It is also helpful to start a question with some background to help the recruiter understand where you are coming from. For example, "In the military, I'm evaluated usually by two people—my immediate rater and my senior rater. They evaluate me on a host of different factors: my written and oral communication skills, my maturity, and knowledge of my job. I'm curious. What are the top three performance criteria for the employees of your company?" Take the time to design your question and formulate it (in relation to your historical background) so the recruiter can better address the question.

As always, be mindful of time. Don't ask questions the recruiter will need 10 to 15 minutes of your 45-minute interview to answer.

The recruiter is not going to accept you on the basis of his or her answers, but on the basis of your answers. While it is important for you to ask quality questions, it also is important to use good judgment in asking questions that can give you information you need but be answered in a concise, succinct manner.

I have been partnering with junior officers in their transition to business for over 45 years. I have seen and experienced just about everything there is in this process and industry. I am always disappointed when I speak with an officer and during the conversation I ask, "Do you have any questions for me?" and he or she says, "No, there is nothing I can think of." Wow! Here this person is thinking about making a transition and speaking with a person who specializes in the process (even wrote a book on it!) and doesn't ask one question. Never suggest you don't have questions. Intelligent, curious people always have questions.

I recall a candidate we had who did really well with a company at the Career Conference and traveled to a follow-up interview at the company headquarters. The company raved about the candidate and wanted to give him an offer. Because one key manager was unable to interview the candidate during the follow-up, the company scheduled a telephone interview between this manager and the candidate (mostly as a formality before giving the candidate an offer). Unfortunately, the candidate forgot the importance of asking good questions and was ruled out. The recruiter just could not believe that a person interested in his company would end an interview without asking some good questions. It did not matter how qualified the candidate was, lack of quality questions ruled the candidate out.

Sometimes a recruiter will use virtually the entire interview and leave you only a couple of minutes to ask questions. Be careful. Just because you are getting close to the end of the interview, you should not say, "I have no questions." This will come across as a negative. A better way of handling it might be to ask one or two questions, and when they ask if you have more you can say, "Yes, I have other questions, but none I need answers to at this time. I can already tell you, I have a very strong interest in your company, and I'll save my questions to be answered in my follow-up interview." Remember, this is only if you are out of time. *This is not a license to forgo questions.*

Today I see more and more company recruiters engaging candidates in a conversational interview in which there is good back-and-forth dialogue versus the structured interview in which the recruiter asks several questions for 30 minutes and leaves time for the candidate to ask questions. In the conversation you have to be ready to ask questions right at the beginning and throughout the interview. Recruiters do this because it is an easy way to differentiate candidates (again by the quality of your questions). You need to be prepared for this type of interview as it is virtually impossible to rescue the interview if you start off with obviously low-weight questions like, "What is a typical day like?" I have seen this happen hundreds of times.

Asking Negative Questions

Some of the questions you might ask are what we call negative questions, such as "Could you give me insight into your employee turnover factor? Could you tell me why your quarterly earnings were down 10 percent? Could you tell me about the tenure of your labor force? What percentage of your products is returned because of poor manufacturing quality? What percentage of your products is delivered to the customer on time?" These questions could have a good foundation for asking. However, they must be asked in a manner that will not come across as negative and suggest to the recruiter that you are a cynical person. For example, "What kind of continuous process improvement initiatives do you have in place to improve the product delivery?" This is a much more in-depth and positive question and will naturally address your curiosity about the percentage of products delivered on time. Make the tone of your questions positive. Take time to develop questions. Word them so they are not negative.

I hope I've made my point. You must be serious about doing your homework and being prepared to ask quality questions.

Researching Companies

In addition to being knowledgeable of overall business trends and concepts, it is critical that you research a company prior to an interview. However, how you conduct that research prior to your interviews depends on two things. It depends on whether you are working with a recruiting firm and where you are in the hiring process.

If you are working with a recruiting firm, check with the firm first. It is usually not necessary to thoroughly research specific companies prior to attending a given career conference. A quality recruiting firm should supply you with definitive information about the particular company, position, and recruiter for each of your interviews. Yes, candidates can do research through a company's Web site, but often they do not know which specific division will be interviewing them or which content from the site is pertinent. We work closely with our client companies to get specific background information prior to any interview with our candidates, removing the need for a candidate to research on the Web for the initial interview.

If, on the other hand, you're going to send out resumes and interview with a company on your own, you must research that company thoroughly. With the Internet today you have a lot of resources, but you also will likely run into information overload. Start with the company's Web site. Most companies have an "About Us" section, and if they are publicly traded, they post their annual and quarterly reports. You should not concern yourself so much with the financials of the reports but more of the qualitative information including statements to investors, letters from the chairman and/or CEO. While this research will give you general information about a company, what is really needed for a successful interview is specific information about the position and/or functional area for which you are interviewing. You need to be able to relate your background and experiences to the requirements and responsibilities of the position. Most companies have a "Careers" section of their Web site as well. Here you will find job postings and descriptions. Search the open positions and read the descriptions, which will usually include a brief summary of the role and then several bullet statements outlining necessary qualifications, both subjective and objective requirements. The "Careers" sections typically also have a description of the culture and what is unique about working at that company. You can use this information to help you make statements of interest in the company during your interview. Other useful Web sites include Wikipedia, Yahoo Finance, Hoovers, and their competitors' sites, and you can also look at company personnel profiles on LinkedIn. YouTube also might have useful videos on the company's products and their application; I even saw a client company's video on YouTube featuring its Six Sigma initiative at a plant. It really helped the candidates put themselves in the positions and understand the production environment. Finally, if you know someone within the functional area for which you are interviewing and he or she is willing to give you specific information, this might be a good way to acquire information.

For initial interviews, research is necessary to help you understand job requirements and responsibilities and formulate quality questions. *However, while this information is important, what you know about yourself is more important than what you know about the company.* The reason for this is that most initial interviews, and for those at our Career Conferences, candidates will have structured interviews for 45 minutes in which the majority of the time is focused on the recruiter asking questions about the candidate. Recruiters want to know about a candidate's abilities and potential. Therefore, although company and position research is important, the most critical research you need to do prior to your initial corporate interviews is research on yourself. Have the ability to communicate that knowledge to a corporate recruiter.

Now, once a second or what we call "follow-up" interview is scheduled, you must do additional in-depth research of the company, whether you are working with a recruiting firm or on your own. You will use many of the same resources I outlined when you are not utilizing a recruiting firm, but you will dive deeper into the information for specifics. Additionally, if it is a consumer-oriented company, go to a retail store and look at the company's product and how it's merchandised. Or if it is a medical device company, see if you can network with family and friends to talk to a surgeon who may use the products or be familiar with them and the procedure for which they are used. If it's a public company, the Investor Relations section of its Web site will be loaded with shareholder information that can give you valuable information on the company and markets. We especially like CEO interviews or quarterly earnings webcasts to provide current information on the company. We like to see candidates who are resourceful enough to research the company in unique ways before their follow-up interview with that company.

Professional Language

I recognize that the military uses salty language and it is a part of the culture, especially in the deployed environment. However, it is not this way in business, and absolutely not acceptable in an interview. I have ruled out candidates because they showed poor judgment and used foul language in the interview. If they will do it with me, you bet they will do it with one of my companies. This is disappointing because it is completely avoidable. I debated whether or not to include this in the book, because in reality, I feel I should not even have to address this. However, since it repeatedly happens, I figured if I addressed this, I could save some precious interviews for military officers.

Remember, companies who hire the military officer are recruiting the future leaders of their company. They want candidates who are mature, demonstrating the ability to communicate with a wide variety of people (customers, suppliers, management, line personnel, peers, etc.). Slang, cursing, and overuse of military phrases will cause the recruiters to rule a candidate out. To avoid being ruled out in an interview due to unnecessary communication mistakes, follow these simple rules:

- Assume you are interviewing with your boss's boss or an O-6 officer and above. Would you say "Awesome," "Cool!" or "Too easy" to an O-6? Probably not, and you should not say them to a recruiter either.

- *No swearing!* It has no place in an interview, and swearing is an automatic rule-out. I mean not only the typical swear words but also those words we all use in their place and think we aren't actually swearing. They are just as bad in an interview—and at home and in the office, too!

- Watch your military phrases. The one that gets me is, "Too easy." This seems popular among Army officers today.

- Do not say, "To be honest with you . . . ." When you say this, you are communicating that up until that point, you have been less than honest! Yet what you really wanted to do was emphasize the following point. You communicate much more specifically and clearly when you eliminate the phrase and just say what you mean.

- Demonstrate mature body language. It's written that 90 percent of communication is through body language. It's as important as any other form of communication, so don't ignore it as you prepare for the interview process. I remember one officer who sat across from me with his arms crossed for 25 minutes. What did that tell me? Regardless of what he was thinking or saying, his body language said to me that he had no interest or did not care what I had to say. Other times, I have had candidates slouch in their chair or have their legs spread far apart. It's just not good body language. Again, how would you sit across from an O-6?

If you are going to interview with leading companies for

development positions, professional recruiters will evaluate you not only on your professionalism but on your maturity as well. Do not waste precious interviews—use your common sense and be a professional communicator.

Colloquialisms and Qualifiers

Military officers win the gold medal for using qualifiers! No one is as expert at using the qualifier as the military officer. I have no idea where it comes from. "I think." "I believe." "Probably." You must understand that the minute you give any type of answer with a qualifier in it, your answer is immediately eliminated. What you've said to the recruiter is, "I'm not really sure, but here's what my guess would be." In an interview we're not asking for your guess, we're asking for the way it is.

I remember I had a young recruiter working for me. I became very frustrated with him over a period of time. It was time to sit down and have a nose-to-nose conversation. He consistently used qualifiers in answering the simplest of questions. I had asked him what time it was. He looked at his watch and said, "I *think* it's *about* . . . ," instead of looking at his watch and saying, "It's 1:09." In other words, he used two qualifiers just to tell me what time it was! As I say, it was nose-to-nose time!

Do not use words such as "yeah," "you know," "roger," "check," and, as I stated before, my least favorite of all, "too easy" for "yes." There is absolutely no reason for you to ever use the words "you know." I quickly remind people that if "we knew," we wouldn't be asking the question.

I remember one individual who began and ended every sentence with "okay." This is not something you can do and call yourself a good communicator. Be very careful of colloquial expressions and qualifiers.

Talking in the First Person

In the military, as in the business world, the most dominant pronoun used to describe actions is "we." However, when describing actions and answering questions in an interview, the only correct pronoun to use is "I." *"I" is the only word in the English language that gives you total ownership of an action.* "We" shares the action, and "you" assumes a philosophical stance or discussion. Please, bend the corner of this page. Highlight every word in this paragraph. The recruiter is interested in knowing about you—not anyone else. He or she doesn't want to know what you might do in theory but rather exactly what you do in reality. This concept is critical to a successful interview and is difficult for most officers to adopt. You must develop the habit of talking in the first person (using the pronoun "I") long before your first interview.

As we accomplish missions in the military and in business, it is only professional to share the success. However, when you are being interviewed, the recruiter is only interested in hiring one person for each position. Therefore, if you sit in front of a recruiter using the pronoun "we," you will fail in the interview. First of all, the recruiter is not interested in hiring all of "we," and, second, it is going to be difficult for the recruiter to determine what you did. If your accomplishment was a group success, you might describe it this way: "My accomplishment was _____. We were successful because I had some great soldiers working for me. Each member of our team made this accomplishment happen. Without them, I could never have had the same degree of success. My role in this mission was _____." Now you proceed in the first person: I planned; I organized; I created; I motivated; I persuaded; etc. Imagine yourself as a puppeteer. You are orchestrating the actions. The key is to give sincere credit to your team while making clear your role, abilities, and responsibilities related to the accomplishment.

Be careful not to be too "I" oriented. Give credit where credit is due. Show that you know the importance of taking care of your team members and that you exercise this. If you don't, you will be ruled out for coming across as being egocentric.

Spouses/significant others, here is a great way to make some money. Fine your spouse/significant other every time he or she uses the pronouns "we" and "you" when he or she should be using "I."

Begin with a one-dollar fine for each misuse, and, if that doesn't work, raise the fine to five dollars. I cannot emphasize enough the importance of developing this habit early in your preparation process. If you wait to practice talking in the first person when it is time to start interviewing, it will be too late.

DON'T USE MY WORDS. USE MY THOUGHTS.

Make sure the answers you give are your answers. Make sure they are well thought out and represent an accurate picture of yourself and your skills. The end result of preparation is that you have intellectualized your answers. You understand yourself, your abilities, your accomplishments. The next step is to deliver them with passion and conviction in an interview. Passion indicates ownership and believability. Be careful—don't miss this point. All the preparation in the world is worthless unless the recruiter believes your answers are genuine.

Involving a Spouse or Significant Other

Should spouses (or significant others) get involved in a career search? *Absolutely!* In all the years I've been in this business, I have encouraged spouses and significant others to attend our Information Meetings, Personal Interviews, and Career Conferences. Changing career direction is one of the most important moves you're going to make in your lifetime. It affects the futures of you and your spouse/significant other. Your career is probably the longest relationship you will have next to marriage.

Examine this critical move as a team. Our Information Meetings include too much information to take home and give in proper context to someone else. Your spouse/significant other needs to be involved in gathering and analyzing information so you can make an informed decision together. You both should have the same degree of knowledge regarding the business world, and you both should have the same degree of commitment to making your lives and career(s) in the business world successful.

Your spouse/significant other can offer constructive critiques and help with interview preparation. He or she should also be involved when you are evaluating offers and making a decision about a position and the company with which you will launch your business career.

When spouses and significant others help with interview preparation, they need to be very honest in their critiques. At the same time, they need to be highly supportive and give lots of positive reinforcement. Effective interviewing is difficult (remember you must be at your best), and preparing to be at your best can be very frustrating. This is not the time for them to be nice or let things slip by. They need to offer help constructively. If your spouse/significant other is too casual in giving critiques, you will tend to make the same mistakes when you interview with a recruiter. While frustrating for you, your spouse/significant other must mention every time you misuse a word, ramble, imply rather than state, and use the phrase "you know." Spouses and significant others should be particularly aware of the believability of the delivery. If answers don't sound sincere, the recruiter will sense the same thing.

Spouses/significant others should ask themselves, "Do I understand exactly what my partner is saying? Does my partner come to the point immediately, give me substance, and answer the entire question? If I were a recruiter, would I like the way the answers were delivered? Is there enthusiasm in the voice and a sparkle in the eyes? Will my partner excite the listener? If I were a recruiter, would I want to hire my partner?" They must detach themselves, be strict and thorough evaluators, and demand quality performance. It is the only way to help candidates improve their interviewing skills.

You can record your answers, and then you and your spouse/significant other can better evaluate what you said. Sometimes, you will want to defend yourself, saying, "That isn't what I said," or "That isn't how I meant to say it," or "I don't think that's what I said." The recording device will play back exactly what you've said and won't lie to you. If you can't articulate or deliver smoothly into a tape recorder, you will not verbalize effectively in front of a recruiter either. These are frustrating methods of preparation, but frustration in front of your spouse/significant other, a recording device, or, for that matter, your recruiting firm will not cost you an interview. Frustration in front of a company will probably cost you a follow-up interview and a job offer.

If working with a spouse/significant other is not possible, work with other officers who are also making a transition. Ask your recruiting firm for names of those on your base or in your area who are preparing for corporate interviews or an upcoming career conference. If you cannot find someone in your area, work with someone via Skype or Facetime. Make a pact to be honest in critiquing one another. Be willing to throw out ideas. Everyone stands to benefit from group work sessions. The sessions will force you to practice articulating accomplishments, and you will receive valuable feedback.

To help your spouse/significant other learn more about the transition process and critical factors, as well as provide assistance in interviewing preparation, we highly recommend that he or she also read *PCS to Corporate America*.

Developing a Habit of Professional Reading

Reading business and self-development books and periodicals is one of the most important steps in preparing for a transition to the business world. Reading increases your knowledge of the business world and provides the foundation for all of your transition and interview preparation. Even if you are simply examining your career options and researching business, start today to educate yourself. Increasing your knowledge of business will increase your ability to make the right career decisions, apply business concepts in your military career to develop connecting points for future interviews, and demonstrate interest in business during an interview.

Corporate America wants broad-minded, well-read people. As a Development Candidate, you must be committed to enhancing your knowledge base and skill package every year. Having the knowledge to step into another area of expertise will open doors for you. Business is a dynamic environment, and the only way to guarantee yourself a leadership role with today's ever-changing and growing companies is to bring to the table a broad skill set. One of the best ways to continually enhance your knowledge base and skills is through a habit of daily professional reading.

Cameron-Brooks alumni will agree with me that reading about business trends and practices is actually pleasurable because we love reading about better ways to run our businesses, motivate our teams, and improve our services, and we love reading about other cutting-edge thinkers and successful business leaders. If you have made the decision to transition to corporate America, I would hope you find reading about business leaders and issues motivating and pleasurable. If you don't, I recommend you reevaluate which career direction is right for you.

I know you are busy with your military career and other obligations, but you cannot use the excuse that you do not have time to read! Every senior military officer and corporate leader will tell you that you don't have time *not* to read. It makes you better.

To cultivate a habit of daily business reading, I recommend you establish reading goals for yourself that are specific. Set aside time every day to read—20 minutes a day, an hour a day, three hours a day (one hour in the morning, a half hour at noon, and one and a half hours in the evening). At a minimum, I recommend you set a goal to read one quality business book each month. Under no circumstances do I believe this to be adequate, but it is a start and will get you headed in the right direction. As your reading habits develop, increase the number of books you read.

To maximize your time, I recommend you power-read business books. Business books do not have to be read like novels. In fact, rarely should a business book be read from cover to cover (it takes too much time). When you read a business book, your goal is to learn five to ten new business tools that you can use at work to augment your productivity and problem-solving abilities. To do this, you do not need to read the book from cover to cover or page for page. Instead, use a Power Reading style. The following is a step-by-step description of Power Reading.

- Read the inside cover to get a good overview of the book. These covers are usually loaded with content.
- Thoroughly read the preface and introduction as well as the first three chapters (80% of the tools in a business book are covered in the first 30% of the book).
- As you identify tools that you like, write a brief summary of the tool/topic on the back inside cover of the book (there are always blank pages in the back of every business book). Ensure you write the page number next to the topic for future reference. If you use an e-reading device, you can take notes using the Notes tool of the device or keep a notebook.
- Return to the table of contents and study the content of the remaining chapters.
- Identify and read three or four chapters on topics that you want to learn more about. As you learn more, add to your notes.
- Skim the remaining chapters for interesting content. Take notes when you find a good concept or tool.

With this approach, not only will you learn five to ten new business concepts, but you will also have good notes for future reference. You can also frequently return to good books in your library to review Power Reading notes.

As a Development Candidate in corporate America, you will be expected to read everything you can get your hands on. Reading for professional development must be a habit, like brushing your teeth in the morning. We want people who like to grow their knowledge base and who understand the importance of doing so. We want people who have a high degree of curiosity. We believe you're never too busy to read. Make reading of diverse subjects a habit!

Also, subscribe to *Fortune* magazine and study every issue cover to cover. I recommend *Fortune* over other magazines because it offers articles describing broad business trends that will help you make good decisions regarding the business world as well as make an impact in your interviews. Additionally, begin a habit of daily perusal of USA Today or the Wall Street Journal, plus a regional newspaper. The idea is to obtain regional as well as broad national news.

In over 45 years of partnering with military officers, I have found that very few read a wide variety of subject matter—business periodicals, national newspapers, or books that have been on the best-seller list for months and months. Many of you read a lot of military publications, and while that is good, we would like to see you read a wide array of material, especially if you are planning to transition to the business world.

You must continue to grow intellectually if you want to consistently achieve. Our client companies demand we bring them knowledgeable people who are willing to grow. Pick up a book for 30 minutes before going to bed at night. If you tell me, "I don't have time to do this," I think you need to reevaluate your career and your life. You cannot spend the rest of your life in a formal academic environment. Therefore, you must read in order to gain knowledge.

A critical part of your transition preparation must include gaining an understanding of the business world and the different careers available to you. You must be able to communicate this understanding intelligently in an interview. Appendix C contains a list of sources I recommend for your personal development and, specifically, for gaining business knowledge. This list is not exhaustive but rather representative of reading material that will give you a broad knowledge of the business world and thus make you better prepared for corporate interviews and a successful business career.

Getting Organized

I've never observed a highly successful person who wasn't organized. Successful individuals are able to juggle numerous appointments, assignments, responsibilities, and dates to remember and still meet their obligations within difficult time limits. Learning to be thoroughly organized should be part of your early development. I see many military officers who do very well at this; however, some do not. Don't wait until others see you as unorganized and forgetful before you develop the professional habit of organizing and planning your time efficiently. I can attest to the fact that some Development Candidates have had setbacks in their careers for just this reason.

I strongly recommend you develop your own planning system. There are many different planning products and systems from which to choose, ranging from smart phones to software programs to hard-bound planning systems. Find what works for you. The business world predominantly uses Microsoft Outlook. I encourage you to become familiar with it if you are not already using it. It's a great way to organize tasks, maintain calendars and contacts, send meeting invitations, and more. It also syncs nicely with most smart phones.

Your Mission

Company recruiters consistently compliment us on how prepared and knowledgeable our candidates are. We work very hard to effectively prepare, teach, develop, and coach our candidates. Some clients describe our development program as a mini-MBA. Our candidates read every book they can, many earn executive education certificates in Six Sigma and Lean, and some get MBAs and other advanced degrees related to business. They learn everything they can about themselves. They learn the best way to have successful interviews. They practice, practice, and practice! These officers make it their mission to maximize their marketability and earn as many interviewing opportunities as they can. In fact, this is exactly the way companies will expect you to approach an objective you attempt to accomplish in your business career. They will expect you to prepare well, do thorough research, and then execute with precision. You cannot expect a recruiter to believe you will prepare well and work hard to accomplish missions for their organization when you haven't done the same for your own interviews and future professional career!

By having a great interview, you will show the recruiter that you prepare well and work hard to accomplish your objectives. A career transition is as deserving of preparation as every other important mission in your life—if not more so.

"One secret of success in life is for a man to be ready for his opportunity when it comes."

—*Benjamin Disraeli*

Take time and invest in preparation—then you will be "ready."

Chapter 4

THE PHYSICAL FACTORS OF INTERVIEWING

O nce you start to work for a company, you'll be measured primarily according to your performance. When you interview, you're going to be judged on every possible factor, including first impressions.

Clothes and Appearance

W hat you wear to an interview is a big part of first impressions. This is especially important when you are interviewing as a Development Candidate. The interviewer is measuring your leadership upside. It's disappointing to hear of someone who has worked hard to secure a good education, build an impressive resume, put in time preparing for interviews, and is then ruled out because of the way he or she is dressed.

If you're outstanding and have done everything right, it's possible, but doubtful, that your clothes will rule you out of a job—unless they are unprofessional. But if the recruiter feels something about you is questionable and that is compounded by a poor appearance, then your clothes will become a major factor.

Someone once said, don't dress for the job you have, but rather dress for the job you want. Go on YouTube and pull up several CEO interviews and notice the way they are dressed. That's your target.

Your physical appearance should imply that you are professional and competent and that you can get the job done. This does not mean you should look dull, but, if you err, it should be on the side of being conservative versus highly fashionable. Remember that you are not trying to please your friends or the fashion experts but rather make a professional first impression on the people who make hiring decisions. These individuals are usually mature and conservative (at least in their business appearance), and care more about what you can accomplish than how good-looking you are.

Please note that my recommendations for dress are solely for the purpose of success in the corporate interview. I'm not attempting to address what you should wear on the job but only what you should wear in the interview. Once you are in a business career, you will have greater flexibility to dress as you please. In addition to my recommendations here, you can also review John Molloy's *New Dress for Success*. Although this was published in 1988, acceptable business attire for men has been established and widely practiced for many years and has not changed. On the other hand, business attire for women is not universally understood, and women can easily make serious mistakes when they take advice from well-meaning people (even clothing store personnel) who do not understand what constitutes professional business clothing for women. Therefore, it is very important for women to read Molloy's *New Dress for Success for Women;* though published in 1996, it is still relevant today.

We recommend that women have two suits for interviewing purposes. Each suit should have a matching jacket and pants or skirt and should be designed in a traditional, conservative style, in solid colors of either black, gray, or navy blue. Some national brands we recommend are Ann Taylor, Brooks Brothers, and Jones of New York. Many styles and colors are available in women's business suits today, and you must select suits of traditional cuts and colors for interviewing. If you choose to wear a suit with a skirt, the length of the skirt should be at the knee or just below the knee. White or off-white tailored blouses are best. They should not be sheer, overly lacy, or made of a fabric commonly worn in social situations. The neckline should be discreet and professional in appearance.

Shoes should be low-heeled (two inches or less is a good rule of thumb) with closed toes and heels. You should be able to stand easily and walk briskly in your shoes. Black, navy, or other dark neutral colors are best. Wear natural-colored hose with no seams or texture.

A woman's handbag should be of small or moderate size and only large enough to carry essentials. It should be what we call "a business purse" that simply gets the job done. Again, black, navy, or dark neutral colors are best.

Women should keep jewelry to a minimum for an interview. One ring on each hand (at the most) and a strand of pearls or a simple gold chain is sufficient jewelry. If you wear earrings, they should be small or fit close to the earlobe. Dangling earrings are not appropriate.

Women should have a hairstyle that is neat and professional. If your hair is below shoulder length, wear it pulled back. A tailored hairstyle is best.

Your makeup should be light—blush and lipstick that are natural looking rather than bright or dramatic. Avoid heavy eyeliner or eye shadow. Your fingernails should be medium to short in length. If you wear nail polish, be sure it is clear. Keep perfumes light or wear none at all.

For both men and women, the rule is to look conservative, professional, classic, and sharp. Everything should be done in moderation. That's why overdoing perfume or aftershave lotion can leave a reminder of you long after you're gone—and not in a positive way.

Men's hair should be cut in a conservative, professional style. If you have a hairstyle that parts, be sure your part is clean and well defined. If your hair is very fine and has a tendency to blow out of shape with the slightest breeze, then use hair spray to hold it in place.

Men should also have two suits. Each should be two-piece and single-breasted with 1½-inch cuffs on the pants. Your suit colors should be navy blue or dark gray. They can be solids or with single white pinstripes ¾ inch apart. The stripe should be very subtle and only visible when you are within arm's length.

Although you might be able to get by with one suit for your job search, I highly recommend two. Then you won't get stuck in a situation that can often occur. You have just returned from an interview and sent your suit out for cleaning, and then you get a call from another company to get on a plane tomorrow for another interview. Now you can use your other suit! One word of caution on cleaning suits–I recommend you have your suits cleaned no more than two or three times a year. I prefer to have mine cleaned only once a year. More cleaning equals faster wear and tear.

Your suits don't need to be extremely expensive, but they should be of good quality. There are several good brands, but we consistently recommend Hart Schaffner Marx and Brooks Brothers. Depending on the line of the suit and the tailoring, we also recommend Jos. A. Bank, which typically has sales for you to build your business wardrobe. All three sell good-quality, moderately priced business suits in styles that are exactly what you need in a business cut. Sometimes, you can find two suits that are acceptable for interviews on sale for the price of one. Your suits should always be extremely well pressed for interviews.

Your shirts should be white because this color projects professionalism and confidence. They also work in every situation with a suit. Blues, purples, pinks, and other colors can create the wrong impression. For example, blue softens a person's presence. This is not what you want to convey in an interview. I usually suggest shirts that are wrinkle-resistant for your job search. You can easily travel with these, folding them in your suitcase and then hanging them up when you arrive, or pulling them from your closet and wearing them immediately. If they have a couple of wrinkles, it will take a quick ironing, or you can use an old business traveler's favorite trick: hang the shirt in the bathroom while you take a hot shower, letting the steam take out the wrinkles. If you do not get the wrinkle-resistant shirt, I highly recommend you wear shirts with button-down collars. I can't tell you the number of times I have seen candidates' collars pointing in the wrong direction! The button-down design overcomes any collar problem. However, if you get the wrinkle-resistant material, you can get the straight pinpoint collar and use quality metal or plastic collar stays to hold them in place. You will absolutely need the collar stays, so if you are forgetful and might leave these at home, go with the button-down version.

Your ties should be "power ties"—bold in color—so that they are the focal point. There's a very simple reason for this. When you travel, you can't take four or five suits with you and change your suit frequently. If you want to switch your tie in the middle of the day, 90 percent of those around you will think you've changed your entire suit.

You can't buy a $25 tie today that will be acceptable for an interview. You will need to spend $30 to $40 or more. Don't ruin an interview for the sake of saving money.

Wear good-quality socks that are over-the-calf; you can buy these types of socks at most major department stores or men's dress stores. You can run in these socks, and they will stay up. Don't wear socks that bunch down around your ankles, as I so often see in interviews.

The shoe I recommend is a wing-tipped or cap-toed lace-up or loafer with a tassel. I recommend a shoe in wine (sometimes called burgundy or cordovan) or black, not the brown or chile-colored shoes that are popular today. They can appear more casual than the wine or black colors. When you travel, you can't carry a lot of different shoes. You can wear the shoes I recommend with a gray or blue suit and a variety of dress slacks. It's an extremely acceptable shoe and is a good choice for interviews and casual wear. Ensure that the shoes are leather-soled. I see many candidates now wearing rubber-soled shoes. Some do shine nicely, but the rule is that you should wear leather-soled shoes with wool pants (the material of your suit pants); you can wear rubber-soled shoes with cotton pants (Dockers, chinos, jeans, etc.). Be sure your shoes are well shined. There is no excuse for any other appearance. There are even small shoeshine kits available that you can carry in your pocket.

Occasionally, a recruiter will ask you to wear "business casual" attire for dinner or meetings other than the actual interview sessions. But what does that mean? There are many different definitions of business casual, especially now that more and more companies have instituted a business casual dress code in the office, either every day or on specific days, like Fridays or when clients are not in the office. For men, I recommend quality slacks, a shirt, a tie, and a sport jacket. (A suit jacket worn with slacks is not a sport jacket.) Today quality slacks and a long-sleeved, collared, pressed shirt without a tie and sport jacket is acceptable, but be careful. If you find your dinner companion isn't wearing a jacket or a tie, it's very simple to remove yours. *It's easy to dress down, but impossible to dress up.*

For women, I recommend a dress or a skirt and blouse with a blazer. Nice pantsuits are acceptable for women today, but again, be careful. You want to portray a clean, crisp, professional look.

No matter what a recruiter suggests you wear for attire, I strongly encourage you to wear the upper end of what is permitted. After all, you are still in the interview process, even though it is not an interview for which you are dressing. Also, if you dress too casually, you are going to feel uncomfortable during the dinner or meeting and less confident. I promise you, you will not be successful feeling this way. Dress for confidence. Dress up rather than down. Let me assure you that if you are in an interview and you're underdressed, you can't make up the difference on the spot. Know ahead of time what will be expected of you. If the company with which you are interviewing does not advise you, ask what is appropriate to wear.

Remember that as a Development Candidate in the business world, you will be expected to lead, not follow. The way you dress and present yourself says a lot, not only about you and your judgment but also about the company or product you will represent. Don't kid yourself. Companies want their employees to look professional and sharp. Today companies want you to be comfortable, but nowhere in the plethora of definitions of "business casual" do the words "unprofessional" or "sloppy" appear.

Remember what you wear when you go to work for a company will be at your own discretion within their professional set of standards. You'll be measured primarily on your work performance, but in a job search, your clothes are a key factor that companies use to evaluate you and your judgment.

Wristwatches

If you wear a watch for your interviews, wear one that is professional-looking, understated, and appropriate for business attire. The watch face and band should be of appropriate size in proportion to your wrist. For metal bands, I recommend a silver or gold color, and for leather bands, black, cordovan, or brown. A general rule is that if you wear a leather band, it should match your belt which matches your shoes. I discourage you from wearing a sports watch, as it is too heavy and bulky and does not look appropriate with a business suit. Additionally, if your watch has alarm or beeps at certain times of the day, ensure it is turned off. It can be very distracting in your interviews.

For all male candidates, I suggest no jewelry other than a class ring, a wedding band, and a business-style wristwatch.

Glasses

If you wear glasses, I advise you to wear professional and conservative-looking frames that will be appropriate with the clothes you wear to your interviews—conservative and confident in appearance. The easiest way to be sure your selection is a good one is to try on the frames while wearing one of your business suits and standing in front of a full-length mirror.

Most importantly, have your glasses fitted properly (by a professional) so that you won't have to push your glasses into place repeatedly during the interview. Candidates often have developed such a habit of doing this that they make the motion of pushing their glasses into place even when they are not wearing them!

Most optometrists will adjust your glasses while you wait, free of charge. Therefore, take advantage of this service and make sure your glasses fit properly.

Being on Time

Few behaviors hinder your climb to the top of the corporate ladder more than being habitually late for commitments. When you are late in arriving for an interview, or any type of event or appointment, or in sending a thank-you note or report, the impression you leave is unsatisfactory. Make it a habit: Never be late.

I encourage you to look at being late for an interview from the point of view of a recruiter. Often, when you are late, you are thinking, "I'll only be a minute late—or, at the most, five minutes late." I encourage you to realize you are the only one who knows this. The person expecting you knows nothing. When you are late by even a minute, the recruiter is placed in the uncomfortable position of wondering where you are. Numerous possibilities present themselves—perhaps you are in the elevator, maybe you have forgotten the appointment, or perhaps you've even had an accident. As the minutes go by, the recruiter doesn't know whether to wait, make a phone call, or leave to do other work. In any case, your action has resulted in the recruiter wasting time.

After you force a recruiter's anxiety level to climb, it may be difficult for you to have an objective interview.

Don't justify being late with excuses. They won't work. The point is this: Consider what being late says about you—nothing good! Being late to an interview, a meeting, an appointment, or whatever it may be implies that you do not care about the commitment enough to plan accordingly (this includes anticipating potential obstacles, like heavy traffic) and arrive on time.

I suggest that you always arrive at commitments five minutes before the scheduled time. Manage yourself and your surroundings such that you can easily meet your commitments. If you value something enough to commit to it, don't let something like being late destroy it for you.

Cell Phone Etiquette

It's time to put cell phone use into perspective. When you carry your phone with you, turned on, you invite interruption, which means you've lost control. I never carry my phone into a business, a restaurant, a retail store, or any other place, and I certainly do not have it with me during an appointment. Therefore, I advise that you *do not* take a cell phone with you into an interview. You are inviting an interruption. Even if you think you will turn it off, there is a high likelihood you will forget. Think I'm wrong? Just ask those people whose cell phones go off during one of my presentations or when I am in church. It's rude, and what it says is, "This meeting is not important and can be interrupted." If you look at your phone or if it rings, dings, or vibrates during an interview, I guarantee you it is an automatic rule-out.

Your cell number will likely be your preferred method for companies to contact you. Your voicemail message should be professional and brief. No one likes having to take the time to wait through a long message and other verbiage to be able to leave a voicemail message. I recommend you have a short greeting stating, "You have reached Roger Cameron's cell phone voicemail; please leave me a message with your name and number and I will return your call." I'm always impressed with a message that says "I'll get back to you within the hour" or one that says "will get back to you today." I don't like it when someone says, "I will get back to you at my earliest convenience." You will get back with me when it is convenient for you? I don't think so. If you can't commit to getting back to someone within the hour or day, at least say, "As soon as possible."

If you have a phone conversation in public (in an airport, waiting room, etc.), talk in a low voice. There is no reason for talking so loud to be a distraction to those around you. Be professional and be courteous and sensitive to those around you.

What To Do and Not Do in the Interview

What are the most common things officers do and don't do in an interview? Probably the best learning experience an officer or any job candidate could have would be to sit in the corner of my hotel room and observe others interview. Members of our team have come with me to military bases to watch as I conduct interviews throughout the course of the day. They each will tell you they were amazed at what they saw candidates do and not do.

Demeanor. Many officers present themselves to company recruiters as if they're carrying the weight of the world on their shoulders. While you may have heavy pressure on you, especially in today's war environment, remember that companies want someone who is open, friendly, quick to smile, and eager to be there, someone who has the ability to make the conversation flow. In a Development Candidate, we want to see a high level of poise and confidence. We expect maturity, and we expect you to be personable and able to interact easily with others. While we certainly understand you have some butterflies in your stomach, you want to show a lighter, more at ease, professional style. It is imperative that you contain your nervousness and demonstrate poise and confidence in an interview. Don't let poor impressions cause you to be ruled out.

Smile. Remember to smile in the interview—a smile attracts a smile. A recruiter will never believe you are interested or excited about an opportunity if he or she never sees you smile during the interview. More importantly, how can you develop rapport with someone without smiling? You will be nervous in an interview, but do not forget to smile. Smiling is an easy thing to do. It takes hardly any effort to smile, and the results can be profound in just about any situation. Try it today. Try it in an interview.

Posture. Often you must sit in chairs that contribute to poor posture. Sometimes the armrests are positioned in a way that you cannot help but rest your elbows on them. When you do, your hands are up in your face. I've seen people come in and talk through their hands, actually leaning on their hands at 9:00 a.m. as if they were tired. Posture is important. Sit up straight in the chair. *Control your environment—don't let the environment control you.* You can change your posture. Don't sit there as stiff as a board. Be natural—but with good posture. And it's okay to cross your legs. Don't sit on the front edge of your chair. Sit back in a professional, comfortable manner. When you want to show enthusiasm, lean forward slightly in your chair. Give yourself room for physical expressions, keeping in mind, of course, that your demeanor and presence must always be professional.

Chewing gum. This is an automatic rule-out. I'm always disappointed when an officer steps in front of me in an interview or at an Information Meeting attempting to communicate with me while chewing gum. It's unprofessional. When I've declined officers for this reason and explained why, they are always quick to tell me they would never chew gum in front of a company. You've got to be kidding! Now, you're telling me you are simply selectively unprofessional! Please, never have anything in your mouth as you talk to others. Watch the news tonight. I assure you that you will never see a CEO on CNBC or a senator on a news channel chewing gum while communicating in a TV interview. They don't, and neither should you. Leaders don't do this.

Smoking. While it is common sense to not smoke in an interview, it may not be common sense to completely avoid smoking within hours of your interview and *never* smoke wearing your interview attire. You will arrive at the interview smelling like smoke, and the interview will be immediately over. Frankly, in today's business environment, smoking is seen as an unsophisticated habit. The costs and health effects are now more widely known. If you smoke, avoid allowing the recruiters to know about your habit. It might be acceptable in certain companies or designated areas, but it is becoming far less so. If that is offensive, please understand that this is just the nature of the environment today.

Foul language. As I outlined in Chapter 3, there can never be an excuse to use foul language in an interview or, for that matter, anywhere in corporate America. What you're saying is that you do not have the ability to express your point of view without it. If you do that, you're telling corporate America everything they want to know about you. There is absolutely no excuse for it. Every time a candidate has used foul language in an interview, I hear about it from the recruiter, and every time, they are declined by the recruiter. I always feel sorry for a person who uses foul language without thinking of the offending message it sends to others. Do yourself a favor and never bring foul language to an interview or corporate America.

Nervous habits. You should be able to come into an interview, regardless of the environment, and concentrate specifically on what you are doing. I've seen interviews take place in almost every location possible—hallways, parking lots, hotel rooms, or on a walk around the block. Don't let nervous habits unconsciously make you look bad. Focus.

For example, in some hotels the room where the interview takes place has a window that looks out on the courtyard or a street. I've had candidates indicate they're more interested in checking out what's taking place in the courtyard or the cars driving by than they are in focusing on the interview. If you're looking out the window, you're losing vital concentration.

Many officers insist on fiddling with pens. There you are, during an interview—fiddling, as if it didn't mean anything, as if it didn't reveal an unconscious nervous habit. Another nervous habit is waving one leg back and forth when one leg is crossed over the other. I had one applicant who did this constantly, so I suddenly took my left arm and began waving it back and forth from my shoulder out. I continued to ask questions. The officer stared at me. I asked, "Am I bothering you?" He said, "Yes, you really are." I then pointed out his nervous habit, which had been distracting me. He sat very still for the balance of the interview and became conscious of a subconscious nervous habit.

You may say, "I would never do that." I have seen many people with nervous habits. Another unquestionably bad habit is when people pop their knuckles. This is rude. When I have brought these bad habits to their attention, they were not even conscious of them. So this isn't something that just happens to a few people or the unfortunate few people. It happens to a lot of people. Be very careful of these negative unconscious habits.

Sometimes I want to say to an officer I am interviewing, "Would you mind sitting on your hands?" Almost every second they're attempting to communicate with their hands. It's okay to do that on occasion. But in the interview you must do everything in moderation. You can't talk with your hands throughout an interview. It gets annoying—and we try to imagine you at a staff meeting or in a company presentation. It becomes so distracting that it's difficult to concentrate on what you're saying.

Many hotels have noisy air conditioning units. But sometimes officers will ignore the noise. They'll still talk in a normal tone of voice instead of lifting their voices to overcome the air conditioning. If I have to turn off the air conditioning in order to hear the officer, I'm going to decline him or her. If they're not aware enough to raise their voice over the noise, then they're really not the kind of person my companies are paying me to find.

Also, there's the problem of what some people do with their rings. I've had officers take off a wedding band and try it on each finger, not even aware of what they're doing. One man got his ring stuck on his thumb and had a hard time getting it off. I have seen a ring fall to the floor and invariably roll under the bed, under the couch, or under the table. It's embarrassing—you're sitting there in your good-looking new business attire. Then, suddenly, you're on the floor, trying to retrieve a ring from under your chair.

Watch your nervous habits.

What to Take to an Interview

Less is more here. When you go to an interview, carry a simple executive folio that has a professional look. Don't bring your work day planner that is overstuffed with papers. We don't think it's good to carry a briefcase. It's just too much and does not a give a good first impression. Keep your folio closed and at your side during the interview; if it's small enough, you can keep it in your pocket. Don't make it the centerpiece of your interview. It's much better to let the recruiter focus on you rather than what you are carrying. You will use the notebook to take down names, addresses (if a company wants you to send them something), or a phone number (if the recruiter wants you to call him or her). If you have a break in your interview schedule, capture as many notes as you can on the day, issues that came up, questions to ask later, etc. Capture names and titles in your notebook (before you forget). So often you will see certain individuals again, and it's great to remember them and your previous meeting. You will meet a lot of people in the hiring and interview process, and good notes will help you remember. Get organized.

Do not be embarrassed about clarifying names, spellings, or other details when you are writing them down. This also holds true for people who call you on the phone during the interview process. It shows professionalism and thoroughness. There is no excuse for missing a name and failing to ask for clarification. This is particularly important if you get into an interview where there are several recruiters. It's critical to write down their names so you can remember them and also send them thank-you letters or e-mails later. Don't be afraid to ask them how to spell their names or to ask for clarification: "Tim? Or did you say Jim?" There is absolutely nothing wrong with that. I know of many embarrassments caused by people forgetting names. Again, you shouldn't keep your folio open on your lap during the interview; it should be readily accessible. It should be clean so you don't have to thumb through pages finding a clean page where you can write a note.

The things you don't take with you into an interview are your laptop computer, cell phone, iPad, or anything else that has no purpose for the interview. Simple is better.

I strongly recommend that you go through a careful self-evaluation after every interview. Interviewing is a skill and can be improved with self-examination and practice. See the interview self-evaluation exercise in Appendix D.

Chapter 5

INTERVIEWING STRATEGY—
FROM PROVING YOUR FIT TO CLOSING

I want to introduce this chapter with some words of motivation. As I explained in the introductory chapter, there are three ways you can transition to the business world—you can either accelerate, step down, or make a lateral move (step across) into a business career.

I've had officers (with whom Cameron-Brooks did not partner) call me after they made the transition to the business world. They tell me they are disappointed with their career, that their leadership and interpersonal skills are not being utilized. Their military experience is not valued. They have less responsibility than when they were in the military. They are not on a track for management development. They tell me they worked hard and were successful in high school, in college, and in the military. They ask me, "Is there anything you can do to help me find a position where my skills are valued and where I will be on a track for upward mobility?" Unfortunately, there is nothing we can do for them. I empathize with them—what a waste of potential—but I do not sympathize. These officers clearly chose the easy way out of the military. Frequently, they tell me, "I had no choice—I did not have time to prepare. I was too busy in the military."

I say, "You did choose." We work every day to help our candidates work smart during their transition preparation. Until their final day in the military, our candidates are top performers.

For months, sometimes even years before they exit the military, they engage in a rigorous transition preparation and development program while excelling in their military jobs. We work with them and help them to be smart workers. They have to produce on both fronts—in their military careers and in their transition preparation. Our candidates actually improve their performance in their military positions while they are enrolled in our development program because the concepts and skills they learn are applied in the workplace. Their marketability improves, and their military career improves, too! None of our candidates will tell you that preparing for a step up into a business career is easy. Choose to challenge yourself and work hard to be at your best for your interviews, and you will be able to compete for positions of enhanced responsibility and upward mobility. Choose the easy way out of the military and you will find a position below you. *If you want a world-class career, you need to do world-class preparation.*

Once you have committed to make a transition, this is the decision with which you are faced: Are you willing to leave the military for a career with less responsibility and opportunity? I wouldn't think so! A transition where you accelerate your career is the only move we are interested in facilitating. And I want this book to take you there. This type of transition up requires hours—hundreds of hours—of hard work, self-examination, research, and practice, but not everyone is willing to make a commitment of this degree. A successful and accelerating transition is not easy.

If you are still committed to accelerating into a business career and competing for development positions, stay with me. Dig into these next critical chapters. Concentrate. Think about what I am saying. Take notes. Get serious about what you need to do. You want to be at your best when you hit the marketplace.

Interviewing Fundamentals

At its most fundamental level, an interview is nothing more than a conversation that follows an agenda. From a recruiter's perspective, the agenda is to make a determination at the end of the interview whether or not the candidate is a "fit." Your agenda, as the interviewee, is to prove that you are a fit with the opportunity.

When I ask most candidates what they think their agenda is in an interview, they often say things like, "My agenda is to determine if I want this job." While this may be a worthwhile objective for a follow-up interview, it has no place in an initial interview. After all, if you invest all your time in determining if you like the job, you waste precious time needed to convince the recruiter of your fit. At the end of the interview, you may come to the conclusion you really want the job, but the recruiter, who owns the interview, rules you out for obvious reasons. *Your mission is to prove your fit.* You will have plenty of time after you get an offer to figure out if you prefer this job over another.

How do you prove your fit? You prove it on three fronts: ability, interest, and rapport. Communicating your fit is the most important strategy for successful interviewing. Make connecting on these three fronts your top priority throughout your interview.

Ability. Are you qualified to do this type of work? Do you have experiences that relate to the job/career for which you are interviewing? As a candidate you need to develop examples from your resume that demonstrate your ability to excel in a business career. Can you imagine hiring someone who was not qualified (unable to do the job)? When you convey points of connection, the recruiter develops an understanding of your qualifications. This may seem obvious, but how do you communicate your ability to lead? How can you communicate initiative? How can you prove to a recruiter that you can solve complex problems? The only way to do this is to develop examples from your past that demonstrate your ability to do the job. Talk is cheap. Just saying that you can lead or assuming that, just because you are a military officer, companies will give you the benefit of the doubt doesn't work.

Interest. Imagine you are interviewing a very qualified person for an important job who does not seem genuinely interested in working with you. What conclusion would you come to regarding his or her fit? A big part of proving your fit is showing interest in the opportunity. You could be completely qualified for a job from an ability perspective and still fail in the interview. A frequent reason for this is that the candidate does not prove he or she is interested. Proving you are interested in an opportunity does not simply mean saying the words, "I'm interested." Much more importantly, it means doing your homework before the interview, developing a good understanding of the business world, asking good questions, showing curiosity, etc. When you do this, the recruiter sees that you have strong interest in the company and the position. You can perform the first step perfectly, but if the recruiter does not fully understand your interest, you will not succeed in an interview.

Rapport. Now imagine that you are interviewing a perfectly qualified person who also has good reasons why he or she is interested. However, throughout the interview you just don't have a good feeling about the candidate as a person. You can't connect with this person. You're having trouble imagining him or her working beside you. You're not sure how this individual will fit in "culturally" with your company. What conclusion would you come to as a recruiter? I can tell you that 100 percent of corporate recruiters will decline a candidate who, in their judgment, is a poor interpersonal fit. This is a very common reason for candidates to fail. If you don't believe me, ask yourself why so many people with great credentials have so much trouble finding great jobs. Generally speaking, this third step gives many military officers great difficulty. Since most people don't do enough preparation for interviews, they are nervous throughout the interview, hurting their rapport-building skills. In some cases your military training hurts you. Most military officers are not comfortable using first names (due to the rank structure), a key part of building rapport in the business world. The military uses employment contracts, diminishing the need for personally connecting with the people in your office or unit. Again, this kind of behavior is completely foreign to most businesses.

You build rapport in an interview through eye contact, the use of first names, a firm handshake, active listening, concise communication, smiling, good energy, and proper posture—all factors in building rapport. Easy to do, right? Not necessarily. Traditionally, the military does not place a lot of emphasis on rapport building and there is not a need to personally connect or build a business relationship with others. As a result, some military officers can improve in interpersonal skills such as using first names, actively listening, smiling, and exhibiting proper posture. You must practice building rapport. You will be nervous interviewing, and this may hamper some of your interpersonal skills. It becomes hard to remember first names and to smile, and sometimes the voice cracks. There will be some nervousness present, but by focusing on interpersonal and rapport-building skills prior to your job search, it will be much easier once you start interviewing. There are several suggestions later in this chapter on how to improve your rapport-building skills and how to build rapport in an interview.

Proving your ability and interest and developing rapport are fundamental to interviewing success. All three have equal weight in the eyes of corporate recruiters. As you prepare for corporate interviews, evaluate all of your interview answers on how they add value on all three fronts of proving fit.

Types of Interviews

Basically, there are three types of interviews in the recruiting world.:

1. Traditional —the recruiter works from a list of prepared questions

2. Resume—the recruiter works from your resume, asking questions about your jobs and accomplishments

3. Conversational—the recruiter exchanges information in an unstructured and conversational manner and may not ask any formal questions

The conversational interview has become much more common today, and for many officers this type of interview is the most difficult. Candidates have remarked to me that they were surprised the recruiters spent 20 to 30 minutes in conversation before the interview actually began. Do not mistake a conversational interview for the recruiter already having made a decision about you and spending time "just to get to know you." Just because recruiters do not ask a lot of questions does not mean they do not expect a lot from you in the interview. They are in fact interviewing you! All interviews are about connecting, and the conversational interview is no different. You will be evaluated from the moment you enter the room. By listening carefully during a conversational interview, you will find that it is easy to identify times you can professionally interject points of connection to prove your fit on the three fronts. Practice the conversational interview with a study partner or your spouse/significant other. The key is to practice, practice, practice!

Time to Verbalize

Military officers are accustomed to moving to the next step based on the observation of past performance. You go to grade school. Your teachers observe you. At the end of that observation period, they grade you. Based upon those grades, you take the next step and move on to junior high. Based on observation and grades, you then move on to high school. The procedure follows you into college, then into ROTC or an academy, and then into the military.

You are observed and graded. You then take the next logical step. However, when you leave the military and make the decision to go into business, you must verbalize these past successes. You're not afforded the opportunity to be observed before being graded—the observation is based on how you verbalize your successes in an interview. No other point makes more officers fail in the interview process. You have never had to verbalize past accomplishments, your leadership style, or your approach to solving problems. You haven't practiced doing so.

It's time to start practicing because in the interview you are expected to verbalize your successes. No one else and nothing else can do it for you. You will not achieve your desired interviewing success if you cannot verbalize your past performance effectively. It doesn't matter that Roger Cameron says you have a solid background of achievements or that you have written records of great performance (very few recruiters want to read your military evaluations), you need to be able to verbalize that performance.

Consider Your Audience

To communicate effectively with corporate recruiters, you need to be careful about using military terms and acronyms. You cannot communicate effectively in the business world using terms such as flight, platoon, division, battalion, TDY, NTC, kinetic, down range, etc. If you would like to verify this, go to any street corner in America, stop the first 10 people, and ask them some questions: "What is the difference between a platoon and a company?" To go even further, ask a Navy officer the size of a division and then ask an Army officer the same question. You will get two completely different answers. It's not that you can't use some of the terms; you just can't use them by themselves. You have to explain or define them. "I led my platoon of 16 people," "I implemented a process for the entire division of 25,000 people," or "I led a maintenance effort for my division of 15 sailors."

In the military you understand these terms. But in a corporate interview, your audience is not the military. Even if recruiters have a background in or are familiar with the military, they expect you to communicate in their language. After all, the purpose of the interview is to gain a position in the business world. In a corporate interview, why would you be talking in any language other than theirs?

Once I was conducting a workshop in Pensacola, Florida, and an hour and a half into the two-hour workshop I said, "Enough. I am going to conclude this workshop unless everyone here agrees to something. Tomorrow morning I want everyone to get up early and read every single article in the *Wall Street Journal* until you are positive you understand the language that corporate America speaks. Then call me and tell me what it is." If you don't know what corporate America's language is, do this exercise yourself. *Corporate America talks in numbers.* Take any article from the *Wall Street Journal*, remove the numbers, and I challenge you to make sense of the article. Learn "corporate speak" if you want to have successful interviews.

You might think this is a minor issue, but take a moment and listen to the conversations around you in the military. How often are military terms and acronyms thrown into a sentence? A lot. Most officers do not even realize that, to most of us, you are speaking a foreign language when you use military terms. It is ingrained. It is time to break this habit and express yourself using language a corporate recruiter will understand.

Learn about the Business World

You cannot be successful in a corporate interview without having an understanding of the world in which you are pursuing a career.

A recruiter is going to be suspicious of your interest in having a business career if you cannot talk intelligently about business. Recruiters want to believe that although you have been successful in the military, you are prepared for the adjustment to the business world and that you will function successfully in this environment. They also want to see that you are excited about a career in business.

Educating yourself about the business world will enable you to make connections between your military background and the business world. You must be able to connect your background and skills to the position for which you are interviewing and demonstrate to the recruiter that you have the ability to do the job.

If you haven't already, make business reading a daily habit. The best way to learn about the business world while you are in the military is through a quality business reading program. See Appendix C for sources I recommend for increasing your knowledge about the business world.

Why Corporate America Hires the Military Officer

Companies hire the JMO for three major reasons: your leadership abilities, your accomplishments, and your objective and subjective skills. Think about these reasons as you prepare for corporate interviews. Be a smart salesperson: *Give recruiters what they want!*

Leadership. The military officer brings the business world subordinate, cross-functional, and "up" leadership experience. Subordinate leadership means that you have full responsibility and full authority. Cross-functional means you have full responsibility but not direct leadership of people; rather, they are your peers. This is found most often in staff positions. If you are a program manager, you have full responsibility to drive the program to a successful conclusion, but you have no authority over the contractors doing the job. "Up" leadership is like cross-functional leadership, but in this case you are leading and persuading those in higher positions of authority than you. Corporate America likes examples of leadership in all of these situations.

Accomplishments. You bring the business world a track record of real-world accomplishments. "Real-world" means bringing important objectives to fruition against time, money, assets, quality, and a major mission. Prior to our wars in Afghanistan and Iraq, "real-world" used to mean combat readiness, but now it includes accomplishments while deployed in operational environments and those that impact readiness.

Objective and subjective skill development. You bring us an enhanced skill set. You have honed your ability to solve problems, to handle multiple objectives simultaneously, and to adapt work effectively in a wide variety of circumstances and with people of diverse backgrounds. This is especially true for those who have served in Afghanistan or Iraq working in ever-changing environments with people of different cultures. Military officers have always been more action-oriented, goal-oriented, and able to do more with less, and you have become even better since the wars in Afghanistan and Iraq.

Know the driving forces behind corporate America's belief in you. You must touch on these factors in your answers and show the recruiter you have what he or she wants. What value would an answer have if it didn't lend credence to the main reasons a recruiter wants to hire you?

Spontaneous and Reflective Questions

Recruiters ask two types of questions in an interview: spontaneous and reflective. Spontaneous questions take about 5 percent of any interview. Examples include the following: Where did you go to college? What was your grade point average? What was your major? Where is your hometown? Obviously, these answers are on the tip of your tongue, and you can quickly, spontaneously answer them.

The most significant and frequently asked question in an interview is the reflective question. This type of question requires more thought than spontaneous questions. Examples include the following: Describe your leadership style. How do you solve complex problems? What motivates you? Give me an example of an accomplishment. Give me an example of a failure. *Your answers to reflective questions are key to securing a recruiter's interest.*

Talking about Accomplishments

A common reflective question asked in an interview is, "Give me an example of a significant accomplishment. Why was it significant, and how did you accomplish it?" Accomplishment questions are the most important questions you will get in an interview because they provide proof of the level of contribution you made to your past organizations. Remember, corporate America likes people who have a track record of making things happen. In other words, the more accomplishments you have, the stronger your track record. Prepare multiple examples of accomplishments in all of your military jobs for a total of at least five or six.

What is an accomplishment? An accomplishment is the attainment of a goal—a time when you set a high, demanding goal and motivated a group of people (whether you had direct authority or not) to make it happen. The best accomplishment examples should come from your work experience when you took the initiative to find better ways to get results. Doing your daily job is not an accomplishment. Working hard by putting in 18-hour days is not an accomplishment. Developing a new maintenance process that improved equipment operational readiness, reliability, and capability is. Leading a team through a shipboard training program that enabled over 90 percent of the team to earn a warfare pin is an accomplishment. Creating an improved budget tracking and approval system that reduced processing time is an accomplishment. The key is to show how you used your leadership to accomplish a goal or an objective that impacted on your organization's performance.

You will know when a recruiter wants to hear an accomplishment answer when they start the question with "Give me an example of a time . . ." or "Tell me about a time . . ." or "Describe a time . . . ."

When a recruiter asks you for an accomplishment, he or she wants to hear about an accomplishment that demonstrates the competencies (consistently demonstrated traits or behaviors, i.e., leadership, problem solving, initiative, analytical skills, etc.) required to be successful in the position for which you are interviewing. It is critical that you understand the position and then understand the question before selecting and then delivering an answer. Your goal is to deliver a significant accomplishment that helps the recruiter envision your success in the position.

A good description of an accomplishment has four key parts:

1. *The accomplishment sentence.* You should state your accomplishment in one succinct sentence. I also like to say: Deliver this Bottom Line Up Front (BLUF). For example, "I developed a new vehicle inspection program that reduced vehicle downtime by 25 percent and increased combat power during 12-month deployments." The vehicle inspection program is the accomplishment (a new way of doing things), and the reduced downtime and improved combat power is proof that the new inspection program made an impact. Remember, it is critical that your accomplishments show impact and bottom-line results (improved capability to do your mission). Deliver your accomplishment with passion and excitement. It's very hard to excite someone else about your accomplishment if you don't sound excited. You need to be succinct. If you ramble and have a lot of excess words, it's hard for the recruiter to hear the specific accomplishment. Make it "mom proof," meaning would your mom understand this? No military lingo, just simple and easy-to-understand terms.

2. *Significance.* Development Candidates lead with a purpose and can accomplish objectives despite obstacles. Recruiters do not want a "doer"; they want candidates who lead with a purpose. In other words, why is vehicle maintenance important, and how does it impact on combat power? I encourage you to explain the big-picture significance of your accomplishment (think like a general or admiral). Remember, you must show how the accomplishment had a bottom-line impact on the primary mission of the armed forces, either combat operations, ability, or readiness. When possible, you should quantify the significance of your accomplishment. Verbally, create a picture using numbers and dollars to get a recruiter's attention and interest. You should also explain the difficulty factor in your accomplishment. Your issue takes on more importance and significance when you have a high difficulty factor. Maybe you had less than normal time, fewer dollars, fewer people, less training, etc.

3. *Planning and thought process.* You read about it every day. Problems made worse, projects gone poorly, product recalls failed, etc. Why? Poor planning. Recruiters want to know what research or analysis you did to frame the issues in the accomplishment. Did you look at historical records, did you collaborate with experts, or did you flowchart a process looking for bottlenecks? What conclusions did you draw from your research? What were the top two or three key issues relating to the success of your accomplishment? Did it have to do with training or reengineering a process? Once you identified the issues, what plan did you develop and who did you involve in the plan? Bottom line: You need to be able to impress a recruiter that you can dig into a problem, understand cause and effect, draw conclusions, understand the issues, and map out a plan to achieve success.

4. *Action.* This is where you show the steps you took to accomplish your objective. In step three you show that you can think through the accomplishment, and in step four you show you can make it happen. For instance, you determine in step three that a key issue is inadequate individual training. In step four you discuss the training program you developed as a solution to the inadequate training. Be careful; don't let the recruiter think your solution to a key issue is simply a Band-Aid (short-term approach). Development leaders put long-term solutions in place as opposed to quick fixes. Also, in this step it is critical for you to show ownership of actions by using the pronoun "I." The more ownership statements you make, the greater the demonstration of your role in making it happen. Finally, wrap your last statement back into the accomplishment (step one) to make a clean closure on your answer.

This is a framework that you can apply to all of your significant accomplishment answers. The more comfortable you become with the framework, the easier it will be for you to develop and deliver examples of multiple accomplishments. Remember, these examples are critical to establishing your track record of making a significant impact throughout your military (as well as high school and college) career. I promise you, evidence of a strong track record will significantly improve your ability to accelerate into a new business career.

Competency-Based Interview

The competency-based interview is a popular interviewing strategy for determining your ability to perform. Some recruiters will use a list of questions or your resume and ask you several competency-based questions in a row. More common is a conversational interview in which the recruiter mixes in competency-based questions throughout the interview. The goal is the same in both—to uncover your behavioral traits, those skills or characteristics that you apply consciously or unconsciously to accomplish objectives.

Examples of questions recruiters will ask in the competency-based interview are open-ended questions that typically begin with "Tell me about," such as, "Tell me about a time you read a book to learn a new skill and applied the concepts you learned to improve a process at work" or "Tell me about a time you were thrown into a new job and achieved results by analyzing the situation and establishing priorities." Remember, when you get these types of questions, you will deliver an accomplishment, and I recommend structuring the answer using the formula outlined earlier. Competency-based interview questions also can be "how" questions, such as, "How do you build a team?" or "How do you build relationships with difficult people?" Recruiters want to hear stories about accomplishments, and in those stories they look for evidence of competencies. They then compare those competencies with the specific traits they require in future leaders for their company.

What is a competency or behavioral trait? It is a consistently demonstrated characteristic. The competencies that companies look for in Development Candidates are determined by analyzing the characteristics of top management. They want Development Candidates with similar characteristics. If you were interviewing for a nondevelopment position, they would focus on functional experience (i.e., knowledge/experience of certain military systems) that is required to perform in that specific position and not competencies.

Many companies will require some of the same competencies. For example, almost every company wants people who are problem solvers, results-oriented, team players, effective communicators, etc. Companies differ on how they prioritize competencies. Some place emphasis on creativity, while others value drive or competitiveness.

Competencies must be demonstrated in your answers; they cannot be stated. Your competencies need to show up again and again in your answers to a recruiter's questions. For example, if one of your competencies is initiative, evidence of your initiative should show up in several answers during the interview. The key here is that unless that trait shows up in multiple examples, it will not be considered a competency or demonstrated behavioral trait.

Unless specifically asked for your strengths or top competencies, it's taboo for you to actually state the trait during a Significant Accomplishment answer. You can't say, for example, that you're "intelligent and competitive." You must illustrate these characteristics by discussing your past accomplishments.

It's critical that you take ownership of your competencies by using the pronoun "I" in your answers. Do not use the pronoun "you" or "we" in your answers. Recruiters want to know about you and what your competencies are—not those of a hypothetical person or of your team.

To prepare for this type of interview, start by analyzing exactly *how you* accomplish difficult objectives. This isn't a five-minute exercise. I envision it taking you several hours—or longer. As you examine past accomplishments, make a list of those *common* behavioral traits that appear in situation after situation. Note how some traits are automatic, or subconscious, and how others require a conscious effort on your part.

List the traits (or characteristics) that appear frequently and that result in outstanding performance. This is a key point. The trait should be developed to a level that results in exceptional achievement; otherwise, the list is meaningless to you. We all organize, manage our time, and interact with others, but do we do it to the degree that we would be considered outstanding in the trait?

Next, I would suggest you prioritize your list of traits and keep them firmly in mind with examples of accomplishments. The end result is that you'll be armed with the information about your most outstanding behavioral traits, and you will be able to give the recruiter concise, articulate descriptions of them.

Here's an exercise you can try that will help you identify the noteworthy traits you possess: Lean back in your chair, close your eyes, and visualize an individual who has worked for or with you and whose performance was outstanding. Think about what you most admired about that individual's performance. When I ask candidates to do this in interview workshops, they consistently mention the same characteristics. The individual they describe is always a hard worker, has a positive attitude, is goal-oriented, is a team player, etc. Now think about the traits you have identified and which of those describe you. Think about situations that have occurred in which you have used these traits and accomplished your goals. Use the tape recorder to record your answer.

Appendix A contains a list of key competencies. Use this list to help you identify those characteristics you think best describe your demonstrated behavioral traits or strengths.

Here are some examples of the characteristics that recruiters want to see in your answers:

- Collaboration with peers, superiors, and team members
- Competitiveness
- Creativity
- Effective, persuasive communication
- Effective use of time
- Goal-oriented
- Innovative
- Leadership, catalyze actions in other people
- Make-it-happen attitude
- Organizational ability
- Pre-problem solution ability
- Prioritization ability
- Sense of urgency
- Strong work ethic
- Success-driven
- Team player
- Technical aptitude

Professional Energy and Enthusiasm

Companies say to us, "We want people who are energetic. We need those who have enthusiasm and catalyze actions in other people." To them high energy and enthusiasm mean the ability of an individual to put out as much work in the eighth hour of the day as he or she does in the first hour. After all, people are paid as much for the last hour as for the first hour.

In an interview we measure high energy in three ways:

1. *Visible high energy—how you walk.* Do you demonstrate a sense of urgency? A favorite recruiter of mine from Texas Instruments liked to stand outside his door about five minutes before the time of an interview so that he could see candidates turn the corner down the hall. If they didn't pick up their pace between the back of the hall and his door, they were on the downhill side before stepping into the interview. Recruiters want to see that you have energy in the way you walk. Keep in mind that you may be observed outside the office where you are interviewed. Maintain a lively pace no matter where you are.

2. *Feeling of high energy—handshake.* When you shake hands, it should be purposeful. You should step into the handshake, whether it's with a man or a woman. The handshake should be firm—full into the hand, showing a physical demonstration of high energy rather than strength. Energy should flow from you to the person with whom you're shaking hands.

3. *Audible high energy—enthusiasm in your voice.* Recruiters want to hear the energy in your voice. Does your voice convey (with changes in its tone and pitch) excitement and eagerness for the work?

I remember listening to a professor of military science talk to an ROTC group at a major southern college. He had a strong voice, but he turned his audience off about five minutes into his speech. They were looking at the floor, out the windows, and at their books and papers. At first, I couldn't understand why his audience was paying so little attention to him. Then I realized he had absolutely no voice inflection. His voice was booming, but everything came out in a monotone, with no modulation of his voice.

Voice inflection and verbal enthusiasm go hand in hand. Too often, companies say to me, "Roger, they said the correct things but not in a convincing manner." If you communicate with enthusiasm— with passion—recruiters are more likely to believe you.

Making Eye Contact

It's critical in developing rapport with a recruiter that you make eye contact as you respond to the questions. Have confidence in your answers. Show that confidence by looking the recruiter directly in the eye.

Often interviewees lose eye contact when it's most important—with a difficult question that may be uncomfortable to answer. That's when I see eyes go to the floor, the ceiling, the window. This shows lack of confidence.

Have you noticed that people "talk" with their eyes? Eyes can sparkle, look bland, or look suspicious. Don't you find you often make judgments based upon what you see in someone's eyes? Don't you question when someone doesn't look you in the eye? You may think, "Are they uninterested, bored, uncaring, or lacking in self-confidence?" Your eyes should show interest, enthusiasm, understanding, curiosity, warmth, and feeling.

Be aware of your eye contact. Where do you look when you talk to someone? Do you look at their mouth or do you look them in the eye? If you are not accustomed to having direct eye contact, it can be awkward at first, but if you concentrate and practice, you will become comfortable with it. Eye contact should be natural, so do not "stare people down." Glance away only about 10 percent of the time.

With good eye contact, you will appear more confident and self-assured. People will listen to you and actually hear more of what you say. Almost all of us can improve our eye contact, so become conscious of yours and find opportunities to improve. I promise you, it will improve your chances for interview success.

Delivering Your Answers

How you deliver your answers is important. Use the following exercises to critique your articulation and speech patterns. I highly recommend that you use a video camera to evaluate your entire communication style, which includes verbal and nonverbal (facial expressions, hand gestures, posture, etc.) communication.

Exercise 1

Prepare an answer to the interview question "Tell me about yourself." This is a very common interview request. You need to explain or present your background (high school, college, and military achievements) to an interviewer in a clear and concise manner. An interview is a *conversation* with the interviewer. Therefore, be very careful not to come across as though you are giving a canned answer or speech. Your discussion about yourself should be sincere and natural.

Have your spouse/significant other or a friend listen to your answer—or record it on a tape recorder. Concentrate on speaking clearly and enunciating your words. Be aware of your voice projection and yet be sensitive to your impact on the other person.

- Are you speaking too loudly or too softly?
- Do you drop the volume of your voice at the end of sentences?
- Do you talk too quickly?
- Do you slur your words together?
- Do you talk more slowly than is normal for a conversation?
- Are you picking your words too carefully?
- How fluid is your delivery?

Have the other person critique you; you can also record and critique yourself.

Exercise 2

Prepare a speech on a subject of importance to you. Present this speech to your spouse/significant other or a friend and record it. The purpose of this exercise is to reveal to you how your speaking pattern varies when you give a speech versus when you are carrying on a conversation. In an interview it is very important for you to be conversational, natural, and sincere. *You should not sound like you are giving a speech.*

Listen to the tape recording of your speech. Compare it to the tape of your reply in Exercise 1. You should notice the differences in your speaking patterns. Do not fall into "giving a speech" in an interview.

Making Things Happen

One of the major points you want to convey in an interview is that you are a make-it-happen, goal-oriented, success-driven person. Think of times you accomplished tough objectives. What were the obstacles you had to overcome? It's not enough to simply tell the recruiter you are a make-it-happen type of person; you must *show* the recruiter that you are by giving the recruiter *proof and evidence* of your ability to make things happen.

I was in Colorado Springs speaking with an Air Force officer whom I had just declined. I asked the young man if there were any insights or help I could give him. He said, "Mr. Cameron, could you tell me in one sentence what recruiters are looking for most in a Development Candidate?" It almost made me think I had made a mistake in declining him. I replied that recruiters are simply looking for an individual who can make things happen—someone who is goal-oriented and success-driven.

Corporations don't want to hire people who rationalize failures with excuse after excuse. Typical excuses include the following: "Oh, I'm sorry I'm late. I didn't know it was going to rain." "I didn't know Ellen was going to take off for four weeks of vacation." "I didn't know the parts were going to come in late." "I didn't know my car was going to have a flat tire." "I didn't know . . . ." Too many people feel that as long as they have an excuse, it is all right to fail. Recruiters and managers disagree. They are looking for people who find solutions to problems and make them successes, individuals who have the desire and ability to overcome adversity and see goals to completion.

Look around you in the military. I'm sure you know people who have a tremendous ability to get things done. You call them go-to people. Those individuals are mission-oriented, the kind of people we want to hire. When you come to corporate America, many times you will be faced with difficult objectives. There are people who throw up their hands and quit when the going gets difficult. This is not the kind of person who is considered a Development Candidate headed to the top of a major corporation. The best compliment I can hear is, "He or she is a make-it-happen type of person, one who gets results despite difficulties."

Certain people have the ability to do it, and others don't. It's one of the reasons we have to interview as many people as we do in a year to find the candidates we want. It's like the individual who interviews with me and has five officer evaluations—all average. Interestingly enough, none of them were the person's fault! In each case, he or she was a victim of circumstance. We may think this can happen on occasion. But if every rater, perhaps five different ones, arrives at the same conclusion, there's little doubt as to what our decision is going to be in this situation.

I remember a young man in El Paso, Texas, who had an appointment with me at 6:00 p.m. He arrived at the door 15 minutes late. As I went to the door, he said, "I'm sorry I'm late; the traffic was bad." It was obvious to me that this individual thought nothing of being late because he had an excuse. I really don't know of any place, including Fredericksburg, Texas, where the traffic isn't bad at 6:00 p.m. Unfortunately, he never recovered from his downhill start with me. If the person was really intent on accomplishing an objective, he would have left early to compensate for heavy traffic.

Are you a consistent make-it-happen type of person? We want to be able to give you tough objectives and know without a doubt that you will bring these tasks back to us successfully completed.

Testing Conviction—The Negative Interview

Some company recruiters will use negative interview questions to test your conviction about career objectives. Company recruiters feel that if they can talk you out of what you want to do, they have proven you have less conviction.

For a manufacturing position, recruiters might ask the question, "What is your opinion of shift work?" Their purpose in asking is that shift work is generally perceived as a drawback, and some people have previously left the company due to working an off shift. It's pretty hard to go into an interview and say, "I'm really excited about shift work." But since most manufacturing facilities run 24-hour operations, you can expect to have an assignment during your career on an off shift, and one of your early promotion levels in manufacturing may be to manage a 24-hour operation. The key to answering a question like this is to give an up-front positive answer and give the interview back to the recruiter. The recruiter only wants to see if you will hesitate or answer negatively. This should be pretty easy for a military officer to answer since many have previously worked off hours. You could say, "I understand the importance of working an off shift and I have a great attitude about it." You do not want to be noncommittal, saying, "I am okay with it" or "I am good with it." Additionally, shift work early in your career can be an ideal way for you to work toward a masters-level degree, working during the evenings and taking classes during the day.

Some recruiters will test your conviction by discussing a position different from the one for which you are interviewing. They may say, "Well, you're an outstanding candidate, and I really feel our company should hire you. However, I feel you would be better suited for position A than the position which we originally intended." Most times, they really do have an additional position and want to consider you for it, but sometimes they may be testing your ability to be committed about the position for which you are interviewing. The problem is that it is hard to tell. I recommend you say to the recruiter, "I am very interested in your company and in the position for which I am interviewing today. However, you are the expert on where to have me start in the organization. I have a great attitude about both positions." This way you demonstrate commitment but also allow yourself to be considered for both positions.

This advice *does not apply to sales interviews*. In general, when recruiters for sales positions ask you this question, they really are testing your conviction. I heard one sales recruiter say to a candidate,

"I think you have strong poise and self-confidence, but you have to understand that, with sales, you're going to have a lot of negative experiences within a day. For example, prospective customers may cancel an appointment at the last minute (when you're already in your car driving there). You're going to end up wasting some time in a day. It's very difficult for you to organize and manage your time effectively. However, I believe you have the ability to handle other positions in our company that are equally outstanding. Would you like me to refer your resume to other departments?" Again, they may simply be attempting to determine your conviction. Be careful; demonstrate your commitment by saying something like, "I understand those challenges, and I understand that every career field has its own unique set of challenges. I have read books on sales and spoken with those in the sales career field. I came into this interview excited about a sales career, already knowing this. Frankly, overcoming those challenges and still achieving goals is one of the things that excites me about sales."

A couple of companies in the follow-up interview process have a designated negative interviewer whose sole purpose is to try to talk you out of the job you're seeking. Unfortunately, not all candidates have listened to me, and they have allowed a company to talk them out of the job. I've actually had candidates come back to me and say, "Roger, I remember what you said, but I'm confident that's not what the company was doing. They actually thought I was better for something else." I moaned! Then, true enough, the candidate was declined for lack of conviction. As a military officer, you're coming out four to eight years or more behind your age group. If you're going to enter the race at that point, you must be committed. You must have conviction. You must know what you want. You must be able to focus and concentrate on that objective. Don't let somebody sway you 30 seconds into an interview.

Occasionally, the negative interview is used to determine poise and self-confidence. Sometimes, recruiters use it "to push on the end of your nose" to see what reaction they will get. While this is rarely used in interviewing today, at the very least I want to make you aware of it. Normally, the type of negative questions you will hear are "A 3.5 grade point average—why wasn't it better?" Notice, it's a negative question on a positive point, which is usually the case. In other words, it isn't for the purpose of embarrassing you. It is for the purpose of determining how you handle a negative situation. In corporate America, just as in the military, you will not always be in a positive situation. At times you'll need to deal with difficult issues. We want to see if you have gained the skill and maturity in the military to be able to do so. We want to see you handle negative situations positively. Do your neck and ears turn red? Do you put on the boxing gloves? Or do you simply square the shoulders, look the recruiter in the eye, and handle it positively? It will potentially come up in interviews. Always remember that the objective is not to embarrass but to determine poise and self-confidence.

Bottom line: Never, never be negative or combative with a recruiter. Avoid using the word "no" in your answers. For example, in answering the question about the 3.5 grade point average, agree with the recruiter. Most candidates immediately want to take the recruiter to task on this grade point average—after all, a 3.5 GPA is better than average. I recommend you begin your response with the word, "yes." "Yes, I recognize a 3.5 GPA is not perfect. I worked very hard for my grades and am confident if all I had had to do in college were academics, I would have done better. I stretched myself to the limit between ROTC and other extracurricular activities, and although I gained valuable time management skills, my GPA was slightly compromised." Deliver your answer without rancor in your voice. Show maturity. Be professional. Never be combative. Recruiters and company managers want to hire individuals who know how to handle negative situations in a positive manner.

Two or More Recruiters

Frequently, two or more recruiters will interview you. Sometimes only one recruiter will actually participate in the interview. Before the interview, determine if all of the recruiters will participate. If a recruiter is placed out of your sight, don't include him or her in the interview. Simply greet all of the recruiters at the beginning of the interview and afterward. Be sure to remember the names of all recruiters present for the interview.

If more than one recruiter interviews you, maintain eye contact with each one when you deliver your answers. Give the recruiter who asks the question the initial and final eye contact. For example, let's say Recruiter A asks you a question. Begin your answer with eye contact with that recruiter. Continue your answer and pick up eye contact with Recruiters B and C, etc. Conclude your answer with eye contact with Recruiter A. If the question is substantive and requires a lengthy answer, you may change eye contact several times, always ending by giving eye contact with the recruiter who asked the question.

Treat each recruiter with an equal amount of attention and respect, regardless of the recruiter's age or gender. I have seen some candidates pay more attention to the male recruiters, even when they have been told that the female recruiter had more hiring influence. Don't let this happen to you. Obviously, it will rule you out.

Always remember that companies are looking for young men and women who have poise and self-confidence. These qualities are important to portray in one-on-one situations as well as group meetings.

Closing the Interview

There are two types of "closes" in an interview. One is an informal close, which you do throughout the interview. The other is a formal close and occurs at the conclusion of the interview. It is critical in an interview that you do both.

Informal closing is making points of interest throughout the interview that demonstrate your interest in the company, position, and industry. This is the best closing method since it is done throughout the entire interview. Ideally a recruiter will never have to ask you why you are interested in an opportunity because you were proactive and found two or three opportunities during the interview to make genuine statements of interest. Finally, good informal closing makes a formal close at the end of the interview easier and more natural.

The formal close occurs at the end of the interview. The most common signals that the interview is nearing its end is when the recruiter looks at you and asks if you have any questions, you hear a knock on the door for the next interview, or the recruiter checks the time several times. This is when you should ask your final one or two questions. Remember—they must be quality questions. This is one of the last impressions you will leave with the recruiter. You want it to be positive.

If you have already had a chance to ask questions, you can go back to an issue discussed earlier in the interview if you feel it can have a positive influence on the outcome of the interview. Let's say you did not feel one of your responses was adequate or you missed an opportunity to give information that is important to your job pursuit. Go back and restate your attitude and provide the information now. Make sure it is a positive restatement or addition to the interview. Again, you want to end on a positive note, not a negative one. Be smart.

How do you formally close the interview? The closing should be a natural exchange—as natural as thanking someone for taking you to dinner or sharing advice with you. In the case of a corporate interview, you close by letting the recruiter *know of your sincere interest in the company and why.*

This is the last statement you want to leave in the recruiter's mind as you exit the interview. It should be positive and unique to that company—not the job! Or, if you choose to close on the job, it should always be after expressing interest in the company. The company is permanent; the job is temporary. If your interview goes the full time, you may have only seconds to deliver a close. You should think about and prepare your close before entering the interview. Again, it must be a statement that is specific to the company and delivered with passion. If your close can be said to more than one company, it will do you more harm than good.

Close the interview by being upbeat. Candidates sometimes walk away from interviews in which they have a high degree of interest without expressing their interest. If you are truly interested in the company and in the position, you cannot afford to leave the interview without letting the recruiter know this.

Typically people are attracted to companies because they like the company philosophy, high-quality products, market share, sales growth, unique customers, market, etc. Share with a recruiter the issues that excite you about the opportunity, back up the issues with detail (i.e., philosophy, products, market share, sales growth, customer base, etc.), and support your statements with why these issues are exciting to you. Make your comments specific. Close with enthusiasm and believability. Bottom line: do not leave the interview without telling the recruiter you are interested!

Military officers sometimes ask me, "Roger, if I am not interested in the opportunity, should I still close the interview?" My answer back to them, "You don't know enough now or even at the end of the initial interview to decide whether you are interested." During your first initial interview, you are developing knowledge of the industry, company, position, and career path. I argue that you have only a thimbleful of information after the initial interview. You don't make decisions in the military based on small amounts of information. You shouldn't in your job search either. I *highly* recommend not closing any doors. Find one reason you genuinely like the company, and remember in most cases it is necessary to conduct follow-up interviews (which allow you to meet other people who work for the company, see the working environment, the location, etc.) before you can determine your interest in a company. Don't rule yourself out by prematurely reserving interest in a company.

We've talked a lot about interviewing strategy and what needs to happen in an interview for you to be successful. Keeping our interviewing strategy and tips in mind, let's turn to the next chapter to learn how to handle the big questions recruiters will ask you in a corporate interview.

Chapter 6

FACING THE BIG QUESTIONS
AND DEVELOPING THE BEST ANSWERS

To deliver the best answers to the significant questions asked in an interview, let's first understand two basic philosophies, which are the basis for 90 percent of the questions you will be asked.

Two Philosophies behind the Big Questions

One philosophy behind a recruiter's questions is to determine the quality or difficulty factor of your successes. How is success judged? By the accomplishment of an objective. We all judge success similarly. What makes us unique are our objectives. How do you judge the quality of a success? Obviously, not every success is of equal quality. Consequently, we judge the quality of success by the difficulty factor. The greater the difficulty, the greater the significance of the accomplishment. You must realize that if success is the accomplishment of an objective, the flip side of the coin is that failure is falling short of an objective or a goal. You can have a slight failure or a catastrophic failure. You can have a slight success or a phenomenal success. Recruiters want to know the quality or difficulty factor of your accomplishments. Verbalize your successes in such a way that the recruiter can determine the degree of success or the degree of failure.

The other philosophy on which a recruiter bases questions is to discover how you perform—your operational methodology. Recruiters want to know "how" you achieved objectives. In other words, they want to know your methodology. Let me give you an example of why this is important. Let's say you led your team of 20 soldiers to increased operational readiness or improved maintenance by 25 percent. You did it by having your team work until 9:00 p.m. each night for three weeks to get it done. Is that method acceptable for corporate America? Absolutely not! Your team members are contractually obligated to do this in the military but not in the business world. They will quit on you in business if you use this method. Recruiters want to know if your methods will fit in their organization and allow you to make a significant positive impact.

Throughout the remainder of this chapter, I will address numerous types of questions recruiters typically ask during an interview. When recruiters ask about a specific example from your past or want to know how you do something, remember, they want to know your operational methodology.

The "Warm Up" Questions

Most interviews are going to start with small talk and some warm-up questions. The three questions below are the most common. They won't get you hired, but they can absolutely end the interview early if you don't handle them right.

"Tell Me about Yourself"

The recruiter says to you, "Tell me about yourself." Often recruiters start the interview with this question. I have had people talk for 15 minutes or more telling me about themselves but not covering the issues in which I had any interest. Some interviewing books encourage you to take 10 minutes for your answer. I disagree. Many corporate recruiters dislike long-winded answers to this question so much that they have changed the question to "Take a few minutes and tell me about yourself." I suggest you answer the question in approximately three minutes. I recommend you divide the answer into three parts:

1. Introduce your early family life in the opening sentence, where you were raised, what was emphasized in your family, and highlights from high school.

2. Discuss your experience in college, reason for choosing your major, and college highlights and accomplishments.

3. Describe key highlights of your military experiences.

The bulk of your answer should come from your time in the military since that is what the recruiter is most interested in. Your answers should cover two things—your goals and your accomplishments. *No rhetoric, just goals and accomplishments.* Your answer to this question should be a "bare bones" outline of who you are.

Interviewers ask this question to attempt to determine if you are at the "helm" of your vehicle (your personal life) and thus, by nature, capable of stepping to the "helm" of the area, department, or division to which you would be assigned within their company. They want to be assured you're solidly in the front seat behind the steering wheel and "driving" your life in the direction you want it to go. Too many people appear to ride in the passenger seat, and, sadly, some seem to be riding in the trunk. Only two words can give the proper perspective to a recruiter—*want (goal)* and *result (accomplishment)*. These two words indicate you are in *control of your life* and are working to make your life successful.

I'll give you an example of an individual who had no understanding of the need to direct his life. Many years ago I interviewed a young officer. His spouse was also present during the interview.

About 20 minutes into the interview, I sensed his spouse becoming uptight. She crossed her arms, leaned back in the chair, and arched her back. I wasn't quite sure what was causing this reaction, even though I hoped I wasn't giving her any cause to be upset with me. Suddenly, she interrupted the interview in an irritated manner, looked at her husband, and, in a stern voice, asked him if he had ever made a decision on his own! Then she said, "I can tell you, I wouldn't hire you!"

I admit I was uncomfortable observing this scenario but not as uncomfortable as I would have been had I been riding down in the elevator with them after I proceeded to decline her husband.

Let's take a look at the interview. I was using the "Why?" interviewing technique. I asked the officer why he chose his college. He told me that he had never planned to go to college, but two of his best friends had talked him into going and so he went where they went. I asked why he selected biology as his major. He really didn't know what he wanted to do, but because he had a good friend whom he respected who chose biology, he thought it would be good for him also. I then asked why he joined a fraternity, and again it was because of a friend. This person's direction in school and in life reflected no goals, no direction. He was not at the "helm" of his life—it was being steered by someone else. His major career decisions were made by circumstance. You can imagine why companies have no interest in hiring people who think this way to lead their company into the next century.

Here is an example of an appropriate reply given by an individual who was asked to tell about himself: "I'm an only child of a Texas farm family. When I went to high school, there were several things I *wanted* to accomplish. First of all, I *wanted* a high grade point average [*goal*] that would allow me to get into the college of my choice. I was accepted by Texas A&M [*accomplishment*]. I wanted to attend Texas A&M because of the strong academics, affordability, and the leadership development offered by the Corps of Cadets. I also knew that I wanted to play sports [*goal*] because I like competition and leading and being part of a team. I was a wrestler and a football player [*accomplishment*]." Remember that we're taking a hard look to see if you are goal oriented and have the ability to make it happen! Notice I didn't say "goal, accomplishment, and detail." At this point, you will not be going into detail as to how you accomplished the goal.

Your explanation of military goals and accomplishments should be brief. *Do not get into every job in the military.* Talk in overall terms of your development during your military experience. Focus on the primary reasons why the business world has an interest in hiring the JMO (leadership, track record of accomplishments, ability to get results, subjective and objective assets). Your answer must touch on these important issues, but remember to keep your response to only three minutes.

As you discuss a point of interest, recruiters may interrupt to ask questions. They will want to know why that goal was important to you and how you accomplished it. Be sensitive to the recruiters and allow them to enter in. This approach allows the recruiters to ask you to elaborate on a point of interest that is important to them. When you're interrupted, it's critical that you remember exactly where you were when interrupted so that when you finish answering the recruiter's question, you can come back smoothly, picking up where you left off. You should never look at the recruiter after elaborating on a point and say, "Now where was I?" After all, it is your story.

"Why Are You Leaving the Military?"

Unfortunately, many officers inadvertently knock the military and come across as negative. They think they have to have compelling negatives in order to explain why they're leaving. *This is not necessary.* Your answer to this question must be positive. In over 45 years of facilitating transitions, I have never seen a candidate succeed who was cynical in interviews about the military or his or her military experience.

It's our position that if you're negative about the military, you're probably also going to be negative about your career in the business world. That's not the kind of person we want to hire.

There is absolutely no reason for you not to be upbeat about the military. You have gained a lot from your military experience. You have developed your ability to lead and work with people like few other civilians your age have been able to do. You have succeeded in an environment that is mission-oriented.

Equally important, you have proudly served our country. My client company recruiters and I believe in the role of our armed forces; we are proud of you! You must also be proud and positive!

Again, in this answer you should be praising the military for its outstanding development of your assets. How could you knock the military on the one hand and then ask corporate America to hire you based on your experience in the military? It sure doesn't make sense to me.

Recruiters want to know why you are leaving the military and transitioning to business. You want to give reasons for both.

Most of you tell me you want to leave the military because your values have changed. This is normal, especially with all of your missions and deployments. For the most part, a change in values is perceived by recruiters as positive. Some of you tell me that now that you have a family, you no longer want to be deployed for a significant amount of time. Some of you say that it has become more important for you to have more control over your career. Some of you feel that you can improve the quality of your life by pursuing a career in corporate America and entering the civilian world. Some of you desire a career where what you do impacts the bottom line every day versus just in wartime. Every one of these reasons is valid. None of these reasons would be perceived as negative or too general or vague. There are a host of other valid, positive, specific reasons as well.

Since our wars in Afghanistan and Iraq, I have heard more and more officers say they are leaving the military due to the deployments and they stop there. While this is understandable and valid, it's not enough to make the recruiter feel good about your decision. After all, you can have a more stable life while teaching, working for a government agency, or going back to full-time school. You will also need to discuss why you feel business is a good fit for you professionally and would provide balance in your life.

An appropriate answer would sound something like this, "While I have enjoyed my time in the military and led teams in multiple deployments, I decided to research other career options due to the multiple deployments. When I researched business, I found that I could have a high-quality career where I could continue to lead, impact results, be in a competitive environment, and have a better quality of life. I do expect to continue to work hard, though, just not deploy for a year at a time."

I am not suggesting you use these words. I'm suggesting you follow this lead, this thought process. Throughout this book I am not trying to put specific words in your mouth—I am trying to guide your thinking and your approach to answering interview questions. You are unique—it is your unique desires, your unique assets, your unique experiences that make up the "package" you will communicate and try to sell to recruiters. Recruiters are not interested in a facade.

"Why Corporate America?"

Many years ago, one of my favorite recruiters ruled out every candidate he interviewed that day. When I sat down with him to review his interviews, I was taken aback and disappointed in what he had to say.

He said to me, "Roger, the reason I come to Cameron-Brooks is that I trust you explicitly. When you tell me something, I just know that's the way it is, but I interviewed nine candidates today who did everything possible to convince me you are untruthful. I asked every candidate why he or she wanted a career in corporate America, and I received nothing but shallow answers. You have told me your candidates read business books and periodicals. But how can candidates read *PCS to Corporate America, Good to Great, Fortune* magazine, and more and still be unable to give me any powerful reasons why they desire a career in corporate America? I have to say I have no interest in people who are not excited about corporate America."

Sadly, I could not argue with him. How could I defend candidates who have studied the business world but could not talk about it in-depth and with enthusiasm?

Look at it from this perspective: Imagine you are interviewing people interested in entering the military. You ask them why they want to enter the military. Their responses are shallow, uninformed. No one seems educated or excited about entering the military. How interested are you going to be about hiring them for a critical opening?

If you are going to leave the military and accelerate into a business career in corporate America, you must read, comprehend, and demonstrate intellect to the recruiters. Read books that will help you talk intelligently about careers, business trends, and operational procedures in corporate America. Gain an understanding of and appreciation for the business world so that you can talk intelligently about it. What's more, convince recruiters you are passionate about a career in the business world. Companies want people who are going to be excited about what they do.

Again, refer to Appendix C for a list of books I recommend for your personal development and, specifically, business knowledge.

The "Why?" Questions

"**W**hy?" is the *most frequently asked* question facing a military officer. "Why?" is a word attached to numerous key subjects, such as "Why did you choose that college? Why that curriculum? Why the military? Why that branch of the military? Why do you want this position?"

I remind you that we're looking for Development Candidates. Development Candidates are ultimately going to spend the bulk of their days making decisions. *We ask the "Why?" questions to determine how you think and reason and to see your ability to come to a quality conclusion.* As you answer the "Why?" questions, the recruiter will listen to how you think through steps and how you come to conclusions.

Every decision breaks down into key issues. A recruiter wants to see the thought process you go through to determine and prioritize these issues, and then how you execute a successful conclusion. The better your ability to convey to a recruiter your thought process and prove its merit with concrete examples, the greater your ability to successfully transition and accelerate your career.

Remember that both you and the company want you to go as high as you can in management. Top managers are paid primarily for their ability to reach quality conclusions. Allow us inside your mind as you talk about how you came to certain conclusions and the method you use to arrive at decisions. We want a manager who is an independent thinker—who can make decisions based on his or her own thinking (after gathering input from others) rather than on a recommendation from someone else. We also want a manager who keeps the end result in mind and who can devise a solid plan of action to accomplish an objective.

The best approach to any "Why?" question is to think in terms of a *comparison*. Compare the positives and negatives of the choice you made with the positives and negatives of your other options—concisely, without rambling.

Tell us, for example, the options you had in financing college—borrowing money from family members or a bank, getting a job, or winning a scholarship. You planned on ROTC being a big part of your college career. Let us know you analyzed all those factors before you came to a decision. I often ask military officers why they chose ROTC. The most frequent response I get is that they had no other way to earn their way through college. That is to suggest to the recruiter that if you can't get into ROTC, you can't go to college. Well, I just don't agree with that. There are many ways to finance your education.

I sometimes ask individuals whose major was history why they chose this field. A typical response is, "Well, I thought I wanted to go to law school." My reply is, "But you're not a lawyer." The person says, "Well, ROTC came along, and with that I had an obligation to the military." I say, "Well, what happened to the objective of being a lawyer?" The reply is that the person changed his or her mind. Now, wait a minute. This person spent four years gearing up to be a lawyer and walked away from the objective with what appears to be a casual thought? No, I don't think so. It's just that the person was unwilling to let me see how his or her mind functions. I have no choice but to walk away from that person, as will any corporate recruiter.

Understand the critical nature of your ability to handle the "Why?" questions. You want recruiters to believe you have the ability to handle complex, high-end positions. Many recruiters will give you nothing but a "Why?" interview. In revealing your thought processes to the recruiter, be succinct. Don't ramble. Remember, the clock is ticking no matter how well the interview is going and no matter how much you and the recruiter are enjoying your conversation.

The "Why?" Exercise

An excellent exercise to prepare for the "Why?" questions is to write down all the major career events in your life and then put the word "Why" in front of each. Record your answers and your analysis of the issues involved in each of the decisions on a tape recorder. Next, listen to yourself. Do your answers reveal strong reasoning? When they do, you're in good shape for handling the "Why?" questions in an interview.

The only way you will become smooth in delivering answers to "Why?" questions is through practice. Lots of practice. Throughout this chapter I am going to give you examples of "Why?" questions and other questions that you will be asked in a corporate interview. I also will give you advice on how to develop the best answers to them. Pay attention. Mark up this chapter. Take notes.

"Give Me an Example" Questions

The most important questions you will be asked in an interview are the "Give me an example" questions. In some instances recruiters use "Tell me about a time . . ." instead. You should have responses to four or five of these questions prepared, and at least one per job that you have had in the military. They are your "hammer" stories that allow you to illustrate the subjective assets, strengths, and experiences that relate to the position for which you are interviewing. Here are two flavors that are common.

"Give Me an Example of a Significant Accomplishment and How You Achieved It"

As we discussed in Chapter 5, putting your successes into words is one of your greatest challenges in preparing for interviews. You must understand the position for which you are interviewing and the required competencies, and then communicate your accomplishments effectively that help the recruiter envision you in the position. You have not had to do this before. You must practice. Recruiters want to see a track record of accomplishments. Follow the four-part formula outlined in Chapter 5 for how to talk about significant accomplishments. Prepare at least five examples of significant achievements you had in the military. You can use these examples for multiple versions of questions about significant accomplishments, though you will have to modify and highlight areas to specifically answer the question. *Ensure you select and communicate the right accomplishments.* You must study the position description and review each sentence to understand what you will do, if hired, and the required competencies and experience. Then listen to the recruiter's question and ensure you deliver the right answer with the details that connect.

Two other common questions are "Give me an example of a significant problem you solved" and "Give me an example of a project you managed." To answer these questions, you will still want to utilize the four-part formula described in Chapter 5 for significant accomplishments, but each will need specific details demonstrating to the recruiter your problem-solving and project management experience and abilities, depending on the question. The questions are similar, but a quote from project management guru J. M. Juran will help you differentiate the two: "A project is a problem scheduled for a solution."

"Give Me an Example of a Significant Problem You Solved"

When a recruiter asks about a problem, he or she is asking about a process that was not working properly or getting desired results, a project that went off track, or a piece of equipment that was not operating correctly. Usually, this doesn't mean a people problem. It's a process problem that had impact on the overall mission. When asking this question, recruiters want to understand your problem-solving methodologies. The mistake most candidates make is that they jump right into the answer by talking about how they solved the problem, never explaining how they came to understand what happened and the root cause of the problem. The recruiter wants to see how you determine the root cause of a problem, evaluate courses of actions, conduct a pro and con analysis or cost benefit analysis on the potential solutions, develop a rationale for selecting the solution, test the solution, and then implement it.

To prepare for this question, list several complex problems you successfully solved. For each problem determine why it was significant and difficult to solve. Next, write down the steps you went through to determine the root cause, how you developed potential solutions (recruiters want to see here that you got your team involved and solicited their ideas), and how you solved it, including the testing, implementation, and lessons learned review with your team. I highly recommend you become familiar with Six Sigma tools—such as DMAIC (Define, Measure, Analyze, Innovate, and Control), Asking "Why?" Five Times, and Fishbone Diagrams—and incorporate them into your answer.

Every problem is an opportunity for innovation. This principle is at the heart of the Continuous Improvement movement that is prevalent in the business world. You need to have several examples of problems that you encountered and how you turned them into lasting solutions that helped the organization turn the crisis or problem into an opportunity for innovation and continuous improvement. Become comfortable talking about how you solve problems. Remember, leaders are problem solvers.

"Give Me an Example of a Project You Managed"

Use the definition of a project by J. M. Juran that I mentioned previously. When you tell the recruiter your project story, the recruiter wants to know what the project scope was, why it was important, and how you managed it from start to finish, including the planning process for testing and implementation and the execution to achieve results. A common mistake, just as in the problem-solving answer, is that candidates completely skip over explaining their thought process and how they planned the project; they immediately jump into the project execution steps.

In describing the planning process, you want to highlight establishing the project objective, communicating it to your team, and developing timelines and milestones. You should be familiar with project management concepts such as project scope, Work Breakdown Structures (WBS), and Critical Path. These project management terms are explained in excellent detail in Heagney's *Fundamentals of Project Management* (4th ed.), which is included in the reading list in Appendix C. You will also want to highlight how you developed and managed the project team and how you delegated project assignments.

In the execution step, recruiters will want to hear how your actions catalyzed the project team's action to stay on time and within budget and scope. Additionally, a critical component that you will need to discuss is how you mitigated risk. What's risk in a project? Instead of a textbook definition, I will share with you how one of our client recruiters described risk: "Anything that could cause the project to deviate from the desired results by going over budget, time, or outside of the scope." In other words, anything that could throw it off track. I smile every time a junior military officer asks me what he or she should say about managing risk because you do this all the time and almost every day! It's just that you are typically looking at it as loss of life, injury, or damage to equipment.

This is not what the recruiters want, but the steps you use are exactly the same. First, evaluate the overall risk, determine all of the risks that contribute to it, and then with your team determine the probability and catastrophic nature of each risk. This will then allow you to prioritize putting in place risk mitigation measures and assigning responsibility to manage it. I cannot emphasize this enough—you must demonstrate how you mitigated risk in accomplishing a project.

Just like the problem-solving answer, I recommend you also explain at the end of the accomplishment the results you achieved and the lessons learned review you conducted with your team to incorporate into future projects.

Occasionally a candidate comments to me that they have really never managed a project. I tell them they absolutely have. They just did not call it that. Let me give you some examples of excellent projects that military officers manage frequently: planned and led a unit and troop movement from one location to another; planned and led training event for 31 personnel that resulted in all sailors becoming proficient in specific tasks; led a $20,000 maintenance effort that repaired a diesel engine in two days. The following are also projects *but not ones that recruiters want to hear about*: planned and organized unit family day; led the unit's Combined Federal Campaign fundraising efforts, exceeding goal by 20 percent; organized a unit fun run, increasing team cohesiveness. While these are projects, they do not relate to corporate America and do not impact the bottom-line result.

For both questions, corporate recruiters will want to hear how you incorporated your team, whether subordinates or peers, into solving the problem and executing the project. Even though the answers must be about your actions, you need to discuss how you asked for their input, developed others, delegated responsibilities, and followed up with them. Finally, you must give them credit for their great work and compliment them in your answer; otherwise, you might come across egocentric (too "I" oriented).

"Strengths and Weaknesses" Questions

Know yourself. Know your strengths and your weaknesses. Feel comfortable in being able to talk about them, knowing that when you put your strengths on the scale, they will far outweigh any weaknesses you might have.

"What Strengths Have You Gained from Your Time in the Military?"

You're frequently going to be asked, "What have you gained from your time in the military?" This is a strengths question that allows you to list the subjective assets that you have learned from your time in the military. It amazes me how officers brush off this question—one of the most loaded questions you're going to get. As I often tell candidates, "Let's take a look at this. Cameron-Brooks only recruits military officers, so we could say that companies coming to Cameron-Brooks to hire know they're going to hire a military officer. It must mean they're coming to us because they want a military officer. Therefore, it must mean they want military officers because of what officers have gained from their military experiences. That makes sense to me. Therefore, unload! Give recruiters the material they are looking for!"

You might respond, "Where do I begin? I have developed the ability to prioritize, organize, effectively manage my time, accomplish difficult objectives, work with a variety of people, and work in different environments—the desert, the mountains, the cold areas, overseas. I've learned how to achieve tough objectives regardless of climatic conditions and circumstances. I've learned how to take difficult objectives and break them down into component parts and how to motivate members of my team to accomplish those objectives, getting tough jobs done with less." My point is this: you have to unload. Recruiters want to know you really have gained something from your time in the military. You might think it is enough to say, "Well, I've gained maturity" or "I've gained the ability to manage assets and people." That's not enough. You must separate yourself from the many other people they will interview. Be careful how you answer this question. This is the one powerful advantage you have over nonmilitary job candidates. Don't brush it off.

"What Are Your Weaknesses?"

This topic was addressed in Chapter 3 but deserves to be mentioned again because it's one of the "big questions." Frequently, recruiters ask the question this way: "If you take all of the assets you have and use on a daily basis, which ones do you feel you can improve upon?" The key word is "can." The attitude we're looking for in candidates is a *drive for excellence*, a belief that they can improve what they're doing and that they hope to be able to do so even at age 98. You can give an excellent speech, but you can give an even better speech. You can have a great command, but you can have an even better command. You can run a four-minute mile, but you can run an even faster mile. We look for people with great attitudes about improving and pushing themselves.

Recruiters will ask the question "Which one of your assets do you feel you need to improve?" This can be a difficult question. Need, by definition, means that you have a significant weakness in that area. I can't imagine General Mills, Johnson & Johnson, Boston Scientific, or any other great company coming to me and saying, "Roger, travel around the world, and let us pay you a fee to hire an individual who has weaknesses." Be careful to distinguish between the words "can" and "need." You must always be honest. If you have deficiencies, be willing and able to talk about those deficiencies. Ideally, you're doing something about them. You can point to a program you are in at that very moment which is helping you correct the deficiency. It's okay to have deficiencies as long as you are doing something to overcome them. A recruiter wants to know that you will take the initiative to improve company processes just as you prove capable of working on the development of your own assets.

Education Questions

If you have a degree that is generally considered irrelevant to business, such as a liberal arts degree, the question is not whether you should or should not have chosen it. The question is, how do you sell it to corporate America? You and I both know that some of the top people in corporate America have liberal arts degrees, but I've never had a company ask me to find them an individual with a degree in liberal arts. It's perfectly all right that you have one. No one would suggest that you couldn't get value out of it. Yet it does not have obvious relevance to most functional career fields in corporate America.

Don't get defensive about your liberal arts degree. We're not suggesting you wasted your time in college or that you're not going to get value from it. However, it seems I spend half my time consoling people who have this degree. I want to help you get over the fact that it is an irrelevant degree—it was not designed for corporate America, for the world of profit. A liberal arts degree isn't as applicable to the business world as finance, accounting, business management, engineering, information systems/computer science, and other curriculums that are directly linked to corporate America.

That doesn't mean a liberal arts degree is bad, but it does mean it will take you months to look through job postings online and in newspapers to find a company looking for a liberal arts degree.

Here's my thinking on how to explain it: "Relative to my decision today to come to corporate America, my liberal arts degree was a mistake. I don't want to suggest that I didn't get things out of political science that will be of value to me, because I thoroughly enjoyed it and feel I developed skills important in the business world, such as problem solving, critical thinking, and communication skills. However, had I known then what I know today of my desire to have a career in the profit-oriented world, I would have earned a more relevant degree."

Stress your determination to enter the business world. Frequently, in asking a person with an irrelevant degree why they want to go into business, we have to say, "You've never shown any indication of interest in business in the 26 plus years of your life."

I draw the analogy that you have a neighbor who has been next door for 26 years. You've left the house every morning and returned every night—but never looked across the fence and said hello. Then, suddenly, one day you lean across the fence and ask the neighbor to marry you. The neighbor answers, "For 26 years you've ignored me. Now you want to marry me. Why?" The neighbor has every reason to ask—and you need to explain. Give proof and evidence. You can't just say, "Betty no longer has an interest in me; therefore, I'm coming to you."

You will have to help the recruiter understand how you decided you wanted a career in the business world. Give proof and evidence of research you did, books you read, people you interviewed, choices you considered—why you've concluded you want to transition to business.

I remember being at Fort Bragg, North Carolina, interviewing an officer with a government degree. I said, "Government degree. I just don't know what I can do." He said, "I'm coming to corporate America whether through you or through someone else. I want to use your company because you have placed four of my friends." He then went on to give me solid *proof and evidence* of his interest. "The reason I'm coming to corporate America is that I have talked with friends in major corporations and have read several books [he stated title and author] about business that have encouraged me to make this choice. For the following reasons [he put his hands up in the air and ticked them off], I have decided to go into corporate America." I listened to him. There was absolutely no question in my mind that this young man had done his homework. He was committed and convincing. I brought him to our Career Conference, and every company fought over him. He now has an outstanding job in the business world, is performing at a remarkable level, and has remained a close friend and ally of mine (he has completed his MBA and continues to have brilliant success).

Recruiters don't care whether you have a less relevant degree. They do care whether you are coming to us for the right reasons. You must bring us *proof and evidence* of the research and the contemplation that has gone into your decision.

"What Is Your Location Preference?"

It is only natural that JMOs wrestle with balancing location preference in a career search. After all, most have been deployed to or have lived in remote locations throughout their careers.

The key is to wrestle with it *before* launching a career search. We recommend JMOs conduct self-evaluation and research to understand how important a location preference is and the associated trade-offs, then develop a strategy to make good career decisions.

Development Candidates and their families need to have geographic flexibility and a good attitude about potential relocation in a career. If you are going to rise to the top of a multinational corporation, you can expect promotions to different cities (maybe countries) during your career. You need to discuss this with your family and determine whether this fits your career plans and whether you can embrace this concept with a positive attitude. I'm always disappointed when, after I have put much effort into working with a candidate for several weeks or months, he or she comes to me and tells me location has become an issue and he or she wants to be in only one or two places. This is not professional conduct. Corporate America and I are very up-front on this issue, and you owe it to yourself to be equally up-front. The time to discuss this issue within your family is before you engage the services of a recruiting firm to work for you.

You will be asked in many interviews, "What is your location preference?" This question has probably caused more recruiters to get an instant sour attitude about a candidate than any other. The most frequent answer is "I'm open." But "open" is not a definition of location. Recruiters don't believe it. *Don't use it.* Verbally, you always need to state a preference. This is different advice than what I recommended you put on an employment application in Chapter 2. On an application, you should always put "open" because there is usually not enough space to explain your answer, as there is in an interview. Just make sure that you are being smart about your verbal answer. You need to connect with the location where the openings are.

There are very few people who don't have a location preference. In fact, my clients understand that you have a location preference, and once you establish yourself as a top performer in your business career, they will try to work with you during your career to help you with your preference(s)—it just can't be a restriction, especially when you are launching a new career. Therefore, in answering this key question, state a regional preference—the Northeast, the Midwest, the Southeast, etc. I do not recommend that you give a city or a state; just specify a region. Giving one city or even one state is a red flag in the eyes of most recruiters. Give the broadest area possible—but one that honestly answers the question.

Be *smart* as well as *honest* in how you answer. If, for example, you're interviewing for a position in Cincinnati and your true preference is the Northeast, say your location preference would be east of the Mississippi River. That will include Cincinnati and the Northeast.

Never waste your time or a company's time by telling them something that is not true. If you're not willing to relocate (i.e., if you're not willing to be open), then say so. Analyze what you're willing to do. Be honest about it—with yourself and with recruiters. However, if you want a development career with a Fortune 500 company, you must be willing to relocate. *Do not assume you can take the good and reject the bad.*

I have a few other thoughts on how to manage location preference during your career search and throughout your career. This will help you develop the appropriate honest answer prior to being asked the question in an interview.

We are all human and if all things were equal, who would not want to be in a familiar location or close to family? The question is not whether you have a location preference, but rather how you will manage location preference with regard to achieving your career goals.

Too few JMO candidates really ask themselves where they want to be in their career 15 or 20 years from now. Do they see themselves as a Development Candidate, investing in their career and growing to the executive ranks of a company? Or do they see themselves as a future middle manager, developing an expertise in a certain area of a business (that is, a Nondevelopment

Candidate)? Both are viable career opportunities, but the first one leads to future leadership and the second to future managers. If you see yourself as the Development Candidate, you have high leadership ambition; if you see yourself in the latter role, you have low leadership ambition.

If you answer that you have high ambition, you should prioritize the quality of your experience, your ability to learn and develop new skills, the investment in your track record, etc. The quality of your opportunity will have a very large role in determining your ability to translate your talent into career success. Using this strategy, geography is a tiebreaker between two equal career opportunities. Location still plays a role, but it is not a leading or a limiting factor.

If you don't see yourself as a future leader, then location can be more of a discriminator for you. In this case, the quality of your location can take the lead over the quality of your career opportunity. There are plenty of people who live near family and are content with simply having adequate employment. They are honest with themselves and realize that they may not be competitive for leadership positions, especially in today's global economy. They understand the trade-off: they may not have the financial reward or all of the future promotional opportunities that come with development careers.

Another way to think about location is using the "Law of the Lid." This concept is borrowed from John Maxwell's popular leadership book, *The 21 Irrefutable Laws of Leadership*. If location is a higher priority than career development, regardless of your talent and leadership skills, you may be putting the "lid" on your future opportunities and potential. Unfortunately, after starting a career with a restricted location, some JMOs realize this trade-off after a year or two of being underemployed in an ungratifying career.

Some candidates tell me they are restricted now, but willing to open up for future assignments. If you want to grow as a leader in the corporate world, pick the best opportunity that will allow you to stretch and learn in your *first* job out of the military. It's hard to get on a development track if you have a slow start in your business career. Once you have a successful business track record, it is easier to navigate your career closer to your geographic preference.

As in the military, the competition increases as you grow in your career. Being willing to relocate to take challenging assignments can help differentiate you from others who won't make this strategic investment. A lot of people talk the talk about being willing to take the hard assignments to invest in their careers. Few people are willing to make the investment. Perhaps that is why so few people grow to be executives in successful companies.

The majority of the Cameron-Brooks JMO candidates accept job offers in their *region* of preference. The reason for this is that good companies have good attitudes about helping people work in a region of the country that meets their personal needs, if at all possible. Your happiness will be important to a good company. This is especially true once you develop a track record in business. There will be times in your business career when you will accept promotions outside your preferred location, as well as times that you will not. The number one reason that business people turn down promotions that involve location changes is due to family considerations. You are free to do this. At the same time, accepting promotions can be excellent strategic decisions. The point is that once you have been in a company and you have a track record of success, you will find that the organization will try to help you balance your professional development with your personal needs.

Here is a suggestion if you aspire to future executive positions in your business career after the military:

1. Define your location preference by region (Northeast, Southwest, etc.).

2. Communicate this preference to your recruiting firm.

3. Identify a couple of other regions in the country where you would consider *excellent* career opportunities (in addition to your preference). If your preference is the Northeast, perhaps consider the Southeast or Midwest as viable second choices, provided the career opportunity is a great fit.

4. Identify areas of the country that you would not consider, even for a good opportunity.

5. Don't bring location back into the picture until you are trying to narrow down offers. Location can be an excellent tiebreaker.

In the end, career decisions have both opportunity and cost. Living outside of your preferred location is a cost, but for the right career move, the opportunity can outweigh the cost and can be a good decision. Educate yourself, focus on the big picture, and avoid making emotional decisions. Try not to let location preferences restrict your ability to realize your full potential in the business world.

Again, be sure you speak with everyone who will be a part of your career decision. After your recruiting firm and interviewing companies have spent time and money to assist in your transition or to hire you, it is very unprofessional to tell them your spouse, fiancé(e), or parents do not want you to leave a certain geographical area. Be a responsible person and discuss location with those involved in the decision before, not after, you engage a recruiting firm or a company. This will help you prepare for the location question prior to an interview and also make good career decisions when you have all of the information about an employment offer—compensation, company culture, career path, nature of the work, company values, and location. The time to think about this is before you interview, not afterward.

"What Is Your Leadership Style?"

You will be asked this question about leadership style in almost every interview. Realize this interview question can come in many forms. For example, all of the following questions are aimed at discovering your leadership style: "How do you motivate people to accomplish objectives? Why do people want to work for you? How do you lead? How do you build a team? How do you lead without authority?" They may even ask you a Significant Accomplishment question, "Tell me about a time you built a team," which indicates that the interviewer wants to hear a specific example illustrating your style.

Company recruiters ask this question because leadership in the military differs from leadership in business. Recruiters want to evaluate your leadership style to determine whether it is compatible with their company's work environment.

Let's first look at the style of leadership corporate America endorses—the involved, collaborative, servant, participative leader. It is critical that you become familiar with the current thought on leadership by reading business books on leadership. This is the only way you will be able to talk intelligently about the way you interact with and lead others.

The perception is that the military style of leadership is designed to be "directive." Some of you are more directive in the way you lead people than others. But in corporate America you can't use rank, orders, or UCMJ as tools. The business world doesn't have any tools like this. Don't think for a moment that these tools are not influential in the military for getting people to agree to certain things or to produce certain outcomes. If you think that this is not used in the military, at least subconsciously, let me ask you this: How long would a civilian friend or your civilian spouse/ significant other stay in a work situation that was unacceptable or negative (for example, if he or she did not get along with his or her boss or if the expectations were unrealistic or the work atmosphere was undesirable)? He or she might stay a day or a week, but probably no longer than that. He or she would simply get up and walk out the door. You and I both know this can't happen in the military. There is this thing called a contract that must be fulfilled. It is this fact that makes leadership in the military acutely different from that in the business world.

You must learn a different style of leadership, be able to talk about different styles, and prove to recruiters that you are capable of exercising a style other than directive. It is critical that while you are still in the military, you start to develop a leadership style that does not rely on telling people what to do. Companies want to see that you are able to lead others in a positive way, creating a pleasant work environment, building consensus, and helping others and their organization become better at what they do. The business world wants leaders who can teach, who help others achieve success and grow. You can't do this by simply "leading by example" or "taking care of my people." You teach others by soliciting their ideas, listening, encouraging, setting goals together, and believing in them.

The number one reason corporate America likes to recruit JMOs is because of their leadership experience. When preparing your answer to this question, reflect on this. You cannot ignore the magnitude of this question. Under no circumstance can you give us textbook answers. You cannot tell us you lead by example, are a situational manager, or manage by objective. This simply is not adequate. *We want to know what you do to motivate members of your team, your peers, and your superiors.*

In the past, leadership was about motivating people to get the job done, and companies loved the military officer who could produce such results despite obstacles. Though objectives were being met, the problem with this leadership was that it was at the expense of their people, the work environment, morale, etc. What has evolved is a more people-oriented leadership style. Today leadership is about teaching. Companies want people who have a track record of improving an organization by growing leaders (helping others realize their leadership potential) throughout the company. In other words, companies want leaders of leaders—people who can develop the leadership talent and other talents in others.

In the military and in business, you cannot implement a new process or make significant changes without being able to get the support of a wide range of people. Because of the military rank structure, if you are simply accomplishing tasks related to your job, you really don't need to use a lot of collaborative and peer leadership; you just tell people what to do and they listen because you are in charge. However, when you take the initiative to make process changes outside of your immediate sphere of influence, you have to be able to "sell" your vision across an organization (team members, peers, senior officers, etc.). The more creative your process changes are and the more initiative you take to make changes, the more you will need indirect leadership skills to build a consensus and make it happen.

Today every recruiter looks for Development Candidates who have excellent interpersonal skills, the ability to develop relationships and build consensus. They want leaders who value people and who believe in coaching others to be more successful. I am not saying that you should forgo your goal orientation, but the business world wants its leaders to have a steel-rod backbone wrapped in a soft exterior.

Describe your leadership style in your own words—and show how it has been effective for you. In listening to your answer about your leadership style, recruiters want to lean back in their chair, close their eyes, and through your verbal picture of your leadership style, envision you going through your day motivating people in the company.

The administrative part of your answer should be less than 30 seconds long. We are much more interested in your motivational and consensus-building skills, which should constitute 80 percent of your answer. The key is to give specifics. For instance, start with the objective you are given. "When I'm given an objective, the first thing I do is take some quiet time to analyze the objective to determine what I'm being asked to do and to identify the time frame for accomplishing it. Then I invite the managers on my team to discuss key issues with me (participate). I share with them (notice I don't say "tell them") what the objective is and the time frame we have to get it done. Now I ask them for their input (participate) as to how they see us accomplishing these objectives. I do this because they are frequently closer to the job than I am, and they usually have very definite ideas about how to accomplish this objective as efficiently and effectively as possible."

"I rely more on asking questions in order to solve problems

rather than offering solutions to the problems. As a leader I focus on the big picture and the objectives we want to reach and seek input from others as to what we need to do to get there. I keep people aware of our goals and vision. I invite their input. I listen. I help people become better at what they do by encouraging creativity and new ideas and by providing a supportive environment in which people feel comfortable proposing and trying out calculated risks."

"I also counsel, mentor, and develop my team members. I provide everyone on my team performance feedback sessions to understand how their performance impacts the team and results. I share with them opportunity areas for improvement. I listen to their goals and interests and identify opportunities for training, development, and increased responsibility. I also find time to mentor high-potential people on my team. I spend some extra time with them outlining a plan for them to reach higher-level goals, achieve promotions, and assume leadership positions."

DON'T USE MY WORDS.
USE MY THOUGHTS.

In other words, what you are doing is listening. As officers tell me about their leadership style, here are the words I hear most frequently: "I *tell* my people what our objective is. I *tell* them the time frame. I *tell* them . . . ."

The goal of participative or collaborative leadership is to make everyone feel part of the decision. The successful leader draws out the best performance in others by helping them think of themselves as a critical part of the success of a mission or objective. Everyone wants to feel important. It's the theory of stakeholders. When people feel their input is valued, they are more likely to be committed to the success of the mission. I doubt you will convince anyone that he or she is an integral part of the decision or mission when you are doing nothing but *telling*. We want people who listen to what others (team members, peers, superiors) have to say.

As you motivate your team members to accomplish these objectives, how do you do it? Are you a positive motivator? If you are, tell me succinctly how you positively motivate. I want to hear such things as "Often I call a team member and express my thanks for putting in a 14-hour day, for getting the job done, and for bringing it in ahead of time." When you describe it in this manner, I can envision you doing that. Share with us how you motivate. We want leaders who can motivate without enlistment contracts backing them up. Contracts allow leaders to motivate through control. We must see your ability to create a positive work environment that encourages people around you to want to be effective contributors. Again, as recruiters listen to your descriptions of your leadership style, they will try to imagine whether or not it would be enjoyable to work with you. They will evaluate your leadership ability and your interpersonal style.

Think through all the situations when you've worked with difficult individuals who have forced you to find creative ways to motivate them. Write down the circumstances of these situations, what was difficult, and what you did to change and motivate the person. Put down at least five experiences. You'll start to see a pattern in these situations—why you've been successful as a leader. Be careful that you are not describing situations in which you used threats to accomplish the motivation. If you tell someone they have to work until the job is done, or that they will have no weekend pass, etc., this is threat leadership and is not what corporate America is looking for in future leaders.

Most recruiters today are adamant about hiring individuals who have the ability to *permanently change behavioral patterns* in their team members. The specific issue is, do you have the ability to develop your team members to continue enhanced performance after you have left the scene? Too often, we suspect by your comments that as long as you're there to "motivate," your team members will produce. It is important for you to demonstrate that you can change behavioral patterns that will lead to permanent substantive improvement in your team members.

To accomplish *permanent* behavioral change, there is a process through which you must lead others. Practice this type of leadership before you leave the military so you can discuss results of the practice in your interviews.

First, identify the behavior that must be changed. Many times it is a behavior that a member of your team was not trained to demonstrate or about which the person has not had a previous knowledge or understanding. If I am trying to coach a member of my team to delegate responsibility better, I first must identify the issue with the person so that together we *agree* that it needs permanent correction. Like any behavioral change, nothing is going to happen if the person making the change does not believe in it. Your role is to help the person see how it will benefit him or her and the team as a whole. In your discussions with this person, remember you're talking about a behavior, not about the person. You want the person to feel positive about making this change. Together you can develop what steps can be taken to start to implement the new behavior. Again, it's a team effort. Let the individual come up with ways to delegate better. Discuss ideas together. Set goals together. Ask questions to help the person see your vision and overall objective. Remember, you need his or her buy-in. Your vision is successful only when it's theirs, too. You are there to help, facilitate, and encourage the change. Lastly, psychologists say you must practice a change for a minimum period of 21 days before it becomes a permanent behavioral change. Individuals appreciate a supportive, positive environment while they are trying to make a change. Your role should be that of a coach and facilitator, providing the positive atmosphere needed to make the change.

As long as the military has contracts, rank, and UCMJ, you can order or tell people what to do, and corporate America isn't going to be interested in this type of leadership. Take this back to the office and execute it so you can give recruiters examples of your successes.

Remember that leadership has a number of key factors. Real leaders must:

- Be motivators
- Be consensus-builders
- Be trustworthy
- Be strategic thinkers
- Provide vision
- Be approachable
- Mentor and counsel team members
- Believe in the members of their team
- Permanently change behavior patterns
- Be givers, not takers
- Develop and mentor others
- Provide performance feedback
- Be willing to tackle the tough issues
- Confront problems, especially people problems, and address those not performing to standard

In conclusion, you must show where your style has gone beyond the guidelines that the military has given you. Companies want leaders who can "stretch the envelope" to allow a company to produce beyond where it has produced before. They want leaders who can motivate others to perform at their best.

The following suggestions will help you examine and improve your leadership ability and better verbalize it in an interview:

1. Read and study about leadership. There are numerous excellent books on leadership (see Appendix C). Also study leaders in the military and in business to identify what you like and want to adopt and what you do not like and do not want to incorporate. Find a mentor who is a strong leader and who can share ideas and best practices with you.

2. Honestly evaluate yourself in the area of growing the leadership capabilities of others. Are you teaching leadership? Are you helping the people around you improve their performance, become better time managers, or make decisions better? How many people have you mentored? Write down the names of three people who are better leaders today because of your influence. Are they growing? Is their performance improving? Are they getting promoted? If so, this is solid proof that you are succeeding as a leader. If not, redirect your leadership efforts to this end. *Great leaders develop other leaders.* Companies want Development Candidates who invest in others, give back, and develop and mentor others. You must be ready to discuss this in an interview. Remember, if you are not teaching leadership, you are not leading.

Again, the best way to adopt a new leadership style is to learn about leadership practices from business books and other leaders. Begin early in your military career to read about and implement new leadership techniques so that you will have results with which to back up your chosen style. Then you must practice the fundamentals of this style so you can discuss the results with recruiters. Simply reading books about and becoming familiar with leadership styles is not enough. Recruiters expect you to have used them.

Answering Questions about Solving People Problems

You will be asked to give examples of specific people issues you have solved as a leader in the military. It is critically important that you give us problems that are performance-oriented.

In other words we have no interest in alcohol, family, drugs, or financial issues. While this can eliminate a significant number of the people problems you face in subordinate leadership roles, they are not good examples to give to a corporate recruiter. We want performance-oriented problems that are operationally or mission related. You must use an example of someone you supervise directly who couldn't prioritize, organize, problem solve, deliver high-quality results, etc. You worked with this individual who was a good worker and had a great attitude about coming to work but just couldn't quite accomplish his or her objectives. Through your personal leadership, training, coaching, and motivation, you turned this average performer into a better performer. Show how you helped facilitate permanent behavior change.

Frequently, when I ask this question I am given an example of a specific people problem someone has solved by terminating the person. The officer either sent the individual to another unit or forced him or her to leave the military. This suggests that your leadership style failed. Why would you give us an example of a problem you solved but during which your leadership failed? Had I asked for an example of a people problem that you failed to solve, then I would have expected this example. Remember, we are looking for individuals who have the ability to take a people problem and solve it in a positive, productive way, with the end result that we have a better performer due to behavioral improvement.

"Give Me an Example of a Time You Counseled Someone" and "Give Me an Example of a Time You Mentored Someone"

Companies want and need leaders who take time to develop their team members. The only way to do this is to spend individual time focused on a person's development. Leaders do this through counseling and mentoring, and as a result, company recruiters will ask for examples of times you mentored and counseled someone.

Mentoring and counseling are significantly different, but a top-performing leader does both. Counseling is consistent periodic feedback focused on enhancing a person's performance. Many think of counseling as negative, though it doesn't need to be, but because people think of it as being negative, you could instead use the term "performance management session." Mentoring is coaching, educating and advising a high-potential person to reach his or her career goals.

When answering the counseling question, companies will want to see that you approached the individual professionally, even though counseling can be considered negative. They will want to see that you focused on performance and the future, developing the expected outcomes and behaviors. Recruiters will want to see that you make it a habit to have consistent, periodic counseling/ mentoring sessions with your team members.

Mentoring involves a mentor and a protégé. The mentor

coaches, guides, teaches, and counsels a protégé to help him or her grow and reach his or her goals. Not all leaders take time to mentor, and to me that's disappointing and selfish. If you are in a leadership position in the military or in business, developing junior leaders is an expected and direct area of responsibility. I can tell you our client companies expect it of their Development Candidates and will want to hear examples from your military career to prove you will also do it in their organization. When answering questions about mentoring, you will want to show that you selected a protégé who had a lot of potential, that you made a commitment to this person, coached and mentored him or her, and then helped that person elevate his or her career. Recruiters will want to see the result. Possibly he or she reached a higher rank, became an officer, attended college, earned a certification, etc.

Questions about Teamwork and Building Teams

As corporate America becomes more participative in its leadership style, as we de-emphasize titles, and as we look harder for those who can lead without being "the boss," we look for people who are team players. A company can reach great heights only when its people can work together successfully as a team. Companies want synergy. I've always said that the success of Cameron-Brooks is a direct result of the quality of our team—the sum of the whole. You achieve a quality team when you have quality team players.

Simply stated, team players are individuals who have as much concern for the success of their peers, department, or company as their own.

Some military officers point out that they have performed in teams their entire tour of duty in the military. We agree with them that, in some cases, this has developed their ability to work as a team player. But not in all cases. We firmly believe that though officers perform on a team, they do not necessarily perform as team players.

Being a team player is easier said than done. Some people find it impossible. While moving up the corporate ladder will always be important to you, a value for individual competitiveness should be subtle at best. The business world expects a philosophy that emphasizes helping others to be successful and to accomplish their professional and personal goals.

I encourage you to examine your team philosophy and look hard at whether you are a team player who works for the good of the team or as an individual who is more concerned about number one. If it's the latter, I recommend you take immediate steps to develop your ability to perform as a team player.

"Do You Micro-Manage?"

Many people miss the rather subtle point made by this question. If you said no to this question, I would have to tell you that few of our client companies would hire you. This statement bewilders many people. Let me explain.

First of all, the question does not ask if you are a micro-manager. If that were asked, I would hope your answer would be no. As explained earlier, the definition of a participative manager is someone with a "steel-rod backbone wrapped in a soft exterior." A recruiter can see the soft exterior but has to ask questions to determine your backbone—questions such as, "Do you micro-manage?"

An ideal response to this question would be similar to this: "Yes—on rare occasions when my commander has given me a critical mission and a short response time. You bet I was looking over everyone's shoulder to ensure mission success."

Corporate America is not a perfect world. There will be times your company will need you to handle crisis situations. Recruiters will want to know you have handled them in the military. With the current military environment and deployments around the world, it is usually pretty easy for a military officer to discuss crisis situations, but not always.

I remember an incident at one of our Career Conferences when a recruiter was discussing one of my candidates whom he had interviewed that morning. He said, "I sure like him. He is bright, intelligent, poised—an excellent communicator. As a matter of fact, if I had a daughter, I would hope she would marry someone just like him." I was feeling very proud until he said, "However, Roger, I'm not going to be able to recommend that our company hire him because he has never had his back against the wall—he has never had to manage a crisis situation." Because I reviewed the candidate's evaluations, I knew he had managed numerous crisis situations closely, but no matter how hard I tried to persuade the recruiter to reconsider, it was too late.

"What Are Your Short- and Long-Term Career Goals?"

The purpose of this question is to determine two things: (1) whether your goals are realistic and compatible with the position and company for which you are interviewing and (2) how you plan to accomplish them. This question is difficult and can quickly get you into trouble. How do you know what is realistic in this particular position and for this particular company? What is the recruiter's definition of short and long term? Two and ten years? Five and twenty years? Therefore, proceed with caution. You want to give answers with depth.

First, define short and long term in years. Recruiters want to know what kind of time frame you expect you'll need to accomplish these goals. These numbers also will help them understand your ambition and drive. I recommend you judge short term to be about three years and long term to be 10 to 15 plus years. In determining your career goals, think of the big picture and empathize.

Think in terms of what a recruiter or company manager would want rather than what you want. It is okay to have "selfish" goals, but keep them out of the interview. What if you believe a long-term goal of yours is to be the CEO of your own company in 15 years? What kind of reaction are you going to get from a recruiter when you state this long-term career goal? It's actually the quickest way to bring your interview to rapid conclusion. The recruiter thinks you obviously have little interest in helping a company grow and succeed. Remember, companies are looking for a good fit between individual and company. Help the recruiter see this fit by connecting your career goals with results for which the company might strive.

In the big picture, how will you make an impact? What reputation will you have? One of a great problem solver? Creative thinker? Outstanding motivator? Strong analyst? Strong visionary?

These are career objectives that benefit your company first and you second. Such objectives are important to any company and demonstrate maturity and empathy.

Exercise: Defining Your Short- and Long-Term Career Goals

This exercise will assist you in identifying and expressing the process you use to establish and attain goals and objectives.

It is important that you be aware of how the business world will analyze and judge your goals. Your goals and objectives should stretch you and make you perspire while reaching them. In the business world, *the more difficult the objective, the more significant the achievement.* Push yourself. Set high objectives, but support them with a plan of action that says they are realistic and can be accomplished. Prove to companies you have the ability to meet their expectations by identifying goals and sharing your plans for achieving them and by giving them examples of goals and objectives you have set and met and yet did so by overcoming difficult obstacles.

Beginning with your short-term goals, write down at least five things (both in your personal life and professional life) you want to accomplish within the next three years.

Now outline how you plan to reach those objectives. Break down each objective/goal into reachable increments. What are the intermediate steps that you need to accomplish along the way? Establish a time frame for the realistic accomplishment of each goal, and use a calendar to remind yourself of each step to be taken.

Think about your long-term goals. Write down five things you want to accomplish within the next 10 or 15 years. Remember, stretch yourself. Do a similar, but broader, outline for how you plan to reach each of your long-term goals.

What short-term goals can you use to reach each long-term goal? Some goals may span 12 months, others several years. Think about how each goal fits into and affects the big picture of your life. Knowing your plan of action—how you are going to accomplish an objective—will help you express your career goals in an interview with confidence and believability.

"What Separates You from the Other Candidates?"

Let's say a company has a single opening and has interviewed three or four candidates. They all look good. Then comes the question "What separates you from the other candidates?" Or "Why should I hire you?"

If you could get inside a recruiter's mind, he or she is really asking, "What makes you better for this position than the other candidates?" The answer I get from most candidates is always the same: "I'm the person who can get the job done. I have the credentials to do the job." That's what everyone says—and it really doesn't impact or make an impression.

I am impressed with an individual who says, "Roger, I'm sure the kind of people you're interviewing all have good abilities and excellent credentials. All of us are confident we can do the job. But let me share with you something I have that I feel is an integral part of me. You won't find anyone with a better *attitude*." This individual supports his or her statement with evidence, explaining further: "If I need to be here at 6:00 a.m. to get the job done, I'll be here. If I need to work through my lunch hour, I'll be here. If I need to work late, I'll be here." And "I'll be here with a positive attitude. Anytime you need anything done, give it to me. I'll get it done for you."

I honestly believe the desire to apply one's ability and a positive attitude about doing the job is more important than just having the ability. It is interesting how many recruiters say, "Bring me someone with intellect and a positive attitude and we'll teach them the skills." I completely agree.

To answer the questions "What separates you from the other candidates?" and "Why should I hire you?" you must use words that have unique impact. I've heard it again and again over the years: "I can get the job done. I have the credentials." But the key is to tell recruiters what makes you unique—your attitude, your creativity, your "stick-to-it-iveness," your ability to learn quickly, your leadership ability, your loyalty, etc. Support your claim with concrete examples. Recruiters want a unique response—they want to know why they should hire you.

Be careful not to put down the other candidates when answering this question. Talk about yourself. Do not compare yourself with others in your examples (remember, we want team players). And don't go on and on. You'll become boring and lose the recruiter. It's so much easier to emphasize with a few words than with many. And remember, when you're asked this and other personal questions, such as why you want a career in corporate America, be emphatic. Give proof and evidence. Put credibility in your answer.

I like to hear, "Roger, I am going to have a career in corporate America." I like someone who is positive and emphatic. An answer will have impact when it is based on solid research and clear thinking. You've reached a conclusion (about what you can offer and why you want a career in corporate America) and can verbalize it. Remember—you must back up your statements with proof and evidence. Bottom line: Be confident, be positive, back up your answer, and be concise.

Other Important Questions

Briefly I want to cover some other questions that appear frequently in an interview. They are interesting and thought-provoking. Take each question, write it down, and formulate your answer following the advice I have suggested. Then, in your study groups or with your spouse/significant other or study partner, practice, evaluate, and critique your answers and delivery.

The questions are divided among the top three reasons corporate America is interested in hiring the military officer. Keep this in mind as you formulate responses.

1. **Leadership**
   - "Tell me about a time you convinced a group of peers to buy into your vision and how you played a significant role in facilitating change."
   - "How do you build relationships with difficult people?" Think about people in all positions, not just members of your team.
   - "How do you lead people when you do not have any direct authority over them?"
   - "How do you build a team?"
   - "How do you lead or manage complex projects?"

2. **Accomplishments**
   - "Describe a creative idea of yours that had a significant impact at work."
   - "Tell me about the biggest risk you took."
   - "Tell me about a complex problem you solved."

3. **Lessons Learned from the Military**
   - "What three words best describe you and why?"
   - "What are your strengths? What are your weaknesses?"
   - "Describe a time you failed."
   - "What is the greatest leadership lesson you learned in the military?"

Every one of these questions should take a considerable amount of time for you to determine an answer and the examples you want to use. Once you frame your answers, make sure you demonstrate your competencies and that you make connections between what you can offer and the reasons the business world has an interest in hiring officers. Remember, you also want to connect on the three levels I previously discussed with you—ability, interest, and rapport. Easy? Not by a long shot! To exit the military and accelerate into a business career takes a significant investment in terms of preparation and self-development, but isn't your professional future worth it?

As I have stated earlier, the delivery of your answers is as important as the content. You must communicate persuasively, convincingly. When you practice delivering your answers to each of the questions presented in this chapter, evaluate yourself using the following questions:

- How expressive is your voice?
- Do you use proper intonation, voice volume, facial expression, and verbal enthusiasm as you talk?
- Do you have the ability to get someone else to respond to your ideas or thoughts because of your enthusiasm—do you excite?
- Can you make your point succinctly without being abrasive or abrupt?
- Do you emphasize key words?
- Do you enunciate and can someone clearly understand you?
- Are you sensitive to the impact of your voice? If you speak too loudly, you will exhaust the recruiter and be abrasive. If you have low voice volume, recruiters will think you do not have the ability to generate enthusiasm and excitement in other people. Be aware of this, and begin to notice how your voice influences others.

Chapters 5 and 6 have given you a lot of interview preparation material. Your challenge is to become an expert on yourself—your strengths and weaknesses and the traits that have made you successful so that, for each question listed in this book, you can prepare answers with depth and substance. Practice your delivery until it is perfect. Do this for each question. It's a lot of work, but your professional future is worth it.

I encourage you to visit the Cameron-Brooks Web site (www. cameron-brooks.com) and utilize our Resource Center. The Resource Center includes tips on interviewing strategy, potential questions that recruiters will ask you, and how to answer them. Many of these tips will also help you communicate more effectively in the military. The sooner you begin tapping into this information and preparing for the transition, the better your performance in your military job, the more marketable you will be when you transition to the business world, and the more successful you will be in your interviews and in your future business career. Use this and all of the information available on our Web site to your advantage!

In the next chapter, I turn our focus to some of the common errors we see in the interview, using actual recruiter comments we've received over the years. Use this next chapter as a reminder of what not to do in the interview.

Chapter 7

CONSIDERING THE REASONS FOR BEING DECLINED

I n previous chapters I outlined what you must do to be successful in the interview. Many JMOs also ask me, "Roger, what are the pitfalls I need to avoid? What mistakes have other candidates made that I should know now so I don't repeat them?" Fortunately, over the many years corporate recruiters have provided me and my team with feedback on their reasons for acceptance or decline. The following are actual recruiter comments describing candidates who were declined—in other words, their pitfalls and mistakes. You will notice that some of the points are similar, but these similarities only emphasize their importance.

As I stated in Chapter 5, you cannot interview successfully without proving your fit on three fronts: (1) ability, (2) interest, and (3) rapport. The reasons for failing to connect on one of these three fronts are noted and fall into one of the following subcategories: *preparation, communication, energy level,* and *leadership*.

Let's look at the following comments and see where previous candidates failed to connect on one of the three fronts and why.

Ability

Preparation

Well rehearsed but not specific when probed. The candidate did not sufficiently prove his ability. He talked in generalizations. For example, to the question "How do you build a team?"

he answered, "I am an involved leader and I really get to know my people." This generalization is not acceptable to recruiters. This candidate did not give specifics that demonstrate "how" he is involved with his team and "how" he gets to know them. He failed to give the recruiter enough information so he or she can visualize him building teams and interacting with others. To do this, you must do your homework.

No competencies. The candidate didn't understand or prepare for the competency-based interview. You must be able to verbally illustrate your key, innate competencies without naming them. This is not easy. You must find the time to prepare multiple accomplishments that you can present to the recruiter to demonstrate your consistent behavioral traits—in other words, traits that show up again and again in your accomplishments. The recruiter is looking for demonstrated competencies (skills). Make sure you take ownership of your competencies by using the pronoun "I" in your answers. The military and corporate America do use the word "we"; however, the interview is about "you" and what "you" did, so you have to take possession of your answer and say specifically what you did by using "I"—for example, "I led my team through a brainstorming session soliciting ideas and courses of action" rather than "We met and developed ideas and courses of action." The "I" statement says exactly what you did. In the second statement, the recruiter can't tell what role you had in generating ideas and courses of action.

Did not connect. The candidate couldn't make points of connection from past performance. Be sure to get involved in a quality business reading program to educate yourself about the business world, the different career fields available to you, and the specific requirements of the career field or position. You must have a solid understanding of the business world in order to relate your skills and military experience to this new environment. Recruiters will rely on you to make this connection, as they have little if any knowledge about your military background. The General Store exercise outlined in Chapter 3 will help you prepare to connect your military experience with business.

Couldn't get anything out of her. This candidate had difficulty discussing her background and qualifications in a pleasant, conversational style. You must be prepared so you can relax in an interview and help the recruiter know the real you. Recruiters want open communicators. To prepare for a discussion of your qualifications, write down your significant achievements that point to relevant skills the position would require, and then practice verbalizing them. Next, practice "interviewing" with good friends. Explain to them that you want the mock interview to be relaxed so that they can help you achieve this goal by giving you suggestions. You can capture your mock interview on video and evaluate yourself. You will be surprised what you see. The point is not to memorize a canned speech but to be able to convey your ability to do the job in an open, conversational style. You do not want to be caught off guard with nothing to say. A recruiter will not pull information out of you.

Didn't know what she wanted to do. The candidate didn't prepare for the interview by analyzing her knowledge, skills, achievements, and objective and subjective assets. She lacked self-insight. Companies want to know you are committed regarding your career direction, and they want to know how you can contribute to their success. The candidate may have thought she could wing it and talk off the top of her head. Be sure you do whatever it takes before the interview to understand specifically how your achievements and skills relate to the different business careers you are seeking and to know that you are confident in your decision to transition to the business world.

Good supervision, but limited success. This candidate had leadership responsibility but could not articulate how he had carried out his responsibilities and produced results. You must log in hours of articulating your accomplishments so you will be prepared in the interview to discuss how your actions as a leader caused positive change and motivated your team to significant accomplishments. This person did not focus on results.

Unrealistic regarding promotion. The candidate stated a requirement for promotion within the first six months, thus projecting himself as expecting too much too soon and not being realistic in his ability to set goals. Nothing will scare away companies faster than for you to make unreasonable demands or to be unrealistic in your goals. He probably didn't take my advice on how to determine short- and long-term goals. It is important to be ambitious but realistic. There are many factors that must be considered for promotion. You will not be promoted overnight. Be realistic in self-evaluation and promotion opportunity relative to your abilities. It is a long, hard road to the top. To reach the top, the road must be filled with significant contributions.

Communication

Couldn't articulate and give specific examples of accomplishments. Had the candidate used a recording device before the interview and listened to herself, this probably would not have happened. No one can speak in a concise, articulate manner without hard work and preparation. Practice articulating your accomplishments, and support your accomplishments with concrete examples.

Didn't give precise answer to question. The candidate's rambling answer indicated that he might not have listened to everything the recruiter asked in his question. Not listening causes the recruiter to question your ability to listen to others in the workplace. You must listen actively to every word before answering a question and take the time to formulate a direct answer, exactly as you would in a work situation with other team members, your supervisors, or customers. Good listening skills are keys to success in an interview, as well as in any professional career.

Talked nonstop; didn't listen and didn't relate background. The candidate didn't look for cues from the recruiter about how the delivery of his answers was being accepted. Be sensitive to the recruiter and listen to what he or she says. Help the recruiter see how your background relates to the career field requirements. To be a Development Candidate, you must reflect, organize, deliver, and then stop. You must demonstrate that you have the ability to listen. Good leaders listen a lot more than they speak.

Rambled; poor communicator. The candidate tried to tell the recruiter too much. He ran out of time and appeared unfocused. Rambling takes up valuable interview time and is never productive. You must decrease the chance that you will ramble when answering questions by spending quality time before the interview thinking about some typical questions that may be asked and how you can answer concisely. When you are asked a question, take a few seconds to organize your thoughts. Answer succinctly, but give answers that have depth. You can give substance concisely.

Energy Level

Reserved; low energy level; not inspirational. This candidate may not have known the importance of selling himself. He needed to show his ability to handle many tasks that require a lot of energy. To make a recruiter believe you can handle a job, you must be excited about the opportunity. You must show enthusiasm and a high energy level. It makes no difference whether you are applying for a position in engineering, logistics, or finance. You are first and foremost a Development Candidate. You must project an image similar to that of the top company leaders. As a leader your attitude is contagious. Would you allow your team to be slow? Low energy? Bored? Dull? You must show your enthusiasm and prove your ability to lead others and go the extra mile.

Leadership Qualities

No initiative. In the fast-paced, competitive corporate environment, you must creatively solve problems on your own initiative. This individual seemed content with the status quo. It is easier to go through life as a follower. This is not what we're looking for in a Development Candidate. You must have the initiative to enhance performance without prompting from others. Again, saying you have initiative is not enough. Give us examples of times when you have demonstrated initiative.

Not a team player. The candidate came across as being too authoritative. Keep in mind what companies look for in their leaders. You want to prove your ability to be a participative leader, one who can be a coach and facilitator, not a leader by directive. Recruiters are looking for candidates who will be able to motivate others by getting their trust versus being their boss. When you prepare for the interview, write down examples of how you have been a team player in any of your school or work experiences. Refer to how you delegated authority and encouraged participation and why others responded to your style. Then practice telling others about these experiences.

Interest

Preparation

Superficial answers. The candidate gave answers that lacked depth, quality, self-insight, and comprehension, all of which demonstrated lack of interest and preparation. Be aware that recruiters are looking for these characteristics. They are the foundation of a Development Candidate.

Same questions as everyone else. The candidate did not listen carefully or gather enough information to ask specific, relevant quality questions. You cannot ask generic questions. They must be relevant to the company and the position. They must have a purpose. The better your questions, the better you will show a recruiter that you have a genuine interest in the career opportunity.

Shallow questions. This candidate showed lack of understanding of (and thus interest in) the position and career. If you've spent the necessary time to get information about the company and type of career field, you'll be able to do some pre-work. Write out your questions before you interview and practice verbalizing them. During your interview, listen carefully to the recruiter(s) so that you will be able to formulate appropriate, open-ended questions that show depth and interest.

Communication

Difficult to hear; lacked conviction. Often recruiters say,

"Roger, I like everything the candidate said, but I'm not convinced that she meant what she said." Sometimes, we have candidates tell us they have consistently been soft-spoken. Their parents and teachers have often asked them to speak up, but they feel it is natural for them to speak softly and that there is nothing they can do about it. I have found it helpful for candidates to record themselves to correct this problem. Place the recording device across the room from you, and then project your voice into it without shouting. Do this for an hour every day. You may read from a book or pick a subject and spontaneously give a speech on it. The test is to project your voice so that soon it will become natural for you to speak in a forceful, convincing manner. You do not have to be soft-spoken for the rest of your life. I am not suggesting that you transform from someone who is mild-mannered and soft-spoken into someone who is loud and obnoxious. I am talking about presenting yourself in a professional, convincing manner. Watch people you know—for example, friends, coworkers, supervisors, and others who have voices to which you respond positively—and watch how they project. Listen to the tone and volume of their voices. If you determine after working on this independently for several weeks or months that this isn't doing the job, then don't be afraid to go for outside help. Go to a diction instructor (someone who can help you use your voice in a better manner) or take a speech course. Do not accept failure in increasing the power and the impact of your voice.

Energy Level

Didn't show interest. The candidate had poor posture and slumped in the chair. She showed very little enthusiasm, both in her voice and the statements she made. Recruiters are looking for candidates who exhibit interest. Be prepared to convince the recruiter of your interest through your body language, which portrays your energy and enthusiasm.

Rapport

Preparation

Programmed/rehearsed answers. Some candidates give answers that appear canned. You must recognize the importance of sincerity in the delivery of your answers. Do your homework in order to digest the information and deliver it in your own personal style. Recruiters want a feeling for who you are as a person. If you talk with passion, recruiters will be more likely to believe what you are saying, to believe in you, and, as a result, to get a good feeling for who you are as a person. Do not memorize your answers! Deliver them naturally with energy and enthusiasm in a conversational manner.

Too rehearsed—said what the recruiter wanted to hear. The candidate's answers demonstrated a lack of confidence and preparation. Recruiters are sharp. They will see through a facade. Prepare. Don't give someone else's answers or deliver them by rote. It will not work. You must prepare in advance to be yourself and to convince the recruiter that you are the right person for the job. Recruiters must determine if you are a good interpersonal fit for the company, and they can do this only when you are yourself in the interview—using your own words, expressing your own thoughts.

Textbook answers. The candidate might have felt that by giving perfect answers, the recruiter would think he was perfect. If you're not comfortable enough or not prepared enough to be relaxed and be your smart self, the recruiter will see right through you. Would you bring someone into your company who you felt lacked confidence or, in fact, was a fake?

Communication

Not an open communicator. The candidate was guarded in his manner and had trouble revealing his true self. How will a recruiter determine your interpersonal fit if your true self is not revealed in the interview? If you have prepared adequately for your interview and have practiced with another person, you will have taken a big step in being able to talk openly with the interviewer.

Being open and relaxed are key components to establishing good rapport with a recruiter.

Was not flexible about location. The candidate took one second to say he was open but then spent five minutes talking about a preference. This contradiction made the recruiter question the candidate's believability. While being flexible about location may be difficult for you, it is important for you to be certain about your willingness to look at your options and to communicate this clearly. Be sure you have a positive, concise way to describe your position, and stick to it. You appear to be indecisive otherwise.

Lectured. The candidate didn't display a natural, easygoing communication style. You must speak with—not to—the recruiter. Strive to have a conversation with the recruiter and answer questions naturally and succinctly so you don't appear to be lecturing.

Overused first names. The candidate called the interviewer by her first name too many times during the interview in an effort to establish rapport. Use first names in moderation. Four or five times during a 45-minute interview is appropriate. It's also important to say the interviewer's name in a sincere and natural way.

Too much slang. The candidate didn't realize that using informal language is not acceptable in a corporate interview. Recruiters are turned off by slang or repeated words, such as "OK," "too easy," "awesome," "cool," "you know what I mean," or "you know." Omit slang or repetitious words from your conversation.

Poor eye contact. By not maintaining eye contact with the recruiter, the candidate did not connect on an interpersonal level with the recruiter and gave the impression of low self-esteem and a lack of self-confidence. Think about your impression when someone with whom you're trying to connect does not look you in the eye. Be sure to practice establishing and maintaining "comfortable" eye contact with other individuals before you interview.

Energy Level

Not natural; too stiff. The candidate was unable to relax and be natural. You should be able to carry on a two-way conversation in an easy, natural, and enthusiastic manner, which will help you establish good rapport with the recruiter. Being natural and relaxed in an interview shows poise, confidence, and maturity.

Overly aggressive. While it is important to be enthusiastic, it is also necessary to observe how the recruiter is reacting to your delivery. Be sensitive to any telltale signs of adverse reaction and adjust. Practice with others before you interview and get feedback about your style.

Too intense. The candidate was too uptight. He was not relaxed. Companies want professional, poised people. No matter what your position in a company, people will respond better if you are relaxed. You must always be comfortable with a pleasant, professional interpersonal style that demonstrates you can work easily with others.

Other Mistakes to Avoid

What follows are some other issues that will get you into trouble during an interview.

"That's a good question." The recruiter does not need to be told that he or she has asked a good question. Unless you say this every time, the recruiter may assume that the other questions are not good ones. Why do people say this? They want to buy time while they're thinking about the answer. It is not necessary for you to say anything. Just take that moment to reflect and then respond.

Evading a question. Do not evade a question. When a recruiter asks a specific question, answer it. Listen carefully to the question and be certain you understand it. For example, if the question is "What is your location preference?" don't reply that you are open. You were asked to give a preference, which is regional, such as the Southeast or the Northwest. I advise candidates to always state their preference in the broadest of terms—for example, "east of the Mississippi River." Do not lose an opportunity just because the location preference you gave was too narrow. Similarly, do not lose an opportunity because you did not answer the recruiter's questions. And do not evade a question by going off on a tangent of that question. This form of evading shows a recruiter either that you lack focus and good listening skills or that you are purposely evading the answer to a question with which you are uncomfortable.

Answer up-front. All responses to interview questions should be up-front, direct, and then followed by any necessary explanation. A question that calls for a "yes" or "no" should immediately be answered with either "yes" or "no," and then with your support for the answer. Too often, when I ask a particular question, the officer replies with rhetoric, and I must sit there and wonder if this is going to lead to a "yes" or a "no." Have the self-confidence to say "yes" or "no" immediately and then support your answer. When an individual sitting in front of me says, "yes," and then explains his or her answer, I know exactly where we're headed with this answer. I don't have to wonder. I don't have to wade through the rhetoric waiting for the answer.

"How did I do?" This is not an appropriate question to ask. A recruiter's job is not to give you instant feedback on whether your interview was good, bad, or indifferent. Some recruiters can't give you an accurate assessment of your performance in the interview until they have finished interviewing all of their candidates. You should know yourself how you did. You should be confident that you answered the questions with substance and depth, developed good rapport with the recruiter, connected your background with the requirements and responsibilities of the position, and conveyed your sincere interest in having a career with the company. Then, as you leave, you know how you did—you know it was a good interview.

———————

In this chapter I have given you the most prevalent reasons recruiters have declined candidates over the years. As you look at these reasons, note that you have total control over the majority of them. In most cases effective preparation would be very beneficial. It's a matter of speaking up with enthusiasm, speaking clearly and persuasively, listening actively, addressing the questions directly, supporting your answers, displaying good self-insight, poise, and confidence, and being concise in what you have to say.

I encourage you to study this chapter carefully during your preparation to remind yourself of what not to do in the interview. Put yourself in the shoes of a recruiter. Ask yourself if you would hire the candidate in each of the situations described above. I doubt you would.

Bottom line: focus your preparation on how to communicate effectively in an interview on all three fronts—your ability to produce results, your interest in the opportunity, and your interpersonal style, all of which will help a recruiter determine if you are the right fit for his or her company.

Chapter 8

AFTER THE INITIAL INTERVIEW

I t's a shame when candidates go through all the work and preparation of buying the right suits, building the right resume, learning how to answer the important questions, and getting through the initial interview, only to fail by not staying constantly alert and thoroughly involved in what happens after their initial interview.

Sending Thank-You Notes

F ollowing your initial interview, make it your practice to write thank-you notes to those companies which have expressed an interest in pursuing you further. The purpose of sending such a note is to restate your strong interest in the company and your desire for a follow-up interview. To help you with this task, here are some guidelines.

1. Pay close attention to your spelling, sentence structure, grammar, and punctuation. If you word-process the letter, do not rely entirely on the spell-check software. Check for errors yourself. Mistakes in these areas will ruin the message you are trying to convey.

2. Never ask a question in your letter that forces a recruiter to respond to your letter. You want to motivate the recruiter to take action and make arrangements for the next step, not increase his or her paperwork.

3. Write your letters immediately, and send them no later than the weekend after the interview. Other job candidates will be sending their thank-you notes promptly, and if yours is delayed, the company could assume a lack of interest on your part.

4. Tell a company when you have chosen it as one of your top companies. Remember how good you feel when you know someone thinks highly of you.

5. Do not start your letter thanking a company for taking the time to interview you. Instead, focus on how much you enjoyed the time spent with the recruiter learning more about the company and the position(s) discussed.

6. Tailor each letter to each individual company. A form letter will do you more harm than good. A personalized letter expresses the sincere interest you have in a particular company. Take a few moments to reflect on the interview and determine why you are excited about that company. Then create a letter that will communicate your desire for follow-up interviews and inspire the recruiter to pursue you further.

7. Try to make your letter unique in appearance. Corporate recruiters or department managers are busy. Most get a lot of mail and e-mail in one day. What's wrong with sending an envelope that is a different color? I just wonder if I got 20 pieces of mail in one morning and 19 of them were white but one was red, wouldn't the red one catch my eye? Did you ever receive an overnight letter and not open it immediately? Please don't be afraid to be professionally unique. Corporate America likes people who are innovative and creative.

8. Should you send a thank-you e-mail instead of a typed or handwritten note? Handwritten notes are more impactful, which is why in general I like them more than e-mail. Just think how many e-mails you get in a day. It could easily be overlooked or deleted. A hard-copy thank-you note is also more personal and, because it takes more time and effort, demonstrates more interest. I do recommend e-mail when it is time sensitive. If, for example, you interviewed with a company that intends to make a hiring decision that night or early the next day, then you should send an e-mail. Better to get it there quickly.

9.   If you're working with a recruiting firm that conveys a company's interest to you and your interest to the company, you don't need to send a thank-you letter since your recruiting firm is following up for you. Always remember that the point is to let the company know you are interested—not to inundate them with irrelevant letters or e-mails to duplicate a point already made. If the recruiting firm is not helping you with follow-up or communication with the company, then you must write these letters yourself.

Follow-Up Interviews

I have observed candidates work very hard and be very competitive in their initial interviews. Once they are invited for follow-up interviews, they think they're over the hump and on the downhill side. *You are never on the downhill side until you have an offer.* We've seen too many times in football games where a team gets out in front. It appears obvious to them they will win. They let up. The next thing you know, they are defeated. You have undoubtedly had this happen to you sometime in your own life. You knew you were in a winning situation. All of a sudden, you found yourself defeated. *When you prepare yourself for a follow-up interview, prepare even harder than you did for your initial interviews.*

I have been excited about candidates I've accepted and looked forward to introducing them to some of my client companies. Three months later I go back to their particular base to work with them on their transition preparation, but this time they just don't impress me. Why? They knew they had been accepted. They assumed once they were accepted they could never be declined—which is certainly not true. You should never let up. You can never feel you are home safe until the offer to go to work for a company is in your pocket.

Once a recruiter has said yes to a candidate in an initial

interview, he or she normally follows up with a series of interviews. You could receive as little as 24 hours' notice of an interview trip, and you need to be ready. Get your suits and your more casual travel clothes cleaned and pressed, shine your shoes, and have your travel essentials easily accessible. Also, organize your corporate information and keep it handy.

Here are some broad guidelines to follow when a company calls you for a follow-up interview:

- *Take notes.* Write down everything. Take the name, number, and title/job of the person calling if you don't know him or her. Write down any specific information that is given. Ideally, add your notes to your personal organizer (i.e., Google Calendar, MS Outlook, smart phone). Express excitement with everyone with whom you interact.

- *Don't assume.* Candidates have been brought in for jobs or locations that were different from those discussed. Company representatives (particularly if they are human resources/talent acquisitions) may not have complete information about you, and they may assume, for example, that you know they are in a certain location when you really do not know their location.

- *Ask questions.* Verify what you "think." The person with whom you are speaking may only want answers to two quick questions and yet may have all kinds of information that would be helpful to you.

- *Close the call.* At the end of the call, confirm you have correctly recorded all the details and verify all the data you gathered from this conversation. Make reservations; call the company back after checking on something, etc. Also, find out what the company will be doing to set up your visit. It would be good for you to have a checklist prepared and handy in the event of these expected and unexpected calls. This way you will not miss a point and need to call the recruiter back. Sometimes this can be embarrassing.

- *Be your smart self.* The person calling could be your future boss! Show energy, enthusiasm, and appreciation for his or her continued interest.

After being notified of an upcoming follow-up interview, you must increase your level of knowledge of the industry, company, and position for which you are interviewing. Quality companies have come to consider an absence of such effort to be indicative of either a lack of interest or a lack of follow-through, both of which are dangerous. You should utilize the Internet for general industry and company research. Visit the company's Web site and instead of only looking at the careers section, which is mostly general information about why the company is a great place to work, go to the section for investors. Read the annual report; listen to or watch some of the analyst conference calls. You will get great insight into recent events at the company such as product launches, competitive activity, market changes, and more. You can also visit industry Web sites and Wikipedia and search the Internet for recent articles regarding the company. Sometimes YouTube will have some relevant videos on the industry, executive interviews, or even the manufacturing process. If it is a consumer-based company, go to a retail store and see the product—how it is packaged, displayed, priced, and differentiated from those of its competitors.

If you know the location for which you are being considered, do some research on the area. Visit the local chamber of commerce's Web site; network with others who may already be living there. Look for the positives or advantages of the area. Don't go into a follow-up interview uninformed.

Travel Logistics

Once you have been invited on a follow-up interview, make sure you have your travel completely arranged and that you understand how you will be getting from place to place. If you will be traveling by air, the company will typically send you the flight itinerary via e-mail. Add the details to your digital calendar or create a folder in your e-mail system for that particular trip. There are also a number of travel-organizing Web sites or apps, such as TripIt, that you can use. If you are flying with an airline and are a member of that airline's frequent flyer program, be sure to get proper credit for your flight. If you don't belong, be sure to sign up before the flight! Some companies will ask you to purchase your own tickets and will reimburse you. In this case you will usually complete an expense report and will be reimbursed before you receive the bill from your credit card company.

Remember that airline tickets are the same as money. If you make any changes to your flights or you do not use a portion of it, ask the airline for an e-mail confirmation and any information on the credit back. The company may be able to use it in the future. If a company asks you to make your own airline reservations, do not book reservations with penalties that restrict changes. On occasion it will be necessary or preferred to arrange the follow-up interviews of two separate companies on back-to-back days, possibly combining the travel plans. It is very important that you take extreme care to divide expenses fairly between the companies involved. You should never see one company on another company's money.

If you will be traveling by car, make sure you have precise directions to prevent you from getting lost and being late. GPS devices, smart phones, and Mapquest are great, but not always right! Once a candidate was late to interview with me in Arlington, Virginia. He blamed his GPS, saying it had sent him two blocks away. It's a poor excuse. A simple Internet search would have helped him avoid being late. If your interview or interviews are scheduled first thing in the morning, always try to arrive at your destination no later than 6:00 p.m. the night before so you will have time to relax and benefit from a full night's sleep.

Now that you have all of your travel arrangements confirmed, you need to verify that every step in the transportation process is covered.

1. *Home to airport.* You may be driving yourself to the airport in your own car, or perhaps your spouse or a friend will drop you off. Whatever your means of transportation, plan ahead so that you make it to the airport at least an hour and a half prior to your flight departure time. Anticipate traffic jams and today's long security lines. If you don't, you will be rushing to make your flight, and you will be nervous before you even start your journey. I have seen people miss their flights due to poor planning, which showed the company that they lacked good judgment. Plan ahead for traffic congestion, gas purchases, a full parking lot, airport check-in process, or any other problem that might come up that would delay you or prevent you from arriving at your flight on time to board the plane.

2. *Airport to airport.* If you are going to have a layover, determine how much time you have between flights. If your first flight has any delays, will that cause you to miss your next flight and, if so, what will your strategy be then? For example, let's say you know you have a 45-minute layover in the Atlanta airport. Sign up for the airline's text messaging or e-mail system notifying you of flight delays, connecting gates, and gate changes. As soon as you land at your connecting airport, you will receive a text or e-mail notifying you of your arrival gate, next flight's departing gate, and how much time you have to make your connection. By doing this, you will know if a short walk or a fast run is required to reach your next plane. If there will be a distance between gates, find out by asking someone or looking at the airline magazine during flight if a shuttle bus/train is available and if it can speed up your time. Always carry all necessary phone numbers with you in case a situation develops that may cause a delay while you are in transit.

Also, ensure you have the phone number and other information of the hotel where you will be staying. You never know what might occur while you are traveling. If your connecting flight is canceled or if you have any other difficulties during travel, you should call the hotel explaining your situation to whomever will be meeting you. As a basic rule, hotel rooms are held until 6:00 p.m. for the arriving guest. To guarantee your room for a late arrival, you will need to give a credit card number to the reservation desk. Therefore, when you get details for your hotel, be sure to get the confirmation number and verify that the room will be held for late arrival. If you will be unable to arrive as planned due to a canceled flight, you must call the hotel prior to 6:00 p.m. and get a cancellation number. Otherwise, your credit card will be charged!

3. *Airport to hotel.* When you confirm your travel arrangements, find out who will be picking you up at the airport. Will it be a taxi? A limousine service? Will there be a company representative there for you? If so, what should you wear? And where will you be met? At the gate? Baggage claim? The curb outside Terminal 2? Will you know what the persons meeting you look like and what they will be wearing, or will they be holding a sign that has your name on it?

You may be picking up a rental car at the airport. If so, you must have a valid credit card issued with your name on it and available credit. You must also have a current driver's license. Be aware that car rental companies have rules that restrict them from renting to individuals unless they meet certain age qualifications. Check with some of the major rental companies to determine current regulations. If you do rent a car, determine how you will get to the hotel from the airport. You must have detailed instructions in hand prior to getting in that car so that you know where you are going. Always carry the phone number of the hotel where you will be staying. The company will usually make your hotel reservations, but occasionally alternative directions will be given to you. Your hotel costs may be billed directly to the company, or the company may ask you to pay and will reimburse you. Again, you will usually complete an expense report.

4. *Hotel to company.* Determine if a company representative will pick you up and, if so, at what time. If you must drive to the company, do you have accurate directions? How long will it take to get there? Should you do a test run to make sure there are no detours or other obstacles? Where will you meet the company representative? In the lobby of the hotel? Outside? Who will it be? Have you met him or her before? Keep in mind that even if this individual may not participate in your actual interview, he or she will still be evaluating you and forming an opinion of you.

Do not leave one step out. Make sure you can address each step so you don't get to the airport in the middle of the night and suddenly realize nobody told you how you were supposed to get to the hotel. If you are given an itinerary over the phone, go over it mentally before you hang up. Also, take at least $100 in cash with you, and keep all your receipts so you can get fully reimbursed. Carry on your luggage. You don't want to arrive without your interview suit and toiletries. It has happened before. Don't let it happen to you!

Make sure to bring the following items to your follow-up interview:

- Your resume
- Company literature
- A copy of *PCS to Corporate America*
- Contact information for three personal and three professional references, including their names, titles, addresses, and phone numbers

Start final preparation for your follow-up interview no later than one night before the interview is to take place. Then, on your flight you can review the material one more time so that you will understand the information thoroughly. Review all of the information you acquire through research and listed above to maximize your chances for success.

Professionalism in the Follow-Up Interview

By the time you get to the follow-up interview, you might start to feel more confident in your interview skills. Be careful. This is when mistakes can happen. While you should be confident, there are some issues to which you have not been exposed that could occur. Approach each interview with 100 percent thoroughness and preparation.

All companies, when hiring a Development Candidate, will want a unanimous decision—having all managers say "thumbs up" to a candidate. It is not good to have even one manager say no to you when, in fact, you might one day work for that individual. It doesn't create the best working environment. *This means every person with whom you interview is an important person in getting an offer from that company.* Therefore, make each person feel he or she is important to the decision. You must go to every interview armed with questions for that interviewer. You cannot ask a question and show no interest in the answer. You should never ask a question when you already know the answer. When you get ready to go on a follow-up interview, you need to have many (30-plus) quality, open-ended questions at your disposal.

During the follow-up interview, it is critical that you make points of connection on all three fronts, proving your ability and your desire to do the job as well as developing rapport with the recruiter so that he or she can visualize working with you. Throughout the interview give the recruiter evidence of your ability, your interest, and your interpersonal fit.

Wrap up every interview in a positive manner. Explain to the recruiter that you want an offer. I don't care what the words are. I don't care how you do it. I've had candidates come back and say, "Roger, I couldn't close the interview because we ran out of time"—or some other such excuse. The candidates say to me, "Roger, you know the interview went up to the last second, and

I didn't have time to close the interview in an upbeat manner." Sadly, I can already guess the outcome of the interview. You must close the interview. *You must let the interviewer know you have a strong interest in the opportunity and that you would be excited if you were extended an offer.*

Please remember, your close must be company-specific. You must give reasons why you are excited about the opportunity. It must also be delivered with believability. Or, again, if it is the company you want to go to work for and you already know that, let the recruiter know it. "This is my top choice—the company I want to work for. I want you to know if I were to receive an offer from your company, I will accept it."

If the follow-up interview happens to put you into an operations environment, such as manufacturing, distribution, transportation, information systems, etc., you must get involved. Many times you feel as if you're simply getting an opportunity to see a particular operating group, but recruiters are going to look for a high degree of interest and curiosity from you. Don't walk through an operational area without asking questions about what you see. One of the most fascinating experiences in the world is to see some of these high-performance environments. I'm not an engineer, but I'm always overwhelmed by what great engineers have done in different manufacturing processes. I could go through a manufacturing plant, and it would take me a week to get all of my questions answered. It's hard to see any of these different functional performance areas without getting excited about what you see. Our alumni will tell you that they were excited about all of the positions we showed them. It makes for a tough decision sometimes when you're standing in the middle of a "candy store." It's that exciting. You must equal this excitement in your demeanor.

If you are interviewing for a sales position, part of the follow-up process will be an invitation to spend a day in the field with the local sales representative. Remember that this person is doing you a favor by taking extra time from a busy schedule to show you the job. Be extremely polite and considerate. Arrive at the agreed-upon destination 15 minutes early. Come dressed in your best interviewing suit unless other attire is specifically requested. (For example, if you are going into a hospital where you may tour surgery areas, ask what attire is appropriate and whether you will need athletic shoes.) If you meet for a meal, there is no need to offer to pay, as the sales representative will put it on an expense report. However, it is important to thank your host. You must get involved. This is not a time for you to simply follow along behind and not interact. Remember, you are being evaluated. Do whatever you can to help out and make the sales representative's day easier. Offer to carry a briefcase, park the car, or anything else you think would be helpful. Take notes of each account on which you call. Who was called on and for what purpose? Write down questions you have of the sales technique used or questions asked and the responses. Do not do anything to interfere with the sales calls. Your social skills will be observed and noted. Be polite and friendly but not obtrusive. When you are back in the car driving to the next sales call, then is the time to demonstrate your curiosity and insight by asking good questions. At the end of the day, remember to ask for the sales representative's card. Then leave a voicemail or write to express thanks again for the valuable time that was spent with you. It is up to you to make that individual comfortable about referring you to the next step.

I have watched candidates spend a day in the field with a sales representative. Never once did they offer to help carry the salesperson's products, marketing materials, or briefcase. They didn't show curiosity and did not even take notes. They forgot the clients they met. You must be involved. You're not out there simply for the sake of observation. You're there for the company to see what your interest is in the position and if you might be a good fit. Show your intelligence and how you perceive the position, the industry, and the company through the questions you ask.

The minute you're on company money, you had better be focused totally on that company.

The minute you walk out of your door at home, the company

is paying every penny of your expenses. Therefore, it is only appropriate for you to give them every ounce of your consideration and concentration.

Dining Out with Corporate Recruiters

Using good manners and good judgment while you eat are also an important factor in the interviewing environment. Generally, dinner is a great time for two-way communication. You want to be prepared with lots of questions. Nothing is worse than awkward silence at a business dinner. You need to prepare to keep up your end of the conversation. I've seen too many candidates lose an offer because of what they did at dinner. This usually comes from relaxing too much and forgetting that you are always interviewing. Always finish your meal. Not eating suggests you are too nervous and lack poise and self-confidence.

Ordering. The company will be paying, so be aware of the cost of what you order. Don't select the most expensive entree on the menu. Generally, you should spend the company's money as if it were your own. When you order, be aware that it is difficult to eat foods with sauces without spotting your clothes. The primary purpose of the meal is to interview rather than eat. Therefore, order foods that are easy to handle, thereby reducing the risk of unsightly stains. You may think it won't happen to you, but I've seen it happen to the very best candidates. It's embarrassing to have a spot on your tie, shirt or pants, blouse or skirt, for the balance of an interview—especially if the spilling happened at breakfast. Getting yourself into that kind of situation suggests you aren't controlling your environment. You're losing sight of the meal's objective—which is to provide an opportunity to interview.

Etiquette. Also, remember your manners. Social interaction is a big part of the business world. Military officers should stand out in this area because this same professional conduct is ingrained in officers from day one in the military. Just remember this simple rule: Always be your best professional self. No exceptions. This will make you stand out in a very positive way, especially given some of the very poor social habits seen among some young professionals who have not had the benefit of military officer training.

Drinking. There are so many negative consequences of having a drink during an interview that there is no good reason to have one during your interview day or meal with a company, even if the recruiter is drinking or offers you one. You are not at your best self when you drink, and your interpersonal interaction is not as good. You are not interviewing to socialize but to prove your fit. If a recruiter or host has a drink and offers you one, you may say, "I do drink on occasion but not while I'm interviewing." You can even say, "This interview is so important to me, I will just have club soda" (or iced tea, water, a soft drink, etc.).

Refer to Appendix D for an interview self-evaluation exercise to use after each follow-up interview.

Chapter 9

MOVING TOWARD THE OFFER

L et's remember who owns the interview—the company recruiter. The recruiter is the only one who can say yes or no; therefore, he or she has total control over the interview.

Basically, every recruiter comes to the interview with a pocketful of offers. Your mission is to gain control of the interview by earning an offer. When and only when you are in the position to say yes or no to an offer does ownership of the interview change hands and you (the interviewee) gain control of the interview.

To accomplish this you must put out 100 percent in every interview. Know you have done everything humanly possible to have a good interview. Sometimes candidates tell me their objective is to convert every interview into an offer. This is simply not going to happen. There are too many variables that go into the hiring process. You and a recruiter might have poor chemistry. I promise you—you won't get an offer when the chemistry is not good. A recruiter might have an interest in you, but during the follow-up process the position might be filled with an internal candidate. No matter how hard you try, you won't be able to convert that interview into an offer either. Don't set yourself up for defeat. Go into every interview putting your best self forward, and you will be proud of the results. This is the best philosophy to help you move toward the offer.

There are several issues I want to discuss that surround a job offer, from package details such as salary to acceptance or decline.

Dollars and Sense

When you're talking with a company recruiter and he or she asks what money you expect, don't say that you're open. You know you're not open. Every time a candidate says that to me, I say, "Fine, we'll pay you $50,000." All of a sudden, the candidate is backpedaling, "Well, that's not reasonable." I reply, "It isn't reasonable that you tell me *you're open.*"

This is an important issue and one that can cause a successful interview to go bad in a hurry. First, it is your responsibility to determine your worth to corporate America by doing adequate research before getting in front of a recruiter. The interview is not the place to experiment. When you determine the salary that you expect, arrive at this figure with objectivity, not emotion.

It takes a lot more than simply wanting a high salary to get one. Wouldn't that be a wonderful world in which to live? You wake up in the morning and determine you want a higher salary. You go to your boss with your wishes, and he or she immediately gives you what you want. I'm sorry—that is simply not the real world! The only way you can earn a top salary is by having strong credentials, conducting world-class preparation, and having successful interviews. Many of our candidates transition into business with significant salary increases. They are always the candidates who do their homework and execute with precision at the Career Conference.

On the Cameron-Brooks application, we ask the question of salary expectations. I use this question as an eliminator. Please don't misunderstand me on this point. I want you to get a competitive salary. After all, recruiting firms are paid a fee based on your salary. However, I expect a candidate to be realistic about his or her salary expectations. I expect you to do your homework and report a figure that is appropriate and earned. To compete for the best salaries, you must be realistic as well as committed to working hard in your transition preparation and being at your best in your interviews.

In the business world you are compensated based on performance. Thus, it makes sense that in the corporate hiring process your salary is determined not only on the basis of your credentials but also on your performance in the interview. Bottom line: prepare to be at your best in your interviews. Hard work will pay off. Research the marketplace. Determine what your value is to corporate America. Then set a fair market value—one appropriate to you and for corporate America.

Pay Raises

There are three ways you can get increased compensation in corporate America:

1. *Annual pay raise.* This raise is just what it says. It is granted annually. There is no specific formula as to how much you can expect in a year (although some companies have a general formula measured on performance). In all cases you'll be evaluated on both objective and subjective performance factors.

2. *Promotional pay raise.* With a position-level promotion, you will receive a pay raise.

3. *Merit pay raise.* A merit pay raise is given for performance above the expected norms. This raise is obtainable; however, it is not easy to receive in a world of high achievers.

Remember, in corporate America you will be paid and promoted according to your performance. We are proud of our dual standard of compensation and promotion. We pay and promote high performers more than others. Top-performing JMO candidates love this concept. They are also frequently the high-end performers in the military; yet they get the same pay as everyone else. "Go-to" people should get paid more!

Being a typical American, you'll never get paid what you feel you're worth. I know individuals in business who are paid

$300,000 a year or more, and they still feel they're underpaid. That doesn't mean they don't wear a smile every day. It's just what human nature is all about, especially for Type A leaders. There is never an ideal world. You will not see outstanding performers at Johnson & Johnson, General Mills, Boston Scientific, and other great companies attempting to move to the military to increase their compensation. Corporate America takes very good care of its top performers. You earn that status first; then it's given to you. You won't get it before you earn it.

Transition Concerns

We are often asked about job "security" in corporate America. This is a fair question relative to the perception of security in the military and the fact we have economic cycles that include recessions. As more than one officer has stated, "I know I will get a paycheck every month if I stay in the military."

To begin with, during the years I have recruited military officers, there have been some who have been laid off for economic reasons, but it has been uncommon. You are being hired as a Development Candidate. Well-managed companies know the importance of developing future leadership and investing in those who are top performers and demonstrate upside potential. The military, regardless of world conditions, continues to produce officers from the academies, ROTC, OCS, and OTS. The same is true in the business world—if we cease to develop leaders, somewhere in the future, we will have a leadership void. No quality company would voluntarily get itself into that situation. This issue alone should give you good security.

You also should realize the tremendous expense of hiring a Development Candidate. It is now estimated that a hiring mistake will cost more than $64,000 if a person quits in the first six months, and this does not include the salary! Anytime a company incurs an "expense," it is never taken lightly. As one Fortune 100 company stated, "We don't hire two to see if one can make it. We hire one and put every resource we have into making sure the candidate succeeds." This is exactly why companies put potential hires through such a rigorous series of interviews and why they require unanimous consent from all managers on extending an offer.

While the above facts offer considerable security, we must point out that, like the military, corporate America is competitive. It is essential that you start your new career eager to succeed, to accomplish difficult objectives, and to work hard and smart. In my lifetime I have yet to see someone successful in the military who couldn't become successful in corporate America. The tools for success are the same regardless of the profession.

Another area of concern is the physical transition itself. Many times, officers have unnecessary anxieties about this. You will find that your company will walk with you through each step. A corporation's normal procedure after a hire is to provide transportation to the new location so that an employee and spouse can search for a house or apartment. While all companies are different, generally speaking, you also will be given guidance on realtors, financial institutions, schools, and neighborhoods. And, of course, all normal expenses will be paid or reimbursed. Always remember that each company has its own policies, and before you create an expenditure, you should determine if it is reimbursable. Also, your company will normally cover relocation expenses that the military doesn't cover. Cameron-Brooks candidates have been extremely pleased with relocation benefits. Corporations know that relocations can cause frustration and unwanted anxieties, and they work hard to eliminate as many as possible.

It is always our desire to help you get answers to specific questions. We encourage you to talk with other officers who have already transitioned. Many times, it is comforting to speak with someone who has been in your shoes. Our Facebook page allows JMOs to reach out to Cameron-Brooks alumni and discuss topics such as this. To benefit from the experiences, insight, and advice of those who have successfully transitioned to the business world, access our Web site at www.cameron-brooks.com and follow the link to our Facebook page. You can also e-mail us at candidates@cameron-brooks.com and we can put you in touch with one of our alumni.

Three Thousand Dollars—The Crucial Figure

When a company does a follow-up interview with a candidate, that company will spend approximately $3,000 or more to cover airline tickets, rental cars, taxis, hotels, and food. Beyond that is the major expenditure of management's time to interview.

By making yourself conscious of this $3,000, you can help a recruiter spend it. Recruiters, like candidates, are protecting their self-interests. Their primary concern, and rightly so, is their success and that of their companies. Many times, recruiters are young people who are willing to sit through numerous interviews. While they do, they're very aware that every time they say yes to a follow-up interview, they have, in fact, signed a company check for $3,000.

They're aware they can't sign too many of these checks and then have upper management decline candidates they've invited back for follow-up interviews. Before long, their "offer to invite" record starts to reflect on their credibility. Too many candidates are unaware of this. You must help the recruiter feel good about spending $3,000 for the follow-up. You can do this only by preparing to give the best possible interview and then making it happen.

If I could get you to write anything on the back of your hand as you go to interviews, it would be this: $3,000. There is probably no factor that should motivate you more to be competitive during the interview than remembering that figure. I suggest you write it on the top of every page of your notes. Think it over. Put yourself in the recruiter's position. If you had $3,000 in your wallet, would you spend that money pursuing the individual you're interviewing? Would you do it if your career depended on this decision?

Some recruiters, on this dollar amount alone, will eliminate a candidate. Today many companies are sending two or more recruiters to interview at our Career Conferences. They feel it is less expensive to get a second and even a third opinion at the conference. Then, when they fly a candidate for follow-up interviews, they are more assured the other managers will agree with their opinions. It's a better decision and less costly to get multiple judgments at the conference before flying that candidate in for a follow-up interview. Also, it assures a higher rate of offer-to-follow-up ratio. Recruiters also like it because it spreads the risk of saying yes and spending company money.

We're finding companies are increasingly aware of recruiting costs. *So remember that $3,000 each time you step in front of a recruiter.*

Don't Overspend

Be alert. Know what amounts you're billing to the company paying for your interview expenses. If you go to the hotel bar and order drinks, you're showing poor judgment. My own judgment, as a company, would be to withhold any job offer.

Think and plan. Don't be like the candidate who traveled to Texas to interview and then found she didn't have the necessary credit card to rent a car from the Austin airport to the client's facility 60 miles away. All she had was cash and a debit card. So she ordered a limousine service for more than $250. You may say, "That was good judgment. She got herself to the company's office." But let me assure you, it was a poor decision to have the plant manager see her pull up in a limousine billed to the company. This candidate did not get an offer. The poor judgment started when she didn't remember to bring her credit card, and all rental car companies will want a credit card in your name. Today traveling to follow-up interviews without a major credit card and no less than $100 cash in your pocket is poor judgment.

Every year, I hear about a candidate getting stuck in traffic and missing a flight for a follow-up interview. There is simply no excuse for this when you are being hosted by a company and they are paying for your ticket. Recently I heard about a candidate who missed his flight and forgot to bring the phone number of the recruiter who was meeting him at the airport, so he could not warn his host that he had missed the flight. Needless to say, the company canceled the interview and declined the candidate. There are no excuses for this type of unprofessionalism.

A company is always measuring your judgment. From the time you leave your door, you're spending the company's money.

You're going to be examined every step of the way. That applies to everything—flights, ground transportation, hotels, and dinners with company recruiters.

Don't let anyone throw you off by saying, "Don't worry. Tonight is just a casual evening. We're going to chat. We'll be evaluating tomorrow during the interviews." Don't believe that for a second. At every event, every person with whom you interact is evaluating you, and there's never any excuse for letting your guard down. Show good judgment at all times.

What Is Your Definition of a Job Offer?

You are not assured of a job offer simply because recruiters smile, request a follow-up interview, show interest, say they will get back in touch, or tell you they like your background.

I frequently ask candidates to define an offer. Some tell me an offer is money, benefits, location, or the position, etc. The answers are usually similar, but I disagree with them. These are components of an offer but still not the clear, succinct definition. An offer occurs only when control moves from the company to the candidate: when the candidate is in the position of saying yes or no to the company. Nothing else constitutes an offer.

I've seen everything in the world happen between a recruiter's smile and the actual offer. Companies have taken a candidate through eight or nine interviews and still not offered. Companies may say they are going to offer, and between that time and when they could phone you, the position was filled by someone else inside the firm. Or sometimes the position is removed from the marketplace because of economics or internal company changes and conditions.

You should never think you have an offer until it is, in fact, in your possession—when you're in control of the interview.

Accepting a Career Position

Accepting a career position is one of the most critical moments. It sets the tone of your new business career. You want to handle your acceptance carefully, thoughtfully, and precisely.

When you accept a position, do so with the primary person—the individual for whom you will be working or who extended the offer to you. *Always accept prior to the deadline—never, ever wait until the deadline.* If you wait until the deadline, the company doesn't know if you're accepting because time has run out or because you want the job.

Be extremely upbeat in accepting. For example, you might say, "I don't need any more time to determine I want to have my career with your company. I accept the position, and I'm extremely excited about getting started. What is my next step?" And the company will go through the upcoming procedures with you.

I want to share a personal story about an employee of ours who has worked for Cameron-Brooks for over 25 years. Originally we interviewed her several times. While on a recruiting trip, I called in and learned that she had accepted. "Is she excited?" I asked an associate. "Well, really, I don't know," I was told. "She said, 'Well, I guess I'll take your job.'" I was concerned about her lack of enthusiasm for the job and even suggested we call her back and withdraw our offer. I wanted someone more enthusiastic about joining our team. Fortunately, we didn't. She has been with us since 1985 and is an integral part of our organization. I wouldn't know what to do without her, but I'll never forget her acceptance, and I've kidded her about it over the years.

A good acceptance has four steps:

1. State the bottom line up-front, something like, "I am calling to accept the offer."

2. State the reason why (it's similar to closing your interview): "I am excited to be a part of a company that has such an extraordinary strong track record of innovation in the medical industry."

3. Address your start date and the logistics of moving to your new company. When you call you should have a planned start date in mind, such as "I would like to start on _____, and I would like conduct my house-hunting trip in the next two weeks. Is that acceptable to you?"

4. Include a sincere statement of appreciation, reiterating your excitement: "Thank you again for this opportunity. I am truly excited to become a part of your organization."

Once you've accepted an offer, you should now write a thank-you message (either a letter or e-mail, but I prefer handwritten notes) to everyone with whom you made contact at that company. Thank them for their part in the hiring process. It would be a shame if you went to work for a company, saw one of the individuals who had interviewed you, and they didn't know you were with their organization. This is where your professional attitude in developing relationships should begin. It's probably one of the most critical steps in starting your business career.

Declining an Offer

When you decline an offer, don't forget your professionalism. Don't forget common courtesy. The minute you know you are not going to accept a company's offer, immediately get on the phone and let the company know. Don't send an e-mail or mail a letter. Those are impersonal, and you can't be sure the appropriate person received the message. Please be conscious of the fact that once an offer goes out on a position, all recruiting for that position stops. While the company may have two or three other people under consideration, they can do nothing whatsoever with them. Of course, the longer those people sit out there without being pursued, the less interest they have in that company and the higher the probability they will be hired by another company. *So never hold an offer when you know you're not going to accept the position.*

When you decline the offer, you should be honest and candid. Declining an offer has five steps:

1. State the bottom line up-front: "I am calling to decline the offer."

2. Let the recruiter down softly and sincerely: "This was one of the hardest decisions I have made in my life."

3. Be honest and tell them the company you decided to join. What's the big secret? You're developing relationships in corporate America. Let them know. Many times it is best just to say, "I have made the decision to go to Company A (tell them the name of the company), where I'll be working in position B."

4. Compliment and thank the recruiter and company: "I was very excited about what I saw in your company, and thank you for the time you and your company invested in me during the recruiting process."

5. Give a subjective reason why you are declining and choosing the other company: "It's just that I felt a bit more compatibility with the other organization. I don't know if I can tell you what it was. I just felt a little bit more comfortable in the other company's environment." A subjective reason is something that is unique to you; it is your feelings or opinions—something that cannot be refuted or changed. Objective reasons include location, pay, speed to promotion, etc.

When you inform a company you are declining an offer, never make location or any other objective factor the primary reason. I'd like to go back and remind you that a company put out $3,000 to fly you in for follow-up interviews. You gave them every reason to believe the location or the compensation you flew out for was totally acceptable to you, so for you to decline later because of location is to say you are dishonest and lack professionalism. The road of life has many curves. You never know when you're going to curve back and run into that person, situation, and company again. How foolish for you to have burned a bridge when you need not have done so. Sometimes it is simply a matter of laziness when you decline a company. What you really meant to say was "I was sincerely open for your location. I had a preference, which I pointed out in the interview. The other company has offered my location preference. It was the only factor that tipped the offer in their favor. It wasn't that your location wasn't acceptable to me. The other offer was just more acceptable." Explain your situation fully. Don't get lazy in declining an offer. Think about what you're saying. Think about your own professionalism of having accepted their money to fly to a follow-up interview. Always be sincere and professional in any move you make in the job search. You want them to feel good about continuing to hire JMOs.

It would be a good idea to follow up a decline of an offer with a professional letter of thanks for all of the costs the company might have incurred for your follow-up interviews and the time its managers took with you. Never burn a bridge. You never know when you may want to walk over it again.

Leave the Military Behind

When you begin your career in corporate America, it is very important that you put your military career behind you. Remember, what's important is not what you did yesterday but what you do today.

Unfortunately, some officers form cliques with other officers within the companies they join. They unknowingly and unwisely create an environment of "them" versus "us." Some officers have done this to the detriment of military officers in general. Companies have told us they hesitate to hire officers because they are becoming too "military." That is foolish. We point out that these people come from different socioeconomic backgrounds, regions, cultures, and military branches. Their backgrounds are similar to those of young college graduates who are hired as Development Candidates. However, because the military officers form a clique to the exclusion of others, a perception of difference is formed. You should be proud of your military background; you should stay in contact with other officers but not to the exclusion of others. Do not decorate your office with an excess of college or military memorabilia. Be more concerned about neutralizing your past and emphasizing today.

Working with the Opposite Gender

This is really more of an issue for the male JMO since the majority of the military is male and many units are only male. If you are a man, it is important in corporate America that you have a positive attitude about working with and for women. There are officers who give us the perception that they can't work with women. Sometimes military officers express opinions in ways that lead us to believe they won't have good working relationships with women as peers, team members, or superiors. Often candidates will say they spoke with "one of my secretaries." When I've questioned them about whether this person said she was a secretary, they say, no, they assumed the woman was a secretary because she answered the phone.

I recall a story of a recruiter who called a candidate and asked him to call a woman in his office to get the details of an offer. When the candidate had received the information, he was to call the recruiter back. He did as instructed and called the recruiter and said, "I called your secretary and got all the details." The recruiter then asked him if the woman had identified herself as his secretary, and the candidate admitted he had just assumed she was a secretary. On the basis of this incident, the recruiter felt he was biased and withdrew the job offer. I'll never defend a candidate who does this. If I feel candidates are being wronged for any reason, I'll go to the wall for them but not when they do things that aren't professional.

Instead of assuming the woman with whom he spoke was a secretary, he could have referred to her position in a generic way. He could have said, "I spoke with your associate," or—better yet—"I spoke with Ms. Anderson (or Jane Anderson) regarding the details." In this way he would not have labeled her with a certain position.

I encourage you to think seriously about the roles of women in business. If working with women is difficult for you or you feel women don't have the ability to compete with you, then don't apply for a position in corporate America.

Hiring and Managing Diversity

Circumstances have greatly improved over my 40-plus years in this business. I can honestly say that today most top-managed companies in corporate America are blind to gender and race. These companies have developed great programs to cultivate and manage diversity within their organizations.

Today there are many leaders from diverse backgrounds in top positions in corporate America. I'm proud to say that many of them are Cameron-Brooks alumni.

I've always felt it is important to be candid and outspoken when discussing issues with diversity candidates. I think it is extremely important that everyone get hired for the right reason—performance—and for no other reason.

Development Candidates must demonstrate the ability to manage a workforce of great diversity of backgrounds, lifestyles, values, and opinions. The "typical" employee is changing and will continue to change. U.S. corporations are challenged by the extraordinary competitive pressures in the world today. To be competitive domestically and globally will be impossible if the talents of all employees are not developed for maximum productivity. Therefore, managers will be measured by their ability to manage a diverse group.

As you prepare for your interviews, be aware that you will be scrutinized for your attitudes regarding others with backgrounds different from yours. Recognize that recruiters will be looking for people who are nonjudgmental, who consider the opinions of others before making decisions, who value people with different backgrounds and values, and who seek to understand and accept them.

Chapter 10

LET'S MEET THE CHALLENGES OF THE FUTURE

Every day, companies bring us more unique, exciting, and challenging positions to fill. As a result, the military officer needs to be even more qualified and ready to hit the ground running upon his or her transition. In the past there were often limited kinds of positions offered to you. Today, because of the powerful success of military officers who have transitioned to business and made significant contributions, the development positions for which we recruit are getting more complex. Because of the wars in Afghanistan and Iraq, there is more awareness of the leadership skills JMOs can bring to corporate America. This success has been well documented in leading business publications such as *Fortune* magazine and the *Harvard Business Review*. However, there are still companies that have little interest in hiring military officers, mostly because of a lack of understanding of an officer's background and training. I have a loud statement for them: "The loss is theirs."

Examples of Available Development Positions

Former military officers have demonstrated success in every industry, in every functional career path, and in every company that has hired them. Let me give you an example of the positions for which our candidates interviewed at a recent Career Conference:

If that is not a compliment for the military officer, I'm not

Business Analysis/Consulting

Business Analyst
Consultant
Contracts Manager
Finance and Accounting
    Manager
Financial Analyst
Internal Auditor
Lean Deployment Leader

Operations Analyst
Process Improvement Analyst
Program Management
Project Leader
Project Procurement Advisor
Senior Consultant
Six Sigma Black Belt

Engineering

Application Engineer
Business Development
    Engineer
Deployment Engineer
Equipment Engineer
Facilities Engineer
Measurement Systems
    Engineer
Plant Support Engineer

Process Engineer
Product Development
    Engineer
Project Engineer
Quality Engineer
Software Engineer
Strategic Marketing Engineer
Systems Engineer

Information Technology

Business Analyst
Corporate IT Auditor
IT Business Consultant

IT Project Manager
IT Team Leader
Program Manager

Manufacturing

Business Unit Manager
Maintenance Team Leader
Manufacturing Management
Production Engineer
Production Manager

Production Superintendent
Team Developer
Team Facilitator
Team Leader

Marketing

Brand Management
Market Analyst

Marketing Associate
Product Manager

Operations/Logistics

Distribution Manager
Logistics Team Leader
Operations Manager
Operations Team Leader

Procurement/Buyer
Supplier Manager
Supply Chain Management
Transportation Supervisor

Professional Sales

Account Manager
Business Development
Industrial Sales
Sales Engineer

Sales Leading to Management
Surgical Instrument Sales
Technical Sales

making my point. The opportunities in the business world for talented JMOs are outstanding!

The quality of these openings demonstrates corporate America's belief in your ability to get results. Each of these positions offers excellent opportunity for advancement. *You have earned the right to interview for these positions.* You have come to our companies with outstanding objective and subjective skills and executed with powerful results. Cameron-Brooks alumni, as I have said, are reaching for the very pinnacle of corporate America, and many have arrived. Every day I receive outstanding reports on what our alumni are accomplishing within our client companies. It is gratifying and well deserved. It's been exciting to see the growing demand for the military officer.

For those of you who make the decision to enter the business world, I admire your desire to make an impact in the private sector, and I would be proud to walk beside you and help you achieve your career aspirations. For those of you who choose to stay in the military, as a citizen I respect your decision to support our great country and wish you continued success in your military career.

Tips for Success

In this last chapter I want to offer a few tips for success in any professional career. Push yourselves to reach great heights in your personal and professional lives, whether you enter the business world or continue to proudly serve and protect our country.

Remember, *you control your attitude.* Nobody else does. All organizations have pros and cons. As a leader, it is up to you to avoid being a critic of the faults in your organization and instead be a light for others to follow. Don't complain about what is wrong with your organization, but instead do something to make it better. Rise above the circumstances of your work. Act like a leader and people will treat you like one.

Deserve your success. How do you do this? Work harder than everyone around you. Go the extra mile, put in the extra hours, sweat the small stuff, and do whatever it takes by putting your heart and soul into everything you do. When you consistently do this over a period of time, you will achieve all the success you deserve. The 10-year or 10,000-hour rule (popularized by Malcolm Gladwell's books) has become very popular in the business world. According to the theory, to master the skills necessary to be successful at your profession, it takes 10,000 hours of dedicated effort or 10 years. There are no overnight successes. Executing consistently for 10,000 hours is how you *deserve* your success.

Leaders are readers. Find any great leader in any organization, and I promise you that you will find a lifelong learner. Read broadly, ask a lot of questions, become a master of your craft, and push the outside of the envelope on your knowledge. You should read one professional book a month (no excuses) to stretch your mind. Do not substitute experience for knowledge (most people make this mistake). Anyone can just show up to work long enough and call it experience, but a leader takes the responsibility to learn and grow to gain knowledge.

Don't become complacent. Anyone can have a few successes, but it takes a true winner to constantly strive for success. Every day you have an opportunity to enhance your track record. Run fast and hard in every race, not just the ones that you perceive as important. Celebrate your successes, but remember that all glory is fleeting. You are only as good as your last accomplishment. Stretch yourself all the time.

Being Professional

To be professional means conducting oneself in a manner that is of the highest standards. We cannot claim to be professional only when it is convenient or timely; to be worthy of the title of professional we must make professionalism a constant in everything we do, in our every thought and action.

Being professional is something over which we have complete control. Thus, we have no one else to blame but ourselves when we act in an unprofessional manner. While we may feel we can fool others and be professional sometimes but not at all times, we only fool ourselves. Everything we do and say portrays our inner self and who we are as a person.

During the course of a normal day, we have many opportunities on an hourly basis to demonstrate professionalism. It begins at home every morning with our spouse or significant other, with our family, with our children, with the service station attendant, with the server at the restaurant, with our fellow employees. The list goes on and on. And it means remembering good manners and being respectful, reliable, gracious, positive, helpful, caring, and nonjudgmental.

In my opinion, way too many conversations happen via e-mail and texting when they should happen either in person or over the phone. Brainstorming, conflict resolution, delivering constructive feedback, providing bad news, etc.—*all* need to be done with a personal touch: verbally. I have a policy: "No bad news via e-mails or text messages." I encourage you to adopt the same policy. E-mail and texting should be for transactional purposes and providing information. Great leaders know how to confront difficult situations to include bad news, conflict, feedback, and more. They have the *courage* to do it personally and verbally, not via e-mail. Additionally, it goes without saying you shouldn't text or e-mail private or confidential information. It can too easily be seen by the wrong set of eyes.

I am sure each of us can recall an experience that involved unprofessional behavior, either ours or someone else's. It is not fun to be on the receiving end of a negative action, and if you were the instigator of such an incident, you are never very proud of your actions in retrospect. Holding ourselves to the highest standards of conduct in everything we do not only makes us worthy of the designation of professional but also gives us a lot of instant gratification; what is more, it makes each day fun! Interacting with others in a professional manner is genuinely enjoyable for both parties. It is a true win-win.

I encourage you to think seriously about professionalism and what it means and takes to be professional in everything you do. Imagine for just a moment what a great environment we would create if everyone were committed to being professional. Make this a goal for yourself at the beginning of every year.

Integrity

Core operating values. Have you taken the time to determine yours? Have you put them on paper? Do you reflect on them periodically? Too many people say they have standards by which they conduct themselves but then act upon them only when it is convenient. Such standards do not make up one's "core" values; rather, they are what I call values of convenience.

What good are values if they are not used consistently? It is one thing to be committed to having values, but the true test is using them consistently. This is integrity. Anyone can assert they have values and integrity; few can assert that they consistently act and make decisions dictated by their core values. It is disheartening to see the excuses people have for shelving their "values" for the moment or when it is not convenient to exercise them.

Unfortunately, not everyone in corporate America has integrity. The financial crisis in 2009 demonstrated what can happen when those without integrity and with the wrong values lead organizations. As a result, today there is an increased emphasis of hiring leaders who operate with integrity and match the organization's values. Companies want leaders who do not quibble but instead shoulder responsibility, those who do not make excuses for any failure for which they are responsible. They want leaders who make the right decisions, even when they are difficult, and who do not allow themselves to get into situations where they must say they are sorry. Those who have to use this word are often those who either cannot or will not make the right choice, and they feel that the "sorry" erases a poor choice. But it doesn't. Poor choices are remembered and will have a negative effect on your career and on your personal life. You are your decisions. If you backslide, even on occasion, you can count on others to remember it—and not in a positive light.

Perhaps the problem today is that people are not weighing the consequences of their choices. Too many people, even elected leaders, appear to be able to get away with actions that are unethical. The reality is that such inconsistencies will catch up to you, if not immediately, then later.

In your professional career, you will be judged on your integrity, not only by people above you who are evaluating your potential, but, even more importantly, by people who work for you. People follow leaders they trust, and making decisions consistent with your values is a big part of this. The first step to integrate your actions with your values is to take time to write down your core operating values and why they are important to you. Then, with every decision you face, get in the habit of checking your options and their consequences against your values. Do they fit?

I encourage you to look at your life in retrospect. I'm sure every one of us can look back and wish we had handled some of our choices differently. After all, we are human. However, we should always strive to make better choices and to become a master of our core values, our decisions, and our actions. We should be proud of our actions; we should feel good every night as we reflect on our day. We should be willing to pound a stake in the ground, draw a line in the sand, as to where we stand on issues that judge our integrity. We should be willing to stand by our values in the most difficult situations, not just when it is convenient to do so.

Recognizing People as Individuals

Learn to use first names. Learn to be a relationship builder. It's important. I remember interviewing in Fort Campbell, Kentucky. I'd been at a hotel near there for three days. With me was a young recruiter who was having a hard time using first names.

The day we left, I told Betty (the server we usually saw in the hotel restaurant) that we were leaving. She burst into tears. Both the other recruiter and I were taken aback.

Then she explained, "Mr. Cameron, I have to tell you how much enjoyment you've given me this week. I wear my name tag, but nobody ever calls me by my first name. Instead it's, 'Hey, waitress.' 'Hey, you.' 'Ma'am.' 'Miss.' What a pleasure to have someone recognize me as an individual." When she left, I saw that my associate was moved, and I've never known him not to use first names since that experience. Today, as president of a company, he still remembers the importance of this issue.

Learn to do this—whether it's your landscaper, a gentleman or a lady at the checkout counter, or a service station attendant. *Recognize them as individuals.* Don't make them feel they are there simply to serve you. It will make you feel better, and I promise you it will make them feel better, too. When I fly, I always ask the flight attendant his or her name. Unfortunately, the reaction I often get is, "What's wrong?" This is sad. Be a nice person. Work to make others feel appreciated. It is a gratifying way to live your life.

Corporate America is a participative work environment. If you don't have the ability to interact positively with people, you frankly don't belong in corporate America. Our client companies are adamant about hiring people with strong BLT (believability, likability, and trust). Does that describe you?

A recruiter at one of our top companies says, "If an individual doesn't have the innate ability to come to work in the morning and say 'Good morning' to the maintenance engineer, he or she is not the kind of person we want working for our company." You must respect others and recognize people—all people—as individuals.

One of the nicest letters I've ever received was from a person I had helped secure a position with Mobil Chemical, a division of Mobil (now ExxonMobil). I will never forget it. He was very happy that he had chosen a great career field with a great company. He realized that with good performance his corporate career would now be essentially secure. He said one of the things he gained from our Career Conference was learning the impor-tance of using first names. He went on to state how proud he was that he addressed by first name the people who waited on him at a restaurant, who worked behind the counter at the local gas station, and who checked him out at the grocery store. Today he never fails to ask others immediately for their names and use their names. I guess I was as pleased at receiving that letter as he was of learning the importance of using first names. Please don't come to us with this excuse: "Roger, it's very difficult for me. I used 'sir' and 'ma'am' all the way through junior high, high school, college, and in the military." I say to you, "That's fine. But that was then; this is now."

Knowing How to Perform Effectively

People are the most important asset a company has. Companies require me to bring them individuals with an outstanding work ethic—people who can execute efficiently and impact the bottom line. These are individuals who get out of bed eager to go to work—with a strong, positive mental attitude and, most of all, the ability to work smart.

It is critically important, as you make a transition to corporate America, to demonstrate the ability to be a *peak performer*. We want smart workers, not *workaholics*. We want workers who are well organized, know how to prioritize, and can effectively manage their time to get their work done in the normal work day. The norm for the military is that working longer hours, no matter how inefficient, equates to peak performance. Is that wrong? No, not really, relative to what the military is seeking, but it is wrong relative to what corporate America is seeking. We want people who work smart and are efficient. We want leaders who allow time to constantly expand their mind, their world, and their vision and have a lot of interests outside their career.

Don't think for a moment that you're not going to work hard. During the phase when you are catching up (with those who started careers earlier)—your initial 18 to 24 months in your business career—you must burn the candle at both ends and in the middle. As you reach the point where you are competitive with your age group, have gained industry knowledge, and have brought your education level to where it needs to be, then it's time to bring your work and family life into balance. Stress the quality of life. Don't burn yourself out on the way to the top. Work smart. Perform effectively. Enjoy your new career.

Controlling Your Environment

As I sit in my favorite seat on Delta or American Airlines (1B or 1C), I watch people come on board. I hear them say to themselves, "What seat am I in?" Then they moan because they are in rows 35 or 39. I often think to myself, "They had an opportunity to tell the airline where they wanted to sit when they made their reservations. Why didn't they?"

Candidates tell me they had a restless night because their room was next to the soda machine or the stairway or the ice machine. I wonder why they allowed the hotel reservations clerk to put them wherever he or she wanted. Don't allow this to happen to you. Control your environment.

WE LIKE "TAKE CHARGE" PEOPLE.

Candidates give excuses about why they didn't accomplish an objective. It's always somebody else's fault. "Somebody prevented me from getting it done. Somebody didn't get back with me or get me the information I needed." I scratch my head and say, "Why aren't you controlling your environment?" Sure, there is no ideal system, no perfect world where we can control everything we do. However, you would be surprised at how many things you can control if you make the effort. It will be difficult to be successful in corporate America if you don't learn to control your environment.

I remember one of the great leaders in corporate America. He would never let a problem come to his office except within a designated time of one half-hour in the morning and one half-hour in the afternoon. If the problem didn't come to him during one designated period of time, he would not handle it until the next half-hour session. He refused to allow problems or circumstances control his environment. He was adamant about controlling his own environment. I have absolutely no doubt that's the reason he had the ability to start his career at a large company and go on to become a great leader at one of the top-managed companies in the country. I learned valuable lessons from him.

Too often, I see officers who have had their lives so controlled by others that they have forgotten how to control their own destiny. So many of you tell me about the difficulty of organizing and controlling your day. I believe that. I know it's typical of so many of your jobs in the military and the uncertainty of military missions and deployments. It is not that one environment is good and one bad. They're simply different. If you intend to come to corporate America and be highly successful, you must control your environment.

> *Your performance characteristics are like staves of a barrel. Your value is determined by the shortest stave.*

Choosing Mentors

Key to success in any professional career is choosing mentors to help guide you in your career. Early in your career develop relationships with people who will agree to work with you as formal mentors.

For those of you entering the business world, I recommend you seek relationships with two interior (within your company) and two exterior (outside your company) mentors. The reason for selecting at least two or more mentors is for you to gain from a diversity of opinions and advice. It is good to have a balance of opinions to measure one suggestion against another. While both viewpoints may be accurate, combining a couple or several opinions will give you confidence about the information you are receiving. For your exterior mentors, I would recommend you talk to your parents, family members, and friends to identify people who have been successful in the business world. If you partner with Cameron-Brooks and become an alumnus, you would benefit from having our organization as one of your exterior mentors. From our vantage point we see what is happening in a wide variety of companies and industries. We share this cross-view of corporate

America with our alumni and make recommendations to them on what to do to continue to succeed in their business careers.

Select interior mentors by the end of your first year in corporate America, if not before. Choose these individuals very carefully. It is important to select people who have had successful careers within your company and a level of experience that enables them to see the "big picture." If they are not successful, it would be difficult for them to give you the guidance and insight that will help you be successful.

Choose people to be your mentors who can give you quality information in a timely manner. I cannot imagine any successful corporate person who wouldn't be honored to give guidance to a veteran and a young Development Candidate. Do not wait until important career decisions are thrust upon you before you seek out knowledgeable people to assist your thought process. Be proactive in establishing mentor relationships before you need them.

Mentors are typically extremely busy people. They are successful professionals with major corporations who make significant contributions to their companies and who accomplish difficult business objectives. Often it is better for you to e-mail them regarding questions you may have; or when you do call them, give them an option of two or three possible times they can speak with you. More than anything else, when your mentor takes time to speak with you or respond with an e-mail, ensure you thank him or her immediately.

Early in your relationship with mentors, let them know what your strengths are, what you like to do, and your high school, college and military extracurricular activities. Give them insight as to what it is you want to accomplish in your career. Let them know what things excite you in a career. It is also helpful to be very candid about your financial status. Any advice given to you must be compatible with your personal financial situation. Prepare a resume and provide copies to your mentors. Keep your resume information current. The more information you can give them about yourself, the more accurate their insight and advice can be.

I encourage you not to miss out on the benefit of having mentors as you pursue a military or business career.

Stop right now and set a deadline for selecting your mentors. Most successful people realize the advantage of mentorship and establish their mentors early in their careers. Take action on this point.

Networking

Networking has become incredibly popular and much easier with Web sites such as Facebook for social networking and LinkedIn for professional networking. Even though Facebook and LinkedIn are useful in their own ways, I want to point out to you that successful individuals go way beyond this. They establish personal relationships with people. For you to do this, you will need to devote effort and time—much more than just clicking "accept" to link with someone. You will need to reach out to others personally for in-person face-to-face or phone conversations. As you develop your network of relationships, you will find that most people enjoy helping others manage their careers and will talk to you and give you information. It's up to you to make the contacts. Look for opportunities with everyone you meet to develop equally beneficial relationships.

For officers planning a career transition, observe other outstanding officers who are establishing careers in corporate America. Make their acquaintance, develop friendships, and, most of all, maintain those friendships. Remember the law of maintaining relationships: "You must give as much as or more than you receive." Think about what you have to offer other people who will contribute real value to their business lives, and develop those capabilities. Too many people wait too late in life to appreciate the value of developing good relationships with others.

As you move into a business career, I would suggest you develop your network in many different career fields, such as engineering, finance, project management, sales, accounting, and manufacturing. At any time in your career, you should be able to contact a close friend who is an engineer or in project management to discuss a technical issue or to contact someone in finance to talk about financial analysis or financial planning for the future. I would recommend that you expand your network to include many companies and industries. This will provide you with a greater diversity of knowledge.

I do recommend when you start your business career that you establish a LinkedIn account, create a network, and join relevant groups. There are a lot of interesting discussions happening within those groups. I also recommend you be selective in deciding with whom you connect and ensure it provides value to you and the other person. If you are going to have a profile, keep it up to date and professional.

Even though Facebook is mostly for personal use, I caution you about the content of your page—make sure it projects the right image. One of my recruiters had to decline a high-quality JMO because of some comments he wrote about enlisted soldiers on his Facebook page. More and more companies are viewing Facebook and other online profiles as part of the background check. It's certainly okay to have pictures of family and friends and personal posts on the wall, but you don't want to have any type of offensive posts or pictures. Be careful. Think, "What would my mom say if she saw this?"

Be smart, be professional, build your network, and remember that your profile on networking sites is a part of your professional image.

Developing a Mastermind Group

Another excellent way to network is to form a "mastermind" group. Many executives and entrepreneurs are members of mastermind groups. You can form personal face-to-face groups or virtual ones. Members meet periodically to brainstorm solutions to issues of importance. The mastermind principle makes it possible for an individual, through association with others, to acquire the knowledge of those individuals without having their education level. For example, a systems engineer expert can explain next-generation computer technology perfectly, but you don't need a four-year computer science degree to understand it. The mastermind concept suggests that there is more opportunity for success in dealing with obstacles to a goal if two or more minds work in perfect harmony toward that goal.

Scarcely a day goes by that we aren't gaining information from diverse, educated, and knowledgeable people, and understanding it—without an equal amount of education. Most of us go through life having informal mastermind alliances, usually in an unconscious state of mind. I'm suggesting you formalize your own mastermind group.

I regret waiting until I was late in my business career to form a mastermind group. I have received many direct benefits, allowing me to save many hours of frustration and to accomplish personal and professional goals more quickly and more efficiently. I hope I have contributed to others in my mastermind groups as well. Don't put the mastermind idea on a back burner. Take advantage of the synergy gained from such an alliance.

One of the major goals of a corporate mastermind group is to help the members do as much as possible to improve their opportunities to have successful careers. For example, your group may want to address specific career opportunities in your field and discuss how members of the group can achieve higher performance.

Be selective about who will be a member of your group. Choose people with similar interests, who have the intelligence and enthusiasm to contribute significantly to the group, and who have been successful in the past. Select people from all geographical areas and career paths. Friends may or may not be appropriate choices. Consider inviting alumni from your college who have worked in the business world to be members, keeping in mind that those individuals must see value in being part of the group.

Early in your career, it is what you know.
Then it becomes whom you know.
Finally, it changes to who knows you.

Your group may want to invite people to speak on topics of importance to you and, afterward, to answer questions from the group. Consider pooling resources and hiring training consultants who deliver business seminars to instruct your group. The opportunities are endless. The point is that as a group you have exciting ideas to explore.

As a member of a mastermind group, maintain a positive attitude at all times. Your goal is to facilitate a supportive, cooperative, and helpful group dynamic in order to encourage information sharing.

Your group can be as large or as small as you like. The larger the group, the longer you need to meet so that everyone can have time to contribute. Establish a specific time to meet each week, every two weeks, or monthly. Development Candidates have busy schedules during the day. Trying to set up meetings during this time will be difficult. Try early morning (6:30 a.m.) or late in the evening (7:30 p.m.) when most of the members might be able to attend.

Let's Get Motivated

I truly believe we have all been blessed with the right to get out of bed in the morning and be happy or unhappy. It's our choice, but there are a lot of people who must not realize they have this choice. Being in the business of recruiting and evaluating people, I observe people wherever I go—airports, hotels, athletic activities, and meetings. I am saddened by people who feel the burden of the world is planted squarely on their shoulders. Whenever I have had that feeling, I have forced myself to lift my head and recognize I have been blessed. I ask myself, "Do I have the right to feel sorry for myself?" Interestingly enough, 99 times out of 100, the answer was no. Everyone at Cameron-Brooks shares this belief. We love getting out of bed in the morning. We love what we do and approach our work with an attitude that reflects this. Everyone on this team loves meeting and working with people. We love the challenges that come to us every day and like the fact that we can meet challenges head on, look them straight in the eye, and rarely fail. It's fun to be successful and alive and to know our partnership with companies and military officers makes a difference. If I visualize what I want, I can get it. I have been given average skills (like many people in our society), but I have performed far above average because of one factor—desire.

I interview many outstanding men and women who have had but a fraction of the success they could have had with all of their great credentials, and I think, "How sad." People come to me and tell me they should be successful because of their great abilities. I'm very quick to point out they can go to any unemployment line in America and find people with equal ability, maybe even more. But because of the lack of desire to apply those abilities, they have difficulty finding and keeping good careers. I believe that 99.9 percent of them are there because they lack the desire to apply God-given abilities. I have an acquaintance who has been very successful and achieved his financial goals, yet he was born with a severe handicap. We read many stories about this type of person—the individual who won't accept a physical handicap as an excuse not to be successful. Many of us complain that we don't have everything we want. We can look around and see those people who have a lot less than we have from the standpoint of intellect, appearance, or physical features, yet they are more successful than we are. Ever wonder why? Do you have any doubt it is simply a greater *desire* to succeed?

Many people never take responsibility for their own actions. They are the people who continually have less than great officer evaluations, and yet not one of these evaluations is their fault. They're the people who will get to the end of life, look back, and feel that life cheated them because they didn't receive everything that was due them. I disagree with all of those thoughts. There is absolutely nothing you can't do if you envision your ability to do it. As I have said earlier in this book, you must have a make-it-happen personality. I often remember the quote "Five percent of the people make it happen, 10 percent of the people watch things happen, and the other 85 percent don't care what happens." I believe there is a lot of truth to this. I stated earlier that, as I interviewed military officers around the world, I accepted 15 percent. I don't wonder why—I know why!

I see too many young officers who feel stuck in their careers but don't do anything about it. I often want to ask them, "Are you cheating yourself? Are you letting seconds, minutes, days, weeks, and months of your life go by and not living your life to the fullest? You're not reaching out to learn, grow, achieve, and succeed. Why did you get up this morning choosing to be unhappy versus happy? What was your reasoning for not establishing your goals and going and getting them? What are you waiting for?"

I remember being at a Career Conference in Austin, Texas. A new corporate recruiter came to me in the middle of the day, and she asked, "Roger, who pays for the candidates to come to the conference?" I said, "The candidates pay their own way." She asked, "Who pays for their room and board?" I said, "The candidates pay for their room and board." She replied, "Well, why would a young man fly all the way to Austin to interview and show absolutely no verbal enthusiasm or excitement in this transition? I had to turn off my air conditioner in order to hear him. He interviewed as if someone should give him an offer just because he showed up! As a matter of fact, I suggested to him that if he thought corporate America was simply going to hire him because of his credentials, then why was he here? Why didn't he just send a resume? After all, we could see his credentials on a resume. We would just send him an offer or a decline through the mail." This is a true story and one that is embarrassing to me. After all, I had recruited him to begin with—obviously, I shared in the failure.

It is hard for me to imagine why anybody would spend $5, let alone $500 or more, to travel across the country and not accomplish the ultimate objective. This young man interviewed with 11 companies, and 11 companies declined him basically for the same reason. He didn't demonstrate in the interviews the leadership qualities to be a Development Candidate. He just didn't act as if he was excited to be alive. I guess he didn't believe he had a choice when he got out of bed in the morning.

As I look at a candidate's interests and hobbies, I smile when

I find an individual who is reading motivational books. When this officer comes in front of me, I'm just a little bit biased. Even before I start interviewing, the candidate is a step up in the interviewing process. In 75-plus years of life, I couldn't begin to count all of the motivational books I have read. I can honestly tell you I have never read one that didn't teach me something new. I also have never read one that didn't remind me of things I had failed to do in my life and give me ideas on how to improve.

Candidates often say, "Oh, I know all that stuff." Knowing it is irrelevant. The question is, "Do you use it? Do you really believe you can be what you want to be? Do you really believe you have the power within yourself to become a tremendous success? Do you really believe you can be a great success—not only in the military but also in corporate America? Do you really believe you can achieve those private goals?" I'm here to tell you that you can—if you really believe.

Individuals have said to me, "Well, I don't believe in motivational books. I am what I am." That's an interesting statement, isn't it? "I am what I am." What these individuals have just said to me and the rest of the world is that they can't improve. Whatever God created them to be, then that's the end of it. This is not true. We can improve ourselves. We can grow. Let me say again—we are adamant about finding people who have potential, people who are eager to become better. They know their success is totally in their own hands. Whatever they want to make of themselves, they can.

I would like to see more officers take advantage of leadership and motivational seminars. I know you take advantage of them when they are sponsored through the military, but I encourage you to attend some additional ones on your own. I am pleased at the number of our candidates who get involved with Toastmasters International. This is a very good program to help you with public speaking as well as your verbal communication skills. I also recommend seminars by Dale Carnegie (www.dalecarnegie.com), Franklin Covey (www.franklincovey.com), and Tony Robbins (www.tonyrobbins.com). These are just a few suggestions, and there are many more available. You don't have to attend a course. You can read books, purchase CDs, download videos, subscribe to podcasts, and watch webcasts. However, I recommend attending the seminars in person. Interacting with others, seeing how others accomplish their goals, and meeting people from other career fields can be an additional source of knowledge and inspiration.

I enjoy working with positive, motivated people. You will rarely see an officer with whom Cameron-Brooks partners who isn't excited, motivated, eager to improve, and professionally self-confident. That's exactly the quality person corporate America is paying us to recruit.

As I reflect on the military officers I have recruited for corporate America, all of them, with few exceptions, have been outstanding. The most dynamic and successful officers take time to grow, learn, and broaden their knowledge base. They don't allow "busy" factors in life to prevent them from doing so.

God only gives us one chance on this earth. If I could motivate just one person who reads this book to reach down inside to find ways to improve, the book will have been a success. I have absolutely no doubt that the book will make people better interviewees, but I would hope for much more than that. I would like to think the book would improve your can-do attitude. I would like to think the book would allow you to choose the better of the two options you have every morning and live it. Remember, when life is over and you look back, no one will have cheated you if you have not accomplished what you had hoped to accomplish. You will have cheated yourself. Don't let that happen. Every day that goes by is a day you will never be able to live over again.

Tomorrow morning, when you wake up and have the choice to make it a good day or a bad day, make the right decision. I know an individual who, every morning when she leaves her bedroom, crosses an imaginary line on the floor outside her bedroom door. As she crosses that line, she is consciously aware it is her choice to make her day whatever she wants it to be. I have rarely seen her not accomplish her objective. Every day is a positive day. She is motivated. She accomplishes difficult objectives. At the end of the day, she feels good about reaching the goals she has established for herself. Put that line outside of your bedroom door. Be conscious of your choices as you step across that line every day.

In conclusion, I recommend you take firm control of your career. Nobody else will care about your career success as much as you will. Remember, success is just as much of a mind-set as it is a goal. Be a catalyst and motivate yourself to accomplish the professional objectives you want for yourself and your family. Find resources like the ones I mention in this chapter to help yourself stay inspired. Most of all, when you wake up in the morning, recognize that you control your desire, success, and happiness.

Marching Orders

Throughout this book I have suggested ways to handle certain questions and situations. *Under no circumstances am I suggesting that you use my words.* Every thought and every idea should be digested and put into your own words, with your own authentic manner of communication. No recruiter wants a person to use someone else's words. There may be certain cases in which words are used from a phrase, but we encourage candidates to be themselves. You are a unique individual, and you must interview as that unique individual.

I want you to remember that you're an outstanding individual in your own right. This book has been designed to help you make a successful transition from the military to business and improve your interviewing ability—not to necessarily change you as an individual. I encourage you to give serious thought as to what you want to do with your life. If that means coming to corporate America or having a career in a different field, this book will help you (regardless of the field).

Remember, you have several selves—you at your best, you at your average, and you at your worst. Transition and interview at your best. To be your best at anything you do, you must be thoroughly prepared. Be committed to what you're doing; focus and concentrate on your objective.

I encourage you to start early to prepare for any difficult

objective. Don't wait until the last minute. Prepare as early as you can in your career for any potential changes you might make. Be conscious, as you go through your military career, of what you do specifically, individually, and uniquely to motivate members of your team. While the military gives you leadership guidance, it doesn't restrict you from personalizing methods of motivation. Be conscious of the individual people problems you have solved along the way. Be performance-oriented. Be conscious of problems you've solved and know how you've solved them. Be aware of the skills you use—organizational ability, prioritizing, consensus-building, time management, etc.—and the procedure you go through each time you solve any problem. Become conscious of your methodology in everything you do. Improve your communication skills by rehearsing and recording presentations ahead of time. Never be embarrassed by the fact that you must practice to be concise and articulate. Preparation for anything you do in life only makes you better. I've never heard of anyone who gained success in becoming a better officer, a better marksman, a better skier, or a better speaker without practice. I've never known preparation to be life threatening or detrimental to health. All I have ever heard in my 75-plus years of living is, "Boy, that person really worked hard to be successful." That's right. That's exactly what it takes.

Pursue your career objectives with a high degree of enthusiasm. Know yourself and be confident. Communicate with poise and enthusiasm so we will not only hear what you say but we will believe it as well.

Know what you have done in the military and what has made you successful. The better you know yourself, the better you know how you have accomplished difficult objectives and the better you can apply that formula to any career objective—in corporate America, the civil service, or your own business. Continue to be self-aware and understand your strengths and deficits and manage them accordingly.

I hope you've enjoyed this book. I hope you feel better prepared now that you have read it. However, no one book makes a well-prepared candidate for stepping up into a business career. I encourage you to read as many books on corporate America as you can get your hands on. You can go to any bookstore (online or on the street corner) and find a host of books to read. Seek out others who have been successful in business and ask for their insight and lessons in success. I've never known anyone in corporate America who wouldn't take the time to explain what the business world is all about. They'll be happy to talk to you and give you some insight. People love talking about what they do. Take advantage of every opportunity. Make things happen.

Best of success to you!

TO ALL MILITARY OFFICERS

W hether you have made the decision to transition to the business world or are simply considering your career options, Cameron-Brooks is available to discuss and evaluate your marketability. When you conduct a Personal Marketability Assessment with one of our recruiters, we will provide you with objective feedback on your marketability, career fields for which you are qualified, the compensation you can expect in your initial starting position, and also if Cameron-Brooks can help you transition. You can be assured of a candid evaluation and extremely knowledgeable, constructive advice.

I strongly encourage you to contact us early in your military career. We will then have the opportunity to suggest certain skill enhancements, additional formal education, specific military assignments, and the best time for you to transition to the business world with your particular skills. Should you decide to remain in the military, the advice we offer will also enhance your military career.

Our proprietary Development and Preparation Program is regarded as the very best career transition training available. The earlier you get involved in our program and the more time you spend with us, the more marketable you become and the smoother your transition will be. We continually receive outstanding comments about our preparation program—not only in terms of interviewing skill development but also for the long-term positive effect it has on your career. Any officer can transition out of the military. Our program helps candidates accelerate into their business careers and make an immediate impact. We give you the tools for a successful transition and for long-term success in your new business career.

Our reputation is established with both military officers and Fortune 500 and numerous other leading companies. We have a track record for successfully working with thousands of officers from all branches of the military and with backgrounds from engineering to liberal arts. We know our business. We know what it takes to conduct a successful career search and transition. We know what kind of talent our client companies are looking for in Development Candidates and consistently bring them the best of the best.

The best measurement of our success is your success. Cameron-Brooks is acknowledged for the professional, caring involvement our entire team devotes to each of our candidates. We sincerely care about you and your career and welcome the opportunity to partner with you and help you achieve your career goals.

Today it is virtually impossible to transition to the business world without being touched by the Cameron-Brooks Alumni Association. Cameron-Brooks alumni offer advice and insight as you prepare for a transition; they attend our Career Conferences to interview and hire you; and they are there to welcome you on the first day of your business career. The Cameron-Brooks Alumni Association boasts successful business people in positions from every possible functional area and with companies from every possible sector of industry. Our alumni have made a powerful impact on corporate America. They have quickly moved up into key positions within their companies, and they have paved a limitless road for success for talented military officers to follow. Our alumni are as loyal to us as we are to them. Together we are accomplishing great things in the business world, bringing new talent to companies and helping great companies become even greater.

Trust Cameron-Brooks to help you maximize your market-ability and position you for a successful professional future. For more information about our career search services, please visit our Web site at www.cameron-brooks.com or call our office toll-free in the U.S. at 1-800-222-9235 or, from Germany, at 0800-85-22670. We are eager to help you in any way we can. Together, we can "make it happen!"

I speak for the entire Cameron-Brooks team when I say, "*Thank you* for your service." Many of you have deployed multiple times to various regions of the world. You and your families have sacrificed a lot for our freedom. We are humbled by the stories we hear about your courage and commitment to defend our freedom. Thank you.

Finally, I want to thank all the Cameron-Brooks alumni, client companies and their recruiters, and those who have worked at Cameron-Brooks for a meaningful career filled with so many relationships with outstanding people. *Thank you!* René Brooks and I have worked for over a decade to grow the leadership at Cameron-Brooks. We have groomed Chuck Alvarez and Joel Junker, contributors to this edition of *PCS to Corporate America,* to assume leadership of our company. They are ready! Additionally, we have several other key leaders in the organization and an excellent team that will continue to provide professional service to military officers and clients for decades to come.

Have a powerful career!
Roger Cameron

Appendices

A. Key Competencies of Development Candidates

The following is a compilation of key characteristics and competencies (consistently demonstrated characteristics) that our client companies look for in Development Candidates. Use this list to help you determine your strengths and, specifically, those that are valued by recruiters. You do not need to possess all of these characteristics or competencies. This list is intended to help you think about and determine the characteristics and competencies you possess as well as the ones you want to further establish while preparing for a transition to business. It will also help you decide which ones are most important to bring to light in an interview.

Action-oriented
Approachable
Assertive
Astute
Business acumen
Career ambition
Caring
Compassion
Composure
Conflict management
Consensus building
Continuous process
  improvement
Creative
Customer focus
Dealing with
  ambiguity
Decision making
Delegation
Develop others
Drive for results
Empathetic
Energetic
Ethical
Fair

Goal oriented
Hard-working
Humor
Initiative
Innovative
Integrity
Intelligence
Interpersonal skills
Leadership
  Change
  Cross-function
  Idea
  Team
Learning agility
Listening
Maturity/emotional
  intelligence
Motivating others
Negotiating
Openness
Organizational
  ability/agility
Patience
Perseverance
Planning
Poise

Positive attitude
Presentation skills
Priority setting
Problem solving
Project management
Self-confidence
Self-development
Self-knowledge
Self-starter
Sensitivity
Strategic thinking
Team-building skills
Technical aptitude/
  learning/skills
Time management
Tough-mindedness
Trustworthy
Understanding others
Values
Visionary
Willingness to learn
  new things
Written communi-
  cation skills

B. Sample Development Candidate Resume

(*Note*: This is a sample resume. Several branches of the military are included in one resume, even though no junior officer would have a background this unique!)

John Q. Citizen
Street Address
City, State and Nine-Digit Zip Code
(Area Code) Home Phone Number
e-mail address (ensure it is professional!)

AVAILABLE: March 31, 2012

EDUCATION
BS Engineering/Math/Science Core Curriculum 2007
Major: Electrical Engineering
United States Air Force Academy
Colorado Springs, Colorado

MBA Finance 2011
University of Maryland
College Park, Maryland

ACTIVITIES

High School: Valedictorian; National Honor Society; Rotary Club Outstanding Senior; Student of Year; Class President; Student Government Representative (Treasurer); Key Club (Treasurer, Lieutenant Governor); Alliance Area Youth Center (President); Varsity Basketball (Captain); Varsity Football; Worked 6 hours per week during school and 60 hours per week during summers.
College: Graduated with Distinction; National Engineering Honor Society; Habitat for Humanity (President); Student Senate; Intramurals (Volleyball [Captain], Football, Softball).

EXPERIENCE

5/07–Present   **Captain, Field Artillery, United States Army**

10/11–Present   Assistant Weapons Officer, USS Springfield: Led 20-member team in operation and maintenance of sonar, fire control, and torpedo equipment on $2 billion nuclear-powered fast attack sub.
- Led 23-member control team as primary mid-watch Officer of the Deck during complex evolutions and overseas deployment, ensuring safe accomplishment of missions vital to national security.
- Compiled/completed USS *Springfield*'s final mission report 8 hours ahead of schedule without incident.
- Researched/analyzed/coordinated/executed uncommon Cape of Good Hope transit with movement through five operational theaters; ensured safe navigation/security, directly contributing to successful deployment.
- Created/coordinated deployment force protection requirements/training; awarded Navy Achievement Medal.

6/10–10/11   Company Commander: Led 135-person infantry team supporting worldwide security/combat operations. Created/trained/developed company from ground up. Maintained $20 million of equipment.
- Planned, resourced, executed, and managed risk for over 40 combat training exercises; achieved 100% of predeployment training requirements and validated company as worldwide deployable.
- Created, implemented, and supervised support and accountability processes for $20 million of equipment; resulted in effective maintenance, resourcing, and accountability during 21 months of continuous training.
- Procured $20 million of equipment and 5,000 square feet of facility workspace through planning and resource forecasting; ensured 135 personnel were adequately outfitted to perform full-spectrum operations.
- Created and implemented mentoring programs to professionally develop personnel; significantly increased professional aptitude, supported professional advancement, and sustained organizational longevity.
- Organized, established, and led 450-person reserve team (30% of battalion); supported 800-person deployed battalion and prepared two companies for deployment; executed duties of Major 6 to 9 years beyond rank.
- Recognized by battalion commander as in "Top 5%" of over 90 company-grade officers observed in 19 years.

12/08–5/10   Chief of Intelligence, Airborne Warning and Control Squadron: Led 4-person intelligence team in Japan supporting airborne combat operations for 140-person squadron in the Asian Pacific.
- Created/implemented aircrew intelligence training, including threat briefs for daily missions and operations.
- Produced first electronic tracker for unit compliance inspection; expedited unprecedented 100% compliance in shortened timeline, meeting 162 criteria in 30 days; no discrepancies found upon inspection.
- Lauded by Group Commander for actions in the North Korean crisis; singularly praised out of 600 people.

5/07–11/08   Brigade Material Management Officer: Coordinated logistics, movement and procurement requirements for 1,800-person signal brigade consisting of 840 wheeled vehicles and 140 major communication systems valued at $300 million. Coordinated facility maintenance and improvements of 49 buildings worth $15 million. Supervised 9.
- Pioneered a Government Credit Card program that was adopted by Corps as model program; saved unit over $200,000.
- Developed first transportation method for military weapons to be moved on a civilian aircraft; resulted in 100% accountability of all weapons and successful transportation.
- Led effort to turn in excess equipment; reduced excess equipment in brigade from 38% to 0% in 7 months.
- Attended 5 months of Logistics Officer Basic Course (Honor Graduate).

C. Recommended Reading

The books recommended below are an excellent starting point to develop your business knowledge and prepare for a transition. However, they are under no circumstances the only ones you should read. Expand your reading program by researching books online through sites like amazon.com or reading reviews of business books and authors in national and regional newspapers. I also recommend an e-reading device so you can always have your reading library with you. Each title below is followed by comments that explain why I feel the book is important.

Built to Last (Collins and Porras). A valuable book regardless of your career path. Discusses with clarity the distinguishing characteristics of the world's most enduring and successful corporations.

Crucial Confrontations: Tools for Resolving Broken Promises, Violated Expectations, and Bad Behavior (Patterson, Grenny, McMillan, Switzler). In my opinion, every leader needs to read this book on how to hold professional conversations with others (subordinates, peers, and bosses) who do not meet expectations. Too often, we sweep problems under the rug because we lack the courage and tools to address them. This book gives you the tools to develop the confidence and courage to professionally confront others who do not meet expectations and promises.

Crucial Conversations: Tools for Talking When Stakes are High (Patterson, Grenny, McMillan, Switzler). From the same authors as *Crucial Confrontations*, this book provides excellent tools on how to listen, persuade, solicit ideas, and control emotions when conversations become heated.

The Fifth Discipline (Senge). An eminently readable book that will give you valuable insight into cutting-edge process improvement and organizational development skills. This is a great read for any JMO.

The Five Dysfunctions of a Team (Lencioni). This is an excellent book on team leadership. Written as a fable, the book is easy and fun to read. It has powerful lessons that you will begin to apply immediately at work and maybe in your family, too!

Fundamentals of Project Management, 4th ed. (Heagney). A lot of what you do in the military is project management; you may just call it something else. If you transition to a business career, you will continue to lead projects. You will be expected to get results and stay under budget, maximizing resources. This book will help you learn the principles of project management.

Good to Great and *Great by Choice* (Collins). Collins is considered one of the best business authors in the last decade. *Good to Great* illustrates management strategies, practices, and disciplines that move companies from average performance to consistently great performance. *Great by Choice* illustrates how great companies manage during turbulent times and continue to achieve success.

The Goal: A Process of Ongoing Improvement (E. Goldratt). This will be one of the best business books you will ever read, and it is relevant to the military as well as corporate America. While written as a novel, it is used as a process improvement model in organizations around the world.

How to Win Friends and Influence People (Carnegie). A classic book on interpersonal skills that still appears on the *New York Times* Bestseller List. Every leader, whether in business, the military, or another organization, needs to read this book.

Integrity Selling for the 21st Century (Willingham). A great book for anyone considering sales. Teaches an effective selling process on how to develop productive, professional, and mutually rewarding relationships with customers.

Lean Thinking: Banish Waste and Create Wealth in Your Corporation (Womack and Jones). A great book on Lean concepts that are being used in companies around the globe to improve process efficiency and eliminate waste in both manufacturing and service industries. To maximize your time, read only the preface and the first five chapters, which outline the Lean principles.

Lincoln on Leadership (Phillips). A one-of-a-kind book that applies Abraham Lincoln's leadership traits to the business environment. This book will help you articulate your leadership experience in business terms.

The New Strategic Selling (Heiman and Sanchez). Considered the best guide for professional selling and large account management. Highly recommended by many Fortune 500 companies.

The 7 Habits of Highly Effective People (Covey). Covey's concepts are used in virtually every major corporation in America. You may also want to read Covey's *Principle-Centered Leadership* and his sequel to *7 Habits*, *The 8th Habit*.

What Is Six Sigma? (Pande and Holpp). If you want to learn how to solve problems, improve quality, and reduce variability in results, you need to understand Six Sigma. Companies continue to implement this continuous process improvement tool to improve their performance. There are many great books and courses available on this subject. I recommend this book because it is short (86 pages) and to the point. You do not need to read this specific book, but you do need to become familiar with the topic.

Wooden on Leadership: A Lifetime of Observations and Reflections on and off the Court (Wooden and Jamison). Fabulous leadership book by one of the most successful coaches in any sport at any level. His advice is simple, yet powerful. My favorite quote: "Success is peace of mind which is a direct result of self-satisfaction in knowing you made the effort to become the best of which you are capable."

If you read these and want to read more, other great business authors include Peter Drucker, Ken Blanchard, Ram Charan, and John Maxwell.

Keep reading and never stop learning!

For additional book recommendations, access our Resource Center via our Web site at www.cameron-brooks.com and also follow out blog at http://blog.cameron-brooks.com, where we frequently recommend books.

D. Interview Self-Evaluation

I strongly recommend that you conduct several mock interviews with someone who can provide you with critical feedback *before* your attend your first interview. Use the tool below to evaluate your presentation before and after any mock or real interview to help immediately identify deficiencies. Companies want to hire top performers with strong communication skills. You demonstrate your ability to become a top performer when you interview close to a Perfect 10 level. You will never have a perfect interview! There will always be opportunities to improve.

- Before each interview, review these key factors and focus on perfect performance.
- After each interview, rate your performance! Analyze how you can improve the next time! Be critical.

When you can confidently rank yourself high on each aspect of performance, you are on the road to success.

Circle a number between 5 and 10 (Perfect = 10)

IMPRESSION		INTERPERSONAL SKILLS	
• Smile	• Energy	• Establish rapport	• Listen Actively
• Appearance	• Posture/Poise	• Relate/Respond	• Sincere
• Handshake	• Eye Contact	• Curiosity	• Approachable
• Walk	• FOCUS	• Connect	• FOCUS
5 6 7 8 9 10		5 6 7 8 9 10	
COMMUNICATION		**CONFIDENCE**	
• Persuasive	• Listen	• Convincing	• Competitive
• Body Language	• Good Questions	• Knowledgeable	• Use Names
• Articulate	• Relate Assets	• Positive	• Eye Contact
• Good Answers		• Self-Assured	
5 6 7 8 9 10		5 6 7 8 9 10	

CLOSE

• Company-specific • FOCUS	How would you rank yourself overall?
• Believable	5 6 7 8 9 10
5 6 7 8 9 10	How would the recruiter rank you?
	5 6 7 8 9 10

Index

competencies of 26–27, 46,
130–132
hiring of, as corporate investment
34
key competencies of 13–14, 68,
255–256
sample resume for 256–260
vs. Nondevelopment Candidates
164
development career
and leadership 165–166
importance of commitment 33–34
vs. career in government 34
vs. nondevelopment career 25–28
vs. starting one's own business
34–35
development positions
and advancement opportunities
230
examples of 227–230
dinners, business 211–212
directive leadership style 168
disappointment
dealing with 80
vs. failure 80
disclosure, full 62
diverse workforce, hiring and managing 226
DMAIC (methodology) 44, 156
drinking 212

E

educational background
discussing, in interview 160–162
on resume 48, 56–57
e-mail
avoiding, for bad news 232
for thank-you notes 200
energy
conveying, in interview 132–133
inappropriate, as reason for being
declined 195–196
low, as reason for being declined
191, 193

engineering positions, examples of
228
Enterprise Resource Planning (ERP)
42
enthusiasm 132–133, 151–152
environment, control of 15, 237–238
etiquette
at business dinners 211–212
being on time 110
cell phone 111
sending thank-you notes 199–201
evaluation inflation factor 39
evaluation process 23–46
excuses 204
Executive Education for Veterans 43
executive folio 115–116
exercises
defining short- and long-term career
goals 180
General Store 70–72, 188
identifying behavioral traits
131–132
interview self-evaluation 260
preparing for "Why?" questions 154
experience. See civilian experience;
military experience
extracurricular activities
evaluation of 40
on resume 56
eye contact 134, 141, 195

F

Facebook 240, 241
failure
confronting 78–80
discussing 76–78
making excuses for 136–137
vs. disappointment 80
family life 147
filters, screening 29
first names 195, 234–236
first person, use of 93–95, 131
Fishbone Diagrams 156
"fit," proving 119–122

Pro Reading: PG 99 → Skim + take notes in cover.
Communication PG 95-96 → use "I" and no fillers
           ↳ involve spouse/sj other to Reprimend.
           ↳ No military terms.